THE SEARCH FOR SPIRITUALITY

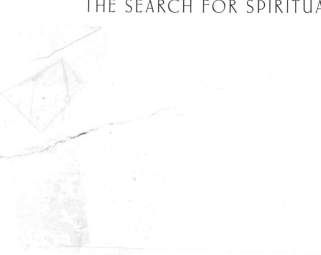

THE SEARCH
FOR SPIRITUALITY

Our Global Quest for a Spiritual Life

URSULA KING

CANTERBURY
PRESS

Norwich

© Ursula King 2009

This edition published in 2009 by the Canterbury Press Norwich
Editorial office
13–17 Long Lane,
London, EC1A 9PN, UK

Canterbury Press is an imprint of Hymns Ancient and Modern Ltd
(a registered charity)
St Mary's Works, St Mary's Plain,
Norwich, NR3 3BH, UK

Published in the United States in 2008 by BlueBridge,
an imprint of United Tribes Media Inc.

www.scm-canterburypress.co.uk

British Library Cataloguing in Publication data

A catalogue record for this book is available
from the British Library

978 1 85311 942 2

Printed and bound in the UK by
CPI William Clowes Ltd, Beccles, NR34 7TL

CONTENTS

With gratitude to my dear family and friends
for their continuing love and support, and
their help in the creation of this book.

PROLOGUE

The great interest in spirituality today stems in part from the general awareness that we live on a planet torn apart by much suffering and violence. Ever more people are in need of healing and in search of a more wholesome life. A profound crisis of meaning has arisen whose roots can be traced to a loss of vision, commitment, and faith—what is in fact a deep spiritual crisis. An immense spiritual hunger exists to find a life of deeper significance than that of material goods, consumerism, and exploitative capitalism. The current global situation with its deep injustices, numerous wars, and threats of ecological disaster calls for new creative thinking and for transformative ways of living. This requires a more reverent attitude toward people and the planet; it also calls for a spirituality that will lead to the reorganization of world economics, politics, education, business, and world governance.

So many people are losing hope and feel depressed when faced with the stark realities of contemporary geopolitics. What can we do, individually and together, in order to ensure the greater flourishing of people and the planet in the twenty-first century? Where can we find moral and spiritual inspiration, guidance, and help amongst global chaos and confusion? It seems that a more ethically grounded and action-oriented spirituality is not just a necessity—it is an imperative if we want to create a world more united and whole.

Why these reflections on spirituality when a wealth of information on spiritual schools, disciplines, and practices, on spiritual guides past and present, on spiritual advice and counsels is widely available? The existing books on spirituality often consider only one particular spiritual perspective or faith tradition; they offer valuable insights without providing a more comprehensive global vision. Too many works on spirituality focus on the inner quest of the individual by advocating personal changes without stressing the need for larger social transformations. Or they deal with particular historical and contemporary aspects of spirituality but do not set them into the larger context of globalization and the now global quest for spirituality.

This book presents contemporary debates on spirituality around the world by setting them in the widest possible context. It tries to capture the major differences that exist between various spiritualities while pointing out the remarkable parallels and sometimes surprisingly convergent developments in the different understandings of spirituality as a lofty ideal and greatly beneficial practice.

Many people rightly ask what spirituality entails. What is the larger context to which spirituality belongs? What language is used, what message conveyed when drawing on discourses of spirituality that are both ancient and modern? Who speaks about spirituality to whom, and with what authority? And how is spirituality lived? How is it taught and caught? Does it really make a difference to people's lives? Can it change the world as we know it?

Some of these questions are taken up in what follows, and some currently available answers are offered for careful consideration. Such answers sometimes compete with each other, so that a discerning reader will have to choose between them. This book makes no claim to present a comprehensive in-depth study or critical assessment of the varieties of spirituality that exist in the contemporary world. Its diverse reflections on a single theme are but a modest introduction to very large, complex realities and experiences. Hopefully it will provide readers with plenty of material for deepening their own thinking, and encourage them to pursue further dialogue and inquiry within and without.

I aim to reach an audience that is passionately interested in spirituality from both an existential and an intellectual perspective rather than readers who consider spirituality merely a subject of academic study and debate. I hope that these reflections will enable readers to expand their own understanding of spirituality. By reading this book you are invited to participate in a deeper dialogue with some of the challenging questions and spiritual minds of our time, and to become inspired in heart and mind to seek and find deeper awareness, enlightenment, and transformation.

May the many perspectives of the global quest for spirituality help readers to make informed choices that will ensure the flourishing of their own lives, and that of many others in the communities and networks to which they belong.

One

SEARCHING FOR SPIRITUALITY

What does the word "spirituality" really mean? While often mentioned in public and private, it is difficult to define since spirituality can be linked to almost any longing of the human heart. Many people do not want to use this rather vague and fuzzy word at all. Does spirituality depend on religion? Or is it something quite different? Does it provide valuable practical help for human life, or is it to be approached with skepticism and doubt? Can there be a spirituality without traditional labels, a secular spirituality not dependent on religion at all? Is spirituality essential for human flourishing, or a luxury one can do without?

Answers to these questions vary enormously, depending on who is being asked. There can be little doubt, however, that spirituality is attracting immense interest in very different, even contradictory contexts in contemporary society. For many in the Western world it is associated with something highly desirable and positive. It is often considered as more appropriate to the demands of modern life than traditional religion, which is seen as more ambivalent, if not irrelevant. How did this change of attitude come about, and why does it influence so many individuals and groups?

While there has been much talk about the growth of secularization in the West, such an amazing reawakening of interest in spirituality has occurred in recent years that even sociologists and economists have discovered spirituality as worthy of investigation. This new fascination may even contradict the view that modern societies are predominantly secular. Although it is impossible to define spirituality in a way that everybody would agree on, it is often understood to be wider than religion, or even quite different from it. Sometimes spirituality and religion are seen as so far apart that they are considered as two separate, independent spheres, exclusive of each other. Yet much can be said for viewing them as closely related and mutually embedded.

Seen from a wider historical and comparative perspective, spirituality is clearly connected with religion, but not exclusively contained by it. When people separate religion and spirituality sharply from each other or even oppose them, religion is then often primarily identified with external, institutional aspects, while spirituality is reduced to something internal, a personal inwardness that has little bearing on social and institutional life. Yet on closer examination it would seem that this represents an impoverished view of both religion *and* spirituality, a loss of vision and a nonrecognition of essential energy resources that can nourish the growth of human life in the fullest sense. Such a sharp separation between spirituality and religion is not helpful for the development of the personal and social transformations so urgently needed if greater flourishing of humans and the earth is to be achieved around the globe.

MEANING OF SPIRITUALITY

Spirituality is spoken of in connection with so many different aspects of contemporary life that its meaning seems profoundly

ambivalent. Sometimes it is invoked with great praise, even a
sense of longing, so that it appears as a highly desirable ideal. On
other occasions its very mention can meet with criticism, resistance, even rejection. Why is this?

The word "spirituality" owes its origin to a Christian context.
Originally it had no direct equivalent in non-Western languages.
Spirituality is now used globally with reference to all religions and
cultures; it thus has become a code word across a wide religious
and secular spectrum to refer to many different experiences and
practices. They all share characteristics that are deemed to be life
enhancing, holistic, and greatly supportive of human well-being
in the widest sense. Numerous voices can be heard speaking about
Eastern and Western spirituality, women's spirituality, New Age
spirituality, secular and esoteric spirituality, interfaith and ecumenical spirituality, children's spirituality, even spirituality and
aging, spirituality and health, spirituality and gender, spirituality
and human well-being. There is also talk of spirituality in management, business, sociology, economics, and geography, even of
spiritual capital in analogy to social and cultural capital. This may
at first seem surprising, but it points to the undeniable fact that, in
its most inclusive sense, spirituality is so all-embracing that it does
indeed touch everything. It can become a true leaven, a fermenting
agent that may deeply influence and shape every aspect of human
life.

Many definitions of spirituality have been suggested, but it is
perhaps more helpful to ask what spirituality *does* rather than what
it *is*. Spirituality can be linked to all human experiences, but it has
a particularly close connection with the imagination, with human
creativity and resourcefulness, with relationships—whether with
ourselves, with others, or with a transcendent reality, named or
unnamed, but often called the Divine, God, or Spirit. Spirituality
can also be connected with a sense of celebration and joy, with
adoration and surrender, with struggle and suffering. A wide

understanding and exploration of spirituality is of considerable interest today, not only to people of religious faith but also to those working in psychotherapy and the human potential movement, to adherents of new religions, to supporters of ecological and peace groups as well as those of the women's movement.

Contemporary understandings of spirituality capture the dynamic, transformative quality of spirituality as lived experience, an experience linked to our bodies, to nature, to our relationships with others and society. It is an experience which seeks the fullness of life—a life of justice and peace, of integrating body, mind, and soul, a life that touches the hem of the spirit in the midst of all our struggles of living in a world that has become ever more globally interdependent, yet is so painfully torn apart.

Like all other human experiences, spirituality exists primarily in the plural. It is thus much more appropriate to speak of "spiritualities" rather than spirituality in the singular. Christian spirituality differs from Jewish, Muslim, Hindu, or Buddhist spirituality. In the past, traditional forms of these spiritualities were often quite different from the way they are understood today. Most important, many contemporary spiritualities have come into existence which are not defined by traditional religions but are secular or newly created, rooted in the experience of a new world. What words do we have to speak about the spiritual, and where do they come from?

WESTERN WORDS FOR THE SPIRITUAL

The "spiritual" is often mentioned when we want to name a reality greater than ourselves, a power or presence that goes beyond the individual person, just as when we speak about the "transcendent" as something that goes beyond. Philosophers, theologians, religious thinkers, poets, and mystics have all sought to clarify the concept of the spiritual, to define it more precisely or describe it in more detail. But this is difficult to do, and their attempts have produced widely varying results. The spiritual dimension is often thought to be an especially defining characteristic of human life as distinct from merely biological life in general. It is closely related to mind and thought, to consciousness, discerning reflection, and self-aware experience.

Different languages and cultures possess many "spirit words" to describe this central human experience. Western thinking on the spiritual has been much shaped by ancient Greek thought, whereas other cultures draw on different sources for thinking about the spirit. The Greeks used four spirit words—*psyche, pneuma, thumos, nous*. Each of these captures a somewhat different reality but also overlaps in meaning with the others. *Psyche* has been called a "breath word," and *pneuma* a "wind word." The first is connected to the animated personal life of the individual made possible through breathing; the second refers to the movement of air in nature, to the power of the wind. For Greek philosophers, these two words—*psyche* and *pneuma*—came to stand for the principle of individual and cosmic life. *Psyche* was the individual soul, whereas *pneuma* related to a transpersonal, cosmic soul, the life of the whole world. It is important to be reminded of this recognition of the existence of an individual and cosmic spirit-soul and their close link with each other, a belief known in ancient times and found again in contemporary discussions about ecological spirituality.

Thumos describes life's vitality, but also will, feeling, and the inner life of spirit and soul. *Nous* is related to mind, spirit, heart, intuitive vision, insight. For the Greeks, *nous* was the spiritual intellect that serves as the instrument of self-transcendence. Over the centuries, *pneuma* and *psyche* came to be more widely used for the conception of spirit and soul than the other two words, at least until recently. The Christian writers of the New Testament took on the spirit word *pneuma* and made wide use of it, as did Christian theologians in subsequent centuries. Their understanding of spirit also draws much on the Hebrew word *ruah*, widely used in the Hebrew Bible. Both *pneuma* and *ruah* are linked to the invisible and intangible movements of breath, air, and wind, which we can feel with and in our bodies, but never grasp or get hold of.

Another important Greek word is *sophia*, which stands for wisdom, an important quality of the inner life of the spirit that can help us find our way in life. Modern Western philosophers from Hegel to Kierkegaard and Nietzsche have written much on "spirit," or *Geist*, in both a universal and personal sense. For the German thinker and poet Goethe, *Geist* was the most important element in human life, "the life of life," but spirit was also "nature's own highest power."

A great tension, even a dualistic opposition, was sometimes perceived between the ideals of the spirit and the demands of vital life in its full embodiment, especially as expressed in human instincts and emotions. Thus the existence of spirit is not so much an obvious fact, as the philosopher Hegel thought, but human beings have to actualize themselves as spiritual beings. In Kierkegaard's understanding, humanity as it exists falls short of spirit; it is more pervaded by "spiritlessness" than spirit. Some philosophers even speak of the displacement of the human spirit in the vast cosmos, where we seek to find a home rather than being at home already. Others see the spiritual dimension of humans as constituted by the activity of loving and valuing. For the French philosopher Gabriel Marcel, all spiritual life is essentially dialogue that brings us together in community.

These discussions show that the spiritual cannot be taken for granted but has to be sought, enacted, and realized. They also make evident that philosophical and religious reflections on "spirit" are closely interrelated, yet also go their different ways.

In the West, the Latin word *spiritualitas* is derived from the noun *spiritus* and the adjective *spiritualis*, whose use can be traced back to the translation of the biblical terms *pneuma* and *pneumatikos*, which St. Paul used in opposition to the flesh (*sarx*), but not to the body (*soma* or *corpus*). The flesh must therefore not be understood as the human body, but it represents everything in human beings that opposes the influence of the Spirit of God. The *pneuma* or *spiritus* in human beings is that power which makes them, by contrast, open to everything that comes from God's Spirit. The first Latin use of *spiritualitas* is found in a letter of St. Jerome from the early part of the fifth century; he speaks about it in the sense of the spiritual life resulting from the grace of baptism. The word was used relatively rarely, but subsequently a shift in the meaning of *spiritualitas* (spirituality) occurred, so that eventually, during the twelfth century, it came to be opposed to *corporalitas* (corporality) and *materialitas* (materiality), even to *carnalitas* (carnality) and *mortalitas* (mortality). It is this oppositional dualism that has remained with the word "spirituality" ever since, a heritage that is difficult to shed and forget.

From about 1500 CE onward we find the word "spirituality" in the English language. According to the *Oxford English Dictionary* it means "the quality or condition of being spiritual; attachment to or regard for things of the spirit as opposed to material or worldly interests." The same reference work defines the "spiritual" as "of or pertaining to, affecting or concerning, the spirit or higher moral qualities, especially as regarded in a religious aspect. Frequently in express or implied distinction to *bodily, corporal*, or *temporal*." These definitions clearly point to the inherent polarity that is traditionally so often associated with spirituality—it is seen as opposite to the physical. The spiritual is often taken as something otherworldly, separate from our bodily and material needs, from time and space. It may also be seen as something distinct from, and going beyond, the psychical experience of the human being.

The German language traditionally uses several words rather

than just one to speak about spirituality; it also employs the word *Frömmigkeit* that stems from the Latin *pietas*. This is originally not a religious term, but it has been used in connection with religion since the nineteenth century. German authors took on the word *Spiritualität* only relatively recently, whereas the French have long made much use of *spiritualité*. In fact, several important works on the history of Christian spirituality come from French writers. They have dealt with the evolution of spirituality, and written on different schools of spirituality, such as Rhenish spirituality, Spanish spirituality, the French school of spirituality, or Russian Orthodox spirituality.

THE SPIRITUAL IN DIFFERENT CULTURES

Each language and culture has different "spirit" words. In Indian religions such as Hinduism and Buddhism the words *moksha* and *nirvana*, sometimes translated as "liberation" and "enlightenment," come perhaps closest to some of the ideals referred to as "spirituality" in English. The Indian languages of Sanskrit and Pali have a rich heritage of spirit words relating to both the ultimate Spirit and the human spirit or consciousness in its many different manifestations. There are such words as *Brahman, atman, citta, purusha*, and many others whose full understanding require long and detailed explanations. Similarly, there exist specific spirit words in Arabic and Japanese, in Chinese, African, and indigenous tribal languages, each with their own connotations. In the colonial contacts between Europe and India it was especially during the late nineteenth century that Hindu religious reformers, such as Swami Vivekananda (1863–1902), frequently spoke of the greatness of Indian spirituality, contrasting it favorably with Western materialism. It was during this time of colonialism that Western interest in many forms of Eastern spirituality first emerged, and that the seeds for closer interreligious encounter and dialogue were first planted.

From a contemporary postcolonial perspective it is obvious that this encounter was limited by its colonial setting. Yet the current critical approach to Western colonial attitudes and the romanticizing perspective of Orientalism, so important for the appropriate assessment and understanding of past historical developments, must nonetheless not blind us to the genuine achievements and real advances made at that time. Within the global history of humanity, it was during this period that the encounter of different religions with their distinct spiritualities first took off. New paths were tried, new ways of thinking evolved. They laid the foundations for a much more inclusive, global vision of spirituality so characteristic of our own time.

Such a vision of a truly global spiritual heritage of humanity found concrete expression in important collaborative studies of spiritualities around the world, both religious and secular, published in the series *World Spirituality: An Encyclopedic History of the Religious Quest* under the general editorship of Ewert Cousins. Consisting of twenty-five volumes, this series presents the different spiritualities of the major religious traditions of the world, but also moves outside them by including studies on spirituality and the secular quest as well as modern esoteric spiritualities.

An impressive achievement and great learning resource, this series is still only the beginning of taking stock of spiritual experiences and histories around the planet. Far more work has to be done to discover what rich spiritual resources of great diversity and splendor humankind possesses as its common heritage. To nurture human well-being and flourishing we can now draw upon the profound wisdom of the religious and philosophical traditions of the entire world. We can discover and learn from a wealth of practical maps for living a good life. We can work more consciously and more effectively for greater human unity than was

possible in earlier historical periods. This unprecedented development is a great blessing for the entire human community. It can
help us to connect with all life on earth and discover the spiritual
as universally present in the midst of life.

SPIRITUAL CONSUMERISM?

But widespread talk about spirituality has now taken on many
trappings of commercial market behavior. Even glossy magazines
and popular talk shows now refer to the latest spiritual fashions.
Spirituality is mentioned in the most unexpected, and sometimes
surprising, contexts, so that its meaning is more confused than
ever. What seems to some a regrettable fad or fringe interest rather
than a serious pursuit has even been branded as spiritual tourism,
on which millions of dollars are spent every year. The extensive
use of alternative, spiritual therapies, fashionable retreat centers,
or popular meditation courses seem to produce little noticeable
change in Western society. Writing in the British newspaper *The
Guardian*, the journalist Libby Brooks reflected on the kind of
questions such spiritual tourism provides answers to. She comments, "These new zealots no longer seek to explain how the universe was created or why war and famine happen. . . . The modern
spiritual preoccupation has shifted from securing a decent stan-
dard of life after death. The focus is on present peace of mind, but
of mind that comes with a hefty price tag." She rightly points out,
"But isn't there a danger of culling the benefits of spirituality without considering the attendant responsibilities? . . . You can't turn
belief on and off like a tap—it should weave itself through a whole
life rather than be seized upon to plug the gap." In the view of the
Princeton University sociologist Robert Wuthnow, such "spiritual
seeking draws criticism because it seems to reflect a shallow consumerist mentality. . . . The concern about such shopping is that

it is driven by a desire for easy answers and an unwillingness to devote hard work to spiritual growth."

A superficial consumerist approach takes away much of the vibrant aspects and depths of what spirituality is about. Similarly, a spirituality exclusively focused on personal concerns such as finding inner peace, one's true self, or a purpose in life—however valuable for an individual—can produce a rather escapist attitude. Perhaps Pope Benedict XVI is right in criticizing the excesses of contemporary individualism and relativism, if this is what spirituality achieves. If it is only about hedonism and personal happiness, or about individual belief systems suited to one's private tastes, then society is in for a downward ride and shock.

A truly holistic, integral spirituality must include both personal and social concerns; it must relate to burning global issues such as the search for justice, peace, nonviolence, and ecological harmony. Rightly understood, a socially aware spirituality will extend to civil society, to economics, business, management, and good governance. People and planet urgently need new participatory and collaborative structures based on worldwide dialogical consultations. Only then can radical social, political, and spiritual transformations emerge. Many signs for the emergence of such processes can already be observed, whether in the work of numerous non-governmental organizations, international aid and development charities, the annual meetings of the World Economic Forum (founded in 1971) in Davos, Switzerland, or those of the World Social Forum (founded in 2001) with its vision that "another world is possible."

PERSONAL SPIRITUALITY

Even a most secular setting, such as a shopping mall, may trigger unexpected experiences or thoughts that might eventually lead to a deeper, more reflective engagement with spirituality. To develop personal spirituality, spiritual nourishment is needed, and this may be obtained in completely unforeseen circumstances outside personal or institutional control. Each of us gathers such nourishment in different ways. Experiences of spiritual insight can occur anywhere, anytime, and can be very powerful and energizing, but also painful and disturbing. People come upon such experiences at the most unexpected moments, amidst their daily round of work, their joys and suffering, loss and grief. It might be when they are confronted with the greatness and beauty of nature, or among the hustle and bustle of cosmopolitan cities, where one encounters the incredible diversity of humankind.

Personally, I remember being deeply moved by some religious settings—the stillness of the great courtyard in the central mosque in the busiest part of Ahmedabad in India, the serene atmosphere of Buddhist temples in Sri Lanka or mainland China, the effervescence of a music festival in a South Indian temple, or the celebration of a Catholic Mass in one of the great European cathedrals. Many people are equally spiritually moved by secular settings, whether the experience of a pop concert on a grand scale, the energetic activities of a local market in Africa or Asia, or the euphoric atmosphere of a great international sports event. Like religion, spirituality comes in many forms that do not have to be separate or exclusive.

Robert Wuthnow's study of the creative spirituality of artists led him to conclude that "creating a satisfactory spiritual life involves taking responsibility for one's own relationship to the sacred. It requires focusing one's attention, learning the rules, mastering the craft, and deploying the imagination. It encourages us to confront the pain that arises from broken relationships and to register the wonder that comes from thinking about love and redemption. In these matters, artists have much to teach us all."

What is crucial in the development of all personal spirituality is the deepening of reflection and an honest attitude toward one-self—an authenticity that recognizes truth and acknowledges a reality greater than oneself. For the French philosopher Simone Weil (1909–1943), born into a Jewish family but much drawn to both Indian thought and Christianity, especially Catholicism, it was above all the cultivation of attention and waiting that are conducive to developing a deep personal spirituality. She wrote, "Attention, taken to its highest degree, is the same thing as prayer. It presupposes faith and love." Attention, whether in education, meditation, or prayer, requires the suspension of one's own self as the center of the world, making oneself available to another person, being open to another reality. For Weil this was the key to both prayer and to doing justice: "Waiting patiently in expectation is the foundation of the spiritual life." For her, there was a special way of waiting upon truth and setting our hearts on it, and one of her most famous works is called *Waiting for God*. She always remained outside the church and never joined any religious group, but her passionate spiritual and social engagement has influenced many other people, some of whom consider her a "patron saint of outsiders."

Simone Weil's reflections show that through mental and spiritual work all activities can be directed to the level of spirit. Her notion of attention bears a certain affinity with what Buddhists call mindfulness. As the Buddhist meditation master Thich Nhat Hanh has said, "Mindfulness is the miracle by which we can call back in a flash our dispersed mind and restore it to wholeness so that we can live each minute of life." Translated into a Christian context one might say that by practicing mindfulness in everything one does, by directing one's full attention to whatever work one is engaged in, all efforts can become a living prayer and be blessed. This is not unlike the motto of the Benedictines, *ora et labora*, "pray and work"—dedication and prayer expressed through work.

Understood in this integral manner, the rich life of the spirit that spirituality encompasses is fundamentally about becoming a person in the fullest sense. It means developing one's capacity for going out and beyond oneself, the capacity for transcending oneself. This ability makes possible all our understanding, pursuit of knowledge, experience of beauty, quest of the good, and the outreach of love toward the other, leading to responsibility and the creation of community.

SPIRITUALITY WITHOUT RELIGION?

An inclusive, all-embracing understanding of the spiritual raises the question whether religion and spirituality are entirely separate and independent of each other. With the privatization of religion in the modern Western world, a number of alternative spiritualities have developed that are completely autonomous and cut off from all religious institutions. The Dalai Lama once stated in an interview, "When I say spirituality, I am not thinking in terms of religious beliefs." This statement basically separates spirituality from religion but also hints at some connection. Today's spiritualities can be a mix of some traditional religious elements that are adapted, reinterpreted, and combined with a strong focus on the pressing environmental and ethical issues that affect the whole planet. And there are other forms of spirituality that are primarily concerned with the discovery and development of the personal self. Most of these are strongly influenced by current psychological knowledge and psychotherapeutic practices. Particularly these spiritualities of the self are now often seen as alternatives to religion. They are considered more healing and wholesome than hierarchical religious institutions that so often seem to reflect the shadow side of religion. It therefore comes as no surprise that some people argue vehemently for the complete independence of spirituality and postulate that it is something entirely distinct from institutional religion.

Seen from this perspective, spirituality can even be understood as a form of resistance to traditional religion. Some writers oppose spirituality and religion so strongly that they consider spirituality as connected with all spiritual orientations and practices *outside* religious institutions, whereas they see religion as what happens *inside* churches, temples, synagogues, mosques, and other religious institutions. By the time the editors of the *World Spirituality* volumes came to the end of their series, the growing influence of alternative forms of spirituality *outside* the traditional religions was acknowledged by including the titles *Modern Esoteric Spirituality* and *Spirituality and the Secular Quest*. The introduction to this last volume contains the indicative comment that "all religious life may be presumed spiritual. . . . Yet not everything spiritual must be religious; there are ways of understanding the world as a cosmic whole and the self as an enduring agent that are not directly indebted to religion." Without providing an uncritical celebration of the secular quest, this book deals explicitly with secular spirituality and is in part organized around the themes Self, Society, Nature, and Culture. It pointedly asks "what followers of established religious spiritualities might learn from their relatively more innovative secular counterparts," and encourages ongoing conversation between the two, so that a religious tradition may appropriate "aspects of what is most celebrated and powerful in secular culture."

These observations illuminate the mutual influence and interdependence of religious and secular forms of spirituality. This is a far more constructive approach than the view of those writers who sharply separate spirituality from religion, opposing them to each other. One must also be aware that far from being an entirely new creation, many modern secular spiritualities are derived from earlier Western and Eastern ideas rooted in ancient, medieval, or early modern sources. Yet these connections remain usually hidden and are rarely publicly acknowledged.

Contemporary secular spiritualities tend to be individualistic, even to the point of self-indulgence. They are widely eclectic but also widely inclusive in their quest for a more authentic life. The Australian writer David Tacey speaks about "a radical split" between spirituality and religion, where religious practice and religious feeling have parted company, so that "spirit" is no longer at home in religious traditions but has been divorced from its traditional "form." That is why he reflects on spirit "without" and "against" form as well as "form against spirit." In his view we are undergoing "a revolutionary crisis where religion and spirituality have changed places," so that spirituality "becomes the new higher authority and the arbiter of social identity and human interaction."

Tacey defines spirituality as referring "to our relationship with the sacredness of life, nature, and the universe," no longer confined to formal devotional practice or institutional places of worship. This is a new paradigm of an "all-inclusive spirituality" that is democratic and nonhierarchical, and thus very different from traditional forms of religious life. Religions have now "been downgraded to subsets of the broader category of spirituality," so that they have to reposition themselves.

In other words, religions are undergoing profound, even radical processes of reinterpretation and transformation, but that does not mean that they can be completely cut off from spirituality. Tacey's discussion is marked by paradox, since a "radical split" would produce a complete separation of religion and spirituality, whereas religions still possess a spiritual core. Although the relationship between spirituality and religion is now inverted, the two are still interrelated in many ways as long as religions are seen as subsets of spirituality.

In a somewhat nostalgic mode the Irish author Diarmuid Ó Murchú reflects on the early spirituality of the human race in prehistoric and early historic periods of human evolution. He speaks about the shift from spirituality to religion that, according to him, occurred with the emergence of religious traditions and the development of patriarchal forms of society. Today there exists a "desire for spirituality-beyond-religion" linked to a new vision of the world and of ourselves which brings forth a new spirituality, seen again as separate and above the established religions.

This picture is too simplistic and dualistic, however. It represents in many ways a backward projection of idealized notions of spirituality onto the past. But these cannot be empirically verified. Such generalizations about the relative importance assigned to spirituality and religion are often based on a rather unitary, ahistorical vision of a distant past that is unfavorably contrasted with the confusing malaise of the present. Yet the present also gives birth to new forms of spirituality that can be more exalted and very different from those of the past.

While challenging and stimulating, such controversial interpretations are of mainly theoretical interest. From a practical point of view the spiritual and religious cannot be separated and contrasted in such a clear-cut, definitive manner. A more conciliatory view is taken by another Australian scholar, Mary N. McDonald, who writes that the "discourses of religion and spirituality represent different, but often overlapping, understandings of self and world." Yet this statement leaves out any reference to an ultimate reality, depth dimension, or divine person, which most religious people would also look for.

Spirituality is now thoroughly pluralized, yet it is doubtful whether it can be seen as entirely, and permanently, divorced from religion. Historically and structurally, in terms of its myriad varieties, spirituality does not function like this. The Dutch psychotherapist Agneta Schreurs considers religion with its teachings and public worship "of enormous significance in nurturing spirituality so that it grows and develops ideally in a healthy and balanced way." She has coined the intriguing expression "spirituality in exile" in order to characterize contemporary spiritualities that flourish without religion. This expression indicates that spiritualities have moved to the margin of religious institutions and exist at their periphery, far removed from the center that religion once occupied in people's lives.

But maybe this is going too far the other way, since this view does not acknowledge the importance of autonomous, alternative forms of spirituality now being nurtured *without* the help of traditional religious institutions, nor does it allow for the innovative work of new religious groups with their radically transformed spiritualities *within* that are emerging all over the world. It is perhaps most important not to separate religion and spirituality too sharply from each other. Their relationship is dialectic and dynamic; they react and respond to each other in their mutual transformations. Tacey uses the excellent metaphor of the "exploding core of spirit," now acting like volcanic irruptions that will free spirituality from its former confinement, and thus transform the entire religious landscape. The impact will be massive. But we must not forget that the religions themselves are also caught up in an immense maelstrom of transformation. To make sense of the world and give guidance to their numerous followers, religions must also make sense of themselves and their own changing situation. For millennia, the ideals and practices of spirituality have been nurtured by the world's religions. While spiritualities have now gained a more autonomous place in people's lives and can exist independently from traditional religious institutions, religion and spirituality are two influential areas of human experience that still remain closely intertwined for hundreds of millions of believers around the globe. But without doubt the understanding of spirituality has radically changed in the West under the impact of modernity, and traditional religion has lost much of its historic authority, so that secular forms of spirituality have grown in unexpected ways, from the onset of modernity to the current wave of postmodernism.

SECULAR SPIRITUALITIES AND CONTEMPORARY CULTURE

The prevailing individualism of modern Western society expresses itself in ever so many ways, from education to politics, popular culture, the media, individual lifestyles, the breakdown of personal relationships, and an excessive celebrity culture. This individualism has been described as the experience of a "homeless mind," fragmented, open to experimentation and eclecticism, celebrating diversity and difference. The existence of such a mind is part of the extraordinary decenteredness and fluid movement of radical change that characterizes what is widely called the postmodernism of our contemporary world. But, like spirituality, postmodernism is difficult to define. As an intellectual and cultural movement it includes the loss of stable meanings and the recognition of diversity; it calls into question the nature of rationality and objectivity, and challenges the use of instrumental reasoning that has so dominated modern science and technology.

In comparison to earlier periods, modernity is perhaps the most one-dimensional culture in human history, and the least open to transcendence that the world has known. It is marked by great spiritual poverty and much alienation. The American sociologist Peter Berger has described the modern world as a culture with no windows on the wonders of life; yet at the same time we are so fascinated by the ever greater "wonders" that scientific research discloses about life's epic history. What a paradox!

It is true that many people no longer possess the sense of a transcendent horizon, nor have easy access to the depth dimension and interiority of human consciousness. Modern psychology, especially depth psychology, is exploring the recesses of our conscious and unconscious mind ever further, yet we seem to have lost a sense of the soul, a sense of the spiritual nature and destiny of the human being.

The postmodern condition of secular society has been likened to both a carnival and a wasteland. Such metaphors aptly capture the sense of spiritual aridity and disorientation, but also the experimental nature of much that is happening. Our image-soaked and information-drenched society can be experienced as a total spiritual wasteland. But its haunting emptiness and superficiality, its frequent lack of substance and depth, is not always totally wasteful, for it also carries fertile soil for new growth. Many contemporaries, bereft of traditional identities, experience the world as a wilderness where firm ground seems lost, and no well-trodden paths can be trusted. Yet this experience opens them up to the possibility of search and experiment, to look for a spirituality less defined and closed, more dynamic and open-ended.

Postmodernism is associated with much fragmentation and experimentation, but also with the idea of creative transformation. Many innovative experiments in art, politics, and literature have unfolded, but also many new explorations into spirituality. In fact, the growing interest in spirituality is very much a hallmark of postmodern consciousness and culture, which provide a new context for *both* traditional religious faiths and new spiritualities. In a world broken into so many fragments, we perceive the "shadow of spirit" with new eyes that can discover many spiritual pointers in our contemporary secular culture.

By now, a considerable number of secular spiritualities have emerged. While these have not necessarily been formulated in opposition to traditional religions, they remain distinct and separate from them. Some are genuine alternatives to religiously rooted spiritualities, whereas others may complement, enrich, or renew traditional religious practices. Some people claim to be spiritual without acknowledging doctrinal or institutional commitments to any of the historical religions. This is not an entirely new development, since noninstitutional strands of spirituality existed in the past, in ancient philosophy for example. However, what is now called secular spirituality is clearly a formation of late modernity and modern secular society.

One can thus speak of a genuinely secular spiritual quest. Here traditional religious and philosophical explanations of the world and the meaning of human life are replaced by powerful new stories that present new conceptions of the self and the cosmos not directly indebted to religion. Instead of the traditional cosmologies and anthropologies, these new narratives are inspired by current understandings of art, nature, science, and the sensibilities of the contemporary world. Alternative secular spiritualities can thus be closely linked to literature and poetry, the performing arts, especially popular music, or certain philosophical stances and social philosophies (even Marxism and spirituality have been found joined together). They also play an important role among adherents of widely supported global movements who campaign on behalf of human rights, women, the environment, or peace and justice issues.

SPIRITUAL RENAISSANCE, REVIVAL, OR REVOLUTION?

Are we then experiencing a new birth and renewal of spirituality? Many spiritual traditions are being rediscovered and newly explored, such as indigenous tribal beliefs, shamanism, Celtic spirituality, or Goddess spiritualities. Yet how far do such "discoveries" indicate a genuine search for a new spiritual vision and an authentic spiritual life? Could the world be on the verge of a spiritual renaissance, as some maintain?

But what do we understand by "renaissance"? The French word *naissance* means "birth," and a *re-naissance* means a birth that occurs once again. Thus it is often understood as a revival, something which existed once before in the past, was then diminished or lost, but is now coming back again. This definition is problematic when applied to contemporary spirituality, for it implies a much too past-oriented concept, often tied to an essentialist understanding of a *philosophia perennis*. Such a "perennial philosophy" tends to consider past spiritual attainments and practices as much greater than present ones. The past is idealized as a golden age when humans were spiritually more perfect, more at peace. This view presupposes that the nature of spirituality is unchanging and remains always the same, rather than being a process that develops and grows dynamically, so that new and fuller forms of spirituality emerge over time.

If the word "renaissance" is, by contrast, more associated with the idea of a renewed interest rather than simply a revival of the past, then it can be understood as not only a renewal of past spiritualities, but also as a new birth where something distinctly original is appearing, with its own life, potential and promise, whose future course cannot be predicted with certainty, although various possibilities can be envisaged. Thus one can speak of "emerging spiritualities" linked to an emergent present and future. This perspective is not an essentialist one, but dynamic and evolving, connected to organic growth and change, to the evolution of life and the world as well as to the powerful flow of time and history. It acknowledges the profound transformation of human consciousness that now reflects on itself in an expanding, growing spiritual awareness tied into the much larger flow and web of life.

There are many signs that we are spiritually progressing, not regressing—that a new spiritual birth is occurring in our contemporary world, which is a new world based on new experience, new vision, and the perception of a new global community. It is a universal, ecological, and mystical spirituality deeply linked to the perception of nature, of the world as a whole, and our place in it. And while this is a new development in human history, its roots are very ancient and go back to the depths of the birth of life and thought. Thus there is both continuity and discontinuity, a renaissance *and* a new breakthrough.

This is a renaissance in the sense of both renewal and new birth. David Tacey goes further still by calling the newly emerging trends a "spirituality revolution," a spontaneous movement in society rising from below, and thus vulnerable to commercial exploitation. This significant new interest in the reality of spirituality is truly existential, and has healing effects on life, health, community, and well-being. Tacey's wide-ranging study, *The Spirituality Revolution: The Emergence of Contemporary Spirituality*, admirably catches the dynamism and vitality of spiritual experimentation among Western and Australian youth, but it does not relate to traditional spiritual practices rooted in specific religious traditions.

From a Western perspective one can easily make the mistake of interpreting the spontaneous new spirituality movements in our highly secularized societies as a revolution. Yet this revolution remains relatively regional—indeed, is it not an exception rather than the rule? The majority of the world's people still belong to religious rather than secular cultures, where this revolution has not yet arrived. Affirming a "spirituality revolution" with such confidence betrays an overly Western-centered position that does not apply globally. Nor is the dominant public behavior of Western individuals, institutions, and nations known to reflect a high ethos and spirituality in its dealings with the rest of the world. Nevertheless, the need for meaning, for a greater awareness of the spiritual nature and oneness of humanity and the universe, exists all over the globe.

Searching for the meaning of spirituality does not produce easy answers. However fascinating contemporary debates about spirituality are, we need to look beyond them at different spiritual ideals and practices to deepen our understanding of spirituality as lived experience in today's world.

Two

SPIRITUALITY AS IDEAL AND PRACTICE

In its most general sense spirituality can be understood as a dynamic method for reaching a particular spiritual goal. Sometimes described as a quest, a search for enlightenment and nirvana, for the Absolute, or for union with God, spirituality is linked to visions of freedom and transcendence, ultimate goodness, beauty and truth, but also to communal hopes of human unity, harmony, and peace. Although spirituality and religion are now often seen as unrelated, this has not always been so. And even today religions still provide impressive spiritual resources and teachings for countless people in the world. Their great spiritual visions and ideals still respond to deep longings of the human heart, although this is less the case in the largely secularized, urban West than elsewhere in the world.

SPIRIT AND SPIRITUALITY

Much talk about spirituality tends to be subjective and individualistic. Inspirational and visionary at best, it often lacks critical discernment and reflection on wider social and global issues. The French Jesuit, palaeontologist, philosopher, and Christian mystic, Pierre Teilhard de Chardin (1881–1955), had a deep interest in the practice of spirituality in the contemporary world. He spoke of the need to study the phenomenon of spirit within the evolution of life just as systematically and critically as all other phenomena in the world. He discussed this in his large study *The Human Phenomenon*, but also in an essay on "The Phenomenon of Spirituality," where he wrote, "Besides the phenomena of heat, light and the rest studied by physics, there is, just as real and *natural*, the *phenomenon of spirit*. . . . The phenomenon of spirit has rightly attracted human attention more than any other. We are coincidental with it. We feel it from within. It is the very thread of which the other phenomena are woven for us. It is the thing we know best in the world since we are itself, and it is for us everything."

Yet in spite of this fundamental givenness of spirit in human experience we do not yet seem to possess an adequate understanding of its nature. For some, spirit seems so small and frail that it becomes accidental and secondary, in fact negligible, when compared to the vast material energies of the universe and the natural world that can be weighed and measured. This empirical-materialist worldview stands in strong contrast to other, more spiritualist-idealist perspectives for which spirit is something so special that it cannot possibly be compared and equated with earthly and material forces. There is a world of souls and a world of bodies, and they remain far apart. This strongly dualistic view of matter and spirit is still often held today and is even present in many religious teachings.

Such dualism has to be revealed for what it is, said Teilhard, since such an implicit opposition of spirit and matter cannot lead to the holistic, integral spirituality that the world needs most today. Instead of opposing spirit to matter, and either belittling or overexalting the place of spirit in the world, he described it as *the* central phenomenon, *the* central strand interwoven with evolution at all levels. In his reading, the whole process of evolution is a continuously expanding movement of spiritual growth. Taken as a whole, the dimensions of spirit "are the dimensions of the universe itself," and "the phenomenon of the spirit is coextensive with the very evolution of the earth." The true name for spirit is "spiritualization," a dynamic process linked to an increasing interiorization, to the growth of consciousness in its movement from the unconscious to the conscious, from the conscious to the self-conscious, leading to a "cosmic *change of state*," to which he gave the name *noogenesis*. This word refers to the birth of mind and spirit, leading eventually to the appearance of the *noosphere*, a growing new layer covering the entire planet, rooted in and emerging out of the biosphere, the planetary layer of life.

Teilhard used the ancient Greek word *nous* for the sphere of mind and spirit, an intuitive spiritual faculty that is able to transcend and integrate multiple realities into a vision of unity. The noosphere is a sphere of human interthinking and interaction, but also a sphere of growing spirit and spiritualization. Teilhard perceived a process of transformation that will bring the universe from the material to the spiritual state. His views were motivated by the passionate concern for a new understanding of spirituality in a vast and fast-changing world. The hypothesis of a cosmos "in spiritual transformation" explained to him most satisfactorily all the features of the world around us. Further proof for this theory, he thought, can be obtained from the experience of mystics and other spiritual seekers who have been strongly attracted to "the phenomenon of spirit" through the ages.

Teilhard de Chardin tried to develop a concrete, practical

spirituality nourished by the experience of the earth and its peoples, rooted in nature, body, and community. The transformative power of spirituality can operate at all levels: it can transform our work, our thoughts, our prayer, our society, our world—the whole planet. The center of spirituality must be animated by the dynamics of love, the only energy capable of transforming the world in the radical way that is now needed if people and planet are to flourish. He criticized the traditional concept of love as too static, too undeveloped in its full possibilities. Love, too, must undergo a change of state and be transformed from a primarily spiritual understanding to practical involvement with world and matter, with the pains of birth, with people's wounds and suffering, their dreams and desires, activities and passivities.

The growth of the noosphere is closely related to the rise and expansion of consciousness, but at its center and heart lies the radically transforming power of spirituality where the source of all energy resides in the fire of love and union. This fire is burning most vividly in the life of mystics and saints, the great spiritual exemplars we meet in so many different religions. Rightly understood, the mystic is the true animator of the world, leading it on the path to spiritual transformation. We can see this in the lives of countless mystics—to name just a few at random: Rabia and Rumi in Islam; Hildegard of Bingen, Teresa of Avila, Meister Eckhart, and Thomas Merton in Christianity; Mirabai and Ramakrishna in Hinduism; the Buddha and so many of his followers, like Thich Nhat Hanh and the Dalai Lama today.

The growth of the noosphere as a progressively expanding sphere of spiritualization, a sphere of growing bonds of love among humanity, is an immensely attractive and energizing vision. But can such a spirituality be taught as an ideal? Can it be lived and put into practice?

SPIRITUALITY AS AN IDEAL

From a historical point of view, different spiritualities are originally expressions of different religious ideals that have grown out of different religious experiences. Their descriptions and concrete embodiment vary greatly from one culture to another. We only have to think of the different ways in which Buddhist ideals of monasticism are expressed in Thailand or Sri Lanka when compared with those of Japan, where monks can marry and follow quite different practices in Zen monasteries and temples. We can reflect on what asceticism means for a Hindu yogi when compared with a Christian monk. Or we can ask what Buddhist nuns have in common with Christian nuns, or whether absolute reality is thought of in human form, and if so, whether this form is visualized as either female or male, or is represented by both genders?

A person of religious faith may consider spirituality as part of the history of divine-human interaction or the experience of transcendence. Spiritual experiences and ideals can be seen as a breakthrough of the spirit into history, a piercing through beyond history into another realm or way of being. The multiform cultural expressions of spirituality are resonant with the longings of the human spirit for the permanent, eternal, everlasting—for wholeness, peace, joy, and bliss. These ideals have haunted human beings throughout history. They have fueled their deepest desires and called them to heroic efforts to transcend the limitations of ordinary human life, seeking to reach extraordinary levels of consciousness, interiority, and intensity of experience enlightened by the fire of spirit.

Each religion and culture has developed a great wealth of different spiritual disciplines and schools, often produced by ascetic and monastic groups, or by especially devout religious individuals. Over the centuries, many different spiritualities have come into existence, and like all things human, they are subject to change and renewal. This means that past and present spiritualities are not the same, not even in the same religion. Today, much past spirituality has come to be questioned because it was created by social, cultural, intellectual, and religious elites who alone possessed the necessary leisure and means for cultivating mind and spirit.

Strikingly, across the different religions of the world two main models of spirituality can be discerned, in spite of all other differences. First, there is the ascetic or monastic model of renunciation spirituality. This is related to physical separation from society at large, the abandonment of worldly goods, and the renouncing of any sexual activity. Followers of this model either live alone or form new communities, as in Buddhist and Christian monasticism. The second model is that of "householder spirituality," for want of a better name. Here asceticism is less dominant, since spiritual growth and perfection are not sought through cutting all ties with the world, but through continuing to live as an ordinary householder, as most people do by getting married, raising a family, and pursuing their daily round of work. Outwardly the householder differs little from other people, but inner attitudes and outer actions are transformed by the adherence to spiritual teachings and disciplines that can be practiced in such a setting. Spiritual striving is combined with looking after day-to-day duties, family life, and the responsibilities of one's work. It is such a more socially involved and ethically engaged "spirituality of living in the world" that seems most needed today.

In Buddhism, Jainism, and Hinduism, the idea of the world-renouncer as model of spiritual perfection is paramount, although parallel examples of householder spirituality also exist. But they are not as highly valued as complete renunciation from the world. Sikhism, Judaism, and Islam, by contrast, focus mostly on the householder model of spirituality and have not developed extreme forms of asceticism or monastic forms of life. Christianity also knows both models, but during most of Christian history the main place for seeking holiness and spiritual perfection was the monastery and cloister, where countless men and women pursued the spiritual life by joining separate religious communities. The history of Christian asceticism and monasticism goes back to early Christianity, but Western monasticism first really took off in a big way with the monastic foundations of St. Benedict in the sixth century.

During the Protestant Reformation in the sixteenth century, many European monasteries and convents were destroyed. The emphasis now shifted from the cloistered life to life in the world, from the celibate to the married state. This gave rise to new spiritual experiments—new forms of spirituality and new religious groups emerged, who pursued different spiritual ideals through their work in society. Among Catholics this led to a new understanding and reformulation of spiritual aims. It also brought about new religious orders that were more world-oriented, beginning with the Jesuit order and the Institute of the Blessed Virgin Mary, founded by Mary Ward in the seventeenth century on the model of the Jesuits. In the following centuries numerous congregations of religious brothers and sisters came into existence in the West which were devoted to an active life in the world, serving in education, nursing, medical care, or missions in faraway places.

Until the late twentieth century the practice of spirituality was mostly taught by different Christian churches, denominations, and sects, whether they possessed special religious communities or not. It is only in relatively recent times that the search for spirituality has openly moved from the religious into the wider secular realm, although certain precursors of this trend first emerged after the beginning of the so-called Enlightenment in Europe. However, this trend has now been greatly accelerated through the fast contemporary means of communication.

The desire for spiritual transformation is deeply rooted in the human psyche, yet the ideals of spiritual perfection, and the paths to reach them, vary widely among different religions. Human beings may long to be united with the Divine or seek union with God as their Beloved; they may strive for oneness with an Absolute, or with what Hindus call Brahman. They may hope to find salvation or liberation, or long to live in paradise. But whatever the ultimate spiritual goals, their understanding depends largely on the teachings and philosophical thinking of a particular religious tradition. Much debate exists about what these goals are and what their true significance is, and also whether they can already be reached in this life or only in another life to come. However, traditional spiritual goals may appear as too otherworldly to many people today whose spiritual aspirations find a more concrete expression in working for human development, the abolition of poverty and violence, the implementation of human rights and dignity, and respect for the integrity of the natural environment.

SPIRITUALITY AS PRACTICE

From a practical point of view, spirituality can be understood as "wisdom for living," as a practice rooted in and growing out of deeply transformative insights linked to particular physical, mental, and spiritual disciplines that have shaped the lives of individuals and communities through millennia. The attainment of concrete spiritual ideals has always been closely connected with philosophical and religious teachings, with beliefs and rituals that have nurtured human beings on their life's journey through the world.

Is that any different today? Do we need a new approach because so many people are unaware of traditional spiritual teachings and have never had an opportunity to learn about them? Or are new approaches to spirituality urgently required because of our fast-changing living conditions and the pressing problems of our global world?

Spiritual practice means following a particular path, often likened to a journey along a special way or a particular discipline under the guidance of a teacher, led by a set of rules and teachings. Jews speak of religious norms as *halakhah*, "the way to go," and the early Christians described Christ's teachings as "the way." For the ancient Chinese, ultimate reality itself was named *Tao* or "the way," whereas Hindus speak of three paths to liberation, those of action or work (*karma*), devotion or worship (*bhakti*), knowledge or meditation (*jnana*). All religions know of particular spiritual disciplines, some to be followed by individuals, others by whole communities, to put particular spiritual ideals into practice and reach specific spiritual goals. Prayer, meditation, religious rituals, the celebration of particular life cycle events such as birth and death, initiation, marriage, the taking of vows, the joining of a religious community, confession of sins, the blessings bestowed during particular events—all of these, when consciously chosen rather than merely practiced out of habit, express a particular spiritual orientation and can become an occasion for spiritual renewal. But spirituality is about more than particular spiritual disciplines and practices. If understood in an inclusive, integral sense, spirituality must affect both personal and social transformation in all spheres of life.

The English author and spiritual director Evelyn Underhill (1875–1941), one of the most distinguished twentieth-century writers on mysticism and spirituality, gave four radio talks on "The Spiritual Life" in 1936 in which she made it quite clear that spirituality is not exclusively tied to religion, but belongs to all of life. According to Underhill, the spiritual life is not "an intense form of other-worldliness" but rather "the heart of all real religion and therefore of vital concern to ordinary men and women." It is "not a peculiar or extreme form of piety" but, on the contrary, it is "that full and real life for which humanity is made." She understood this so realistically that she could even argue that "the prevalent notion that spirituality and politics have nothing to do with one another is the exact opposite of the truth. Once it is accepted in a realistic sense, the spiritual life has everything to do with politics. It means that certain convictions about God and the world become the moral and spiritual imperatives of our life, and this must be decisive for the way we choose to behave about that bit of the world over which we have been given a limited control."

No plainer statement could be made to express that spirituality is not an end in itself, but rather a means for transforming ourselves and the world. It is connected with our life at every level and affects our relationship with everything else. The inclusive definition of spirituality as an exploration of what is involved in *becoming* human is helpful here since it remains completely neutral as to the place of religion in the practice of spirituality.

Spirituality has also been described as an attempt to grow in sensitivity to self, to others, to nonhuman creation, and to God. Such an understanding brings religion into view, to some extent at least, since it mentions God. It seems helpful, though, to realize that by being born and growing up into adulthood we are human, yet that there is still much more to the fullness of *being* human than this biological, psychological, and mental maturation process. To help human beings on their life's journey toward maturity, to a plenitude of life in the widest sense, spiritual goals and ideals of perfection have been recommended by countless seers, philosophers, religious founders, and counselors through the ages. But are they appropriate for today?

The essential, most urgent question for twenty-first-century humanity seems to be whether appropriate spiritual paths and practices can be found to help us solve some of the great spiritual challenges of the present time. We cannot simply follow the old, long-laid trails of the past, since they are bound to be insufficient for guiding us to new goals. Who is there to guide us across some of the new, uncharted territory of our world and the chasms of our lives?

SPIRITUAL GUIDANCE

In the traditional settings of the past, spiritual guides and teachers existed to provide guidance with authority, nurtured by wisdom and experience. The spiritual guide, guru, shaman, or director is a very ancient figure who in one form or another is found in most religious traditions and cultures. The spiritual preceptor has walked the spiritual path before and knows its stages. Such a person, whether of special charisma, saintliness, or unusual experience, an ordained figure or a layperson, helps and advises others, and can assess what progress disciples are making in their spiritual life.

Judaism knows the rabbi as teacher, whereas in Islam the role of the spiritual guide is taken up by the *shaykh* or *pir* who guides his followers on the Sufi mystic path. Buddhism knows the figure of the spiritual guide as "good and virtuous friend" (*kalyana mitra*) in Theravada Buddhism, as *lama* in Tibetan Buddhism, as *roshi* in Zen Buddhism. Yet perhaps nowhere is the figure of the spiritual teacher more important than in Hinduism where it has existed ever since the ancient times of the Upanishads. In fact, the figure of the *guru* is so central in Hinduism that the term "guru" has been transferred to teachers of other religions and to masters of other areas of expertise, such as singing, dancing, and other skills. In the modern West, we now even speak of "lifestyle gurus" in a completely secular sense.

In the Upanishads, the guru is a person who has reached the highest state of spiritual realization, and who is able to lead other people to the same goal. Hinduism knows a particularly close relationship between the guru and the disciple whose spiritual growth is dependent on the complete surrender to the teacher. Starting with Swami Vivekananda in the late nineteenth century, Hindu gurus began missionizing in the West, and many became well-known figures in North America, Europe, and other parts of the world. During the second part of the twentieth century Maharishi Mahesh Yogi preached Transcendental Meditation, A. C. Bhaktivedanta Swami Prabhupada founded the International Society of Krishna Consciousness, better known as the "Hare Krishna Movement," and the controversial spiritual teacher Bhagwan Shree Rajneesh, later called Osho, developed the influential Osho Movement with its new forms of active meditation and a large international following. Another remarkable development has been the emergence of female gurus in India in contrast to the past, when the teacher-disciple relationship was traditionally always handed down along exclusively male lines. In India today one can find quite a few influential women gurus, and some have become well known internationally, like "the mother of bliss" Anandamayi Ma, or Dadi Janki, one of the leaders of the Brahma Kumaris movement. Yet some famous Hindus do not have a guru at all; Gandhi had none but followed his inner voice.

Christians know the figure of the spiritual director, especially within a monastic and retreat context. In Orthodox Christianity spiritual guidance is provided by an elder, called *staretz*, a figure made widely known through its prominence in Dostoyevsky's novel *The Brothers Karamazov*. People following the "Christian way" have always considered Christ himself first and foremost as the supreme teacher. His life and teachings have provided the primary example, and "the imitation of Christ" has produced a rich harvest of devotional and spiritual literature in the Christian West and East, augmented by innumerable cultural expressions of spirituality in drama, music, and the visual arts. All of these have nourished Christian spirituality through many centuries, just as Hindus, Buddhists, Jews, Muslims, and members of other faiths have been sustained by theirs.

The religious and cultural examples of spiritual practices are legion. Yet again we must ask how far the rich diversity of these practices, the many teachers and teachings, can provide the right guidance today to develop life-enhancing spiritualities for personal and planetary transformation in a far more complex and interconnected world than any known in the past. Since the meteoric rise of psychoanalysis during the twentieth century many people seek guidance for their lives and find healing and integration through the help of professional psychoanalysts, therapists, and counselors. Have these to a large extent replaced traditional spiritual guidance, or is the pursuit of spirituality in search of the powers and energies of the spirit something quite different from exploring the depth of the individual psyche?

Who are the spiritual guides for today, the pathfinders of the spirit who can help us find our way through the spiritual maze of our lives and our world? There exist relatively few spiritual personalities whose visions are sufficiently large and inclusive to encompass both personal and planetary transformation; and in some ways it is easier to trace the influence of spirituality through the stages of an individual's life than as a force of change in our great collective institutions on the planet. But that will eventually have to come as well.

In the general introduction to his series of books on *World Spirituality*, Ewert Cousins speaks of spirituality as being concerned with the inner movements of the human spirit towards the real, the transcendent, the divine. Spirituality is wisdom and wise counsel that can help human beings follow a path, thus guiding their journey to spiritual realization. This is spirituality understood as experience, discipline, and practice. But today the word "spirituality" refers also to an academic discipline of critical study and reflection, a new field that has grown greatly over the last few decades. It analyzes and reflects on spiritual traditions and practices, but in turn can enrich these and take them to new levels.

SPIRITUALITY AS A SUBJECT OF STUDY

Since the late twentieth century spirituality has increasingly made its appearance in many areas of contemporary culture, whether it is simply being mentioned or taken more seriously. Examples are found in contemporary music, art, literature, education, sport, geography, economics, business, counseling, nursing, and health. At the same time a growing number of scholars have come to recognize spirituality as a serious subject of study which may be pursued within, and also independent from, the study of religion. Thus spirituality is a relatively recent, new interdisciplinary field that examines the history and practice of spiritualities in a wide range of traditions, cultures, and contexts. A wealth of publications has been produced in this field, from large historical surveys, reference works, and handbooks to detailed studies of particular spiritualities, spiritual experiences, and spiritual personalities in different religions and within the secular world.

In the past, spirituality was always closely connected in the West with theology, especially Christian theology. In fact, before the Second Vatican Council (1962–1965) the word "spirituality" was an almost exclusively Roman Catholic term describing "the practice of the interior life," as it was then called. But spirituality as a word and important topic of concern was then also gradually adopted by Protestantism, Judaism, and many other religions, and eventually also by various secular groups and movements.

This wide general usage of "spirituality" was accompanied by a shift in emphasis from earlier theological and historical approaches to a predominantly anthropological approach toward spirituality. This perspective emphasizes that the spiritual is a dimension within each human being, a potential that can and should be drawn out and developed in every person. It focuses on the human dimension of spirit rather than on a nonhuman or divine spirit. This represents a marked shift of emphasis when compared with traditional approaches to spirituality, whose primary focus was the One, God, and transcendence. This is as true of the philosophical approaches of Plato and Plotinus as it is of the theological and mystical approaches of Christian saints and theologians. Today the starting point is the question of how people can transcend themselves and fully actualize their spiritual nature. Spirituality thus refers primarily to a person's experience of transcendence, but the nature and dynamic of this transcendence remains undefined and is differently determined, depending on the different perspectives of one's worldview, religious faith, or secular beliefs.

Three distinct but interdependent understandings of spirituality have been developed in the contemporary study of this new field. First and foremost, there is spirituality as lived experience, whether in traditional religions, new religious movements, or in a secular context. This experiential ground provides the foundational context for all spirituality—the transformative experiences on which all subsequent reflections and teachings are based.

Second, there is a body of teachings, counsels, and particular practices that have grown over time out of these foundational spiritual experiences, and influence them in turn. The teachings on spiritual disciplines, counsels of perfection, rules of living, forms of behavior, or newly developed spiritual guidelines are systematically grouped together in writings that can be studied and handed down from one generation to the next. Here we can distinguish between the classic spiritualities of traditional religions, the newly emerging forms of contemporary spiritualities within existing religions, but also the new forms of spirituality that have developed as alternatives to religion.

A further, third level of understanding moves from the first (experience and practice) and second (spiritual disciplines and teachings) to spirituality as a focus for formal study. The systematic, comparative, and critical study of spiritual experiences and teachings has developed over recent years in quite new ways and is now carried out in different educational institutions, including universities, colleges, and schools in North America, in Europe, and in some parts of Asia and South America.

A human-centered, developmental approach to spirituality is also favored by some contemporary psychologists and psychotherapists who want to link psychology and spirituality in their interpretation of the human sense of self or wish to integrate a spiritual dimension into their therapeutic practice. The American psychotherapist Victor L. Schermer speaks about a new "psychospiritual paradigm." He argues that such a new integrative approach has become possible in the last twenty years through new perspectives in science, psychology, and medicine. Thus he approaches spirituality from a psychological rather than from a metaphysical or theological perspective, relating it to the context of an embodied, distinctly human psyche. Spirituality is not something added on to our life, emotions, instincts, but it is integral to the dynamic development of our psychospiritual self that seeks realization in life's journey. "It is our lives as lived that constitute our spirituality," Schermer says, and this approach also emphasizes the practical dimension of spirituality.

As the crying spiritual needs of many people are now more clearly diagnosed, the general interest in spirituality is growing, and the repercussions of spiritual attitudes on all parts of life are becoming more recognized. If spirituality is understood in a general sense as a "vision of the whole," it is obvious that most human beings are mostly not whole, but more often fragmented, wounded, broken. Since human beings as a species have not yet reached maturity and fullness, we continue to grow, expand, and yearn for greater being, more depth, or simply for "wholeness" and "plenitude."

A vision of the whole may be what has been called "the original vision" that some people seem to experience in childhood or youth. Others carry deep within an intuitive calling to go beyond the immediacy of ordinary daily life to find a deeper meaning, a greater task, an experience of love and union, of peace and happiness, of surrender and contentment. Philosophers and religious thinkers usually refer to this in a more general sense as the human search for transcendence that seems to be seeded into our consciousness as an integral, perennial element of the reflective awareness of being human.

In the past, spirituality has often been closely connected with institutionalized religion, but today this link is by no means self-evident. What spiritual insights and help can religion still give us, and where do we need to develop new paths that go far beyond past spiritual beliefs and practices? Traditional teachings, texts, and experiences need to be approached with a fair amount of suspicion and critical questioning, since their helpfulness for a vastly changed world with its new problems and opportunities can by no means be taken for granted.

What are the spiritual needs and resources of a global world? What can feed our zest for life and ensure the continuing flourishing of humans and the earth?

Three

SPIRITUALITY IN A GLOBAL WORLD

The traditional meaning of spirituality seems to be more linked to a personal sense of "soul" or "self" than to the needs of society or the whole earth community. Ideals of individual holiness, of a genuinely "spiritual" person, abound in the sacred writings of the world. Occasionally, though, we also catch glimpses of another vision, that of a transformed society. Hindus call this *dharmaraj*, the reign of righteousness, whereas Christians refer to it as *basileia* or the "kingdom of God." The longing for a more just and peaceful society, a more harmonious and redeemed world, runs very deep in human history and cultures. Among Muslims the notion of *ummah* refers to the community of all believers, but the Qur'an also contains the larger vision of the intrinsic unity of humanity as a single community.

Spiritual needs are basic to humans. Everyone has such needs, even when not clearly articulated. All human needs, whether physical, mental, psychical, or moral, are deeply intertwined with the spiritual, since anyone fully alive has to forge meaning out of the labors and trials of human existence. We all seek happiness and joy; we all recognize spiritual nourishment and elation. And each of us has to cope with pain, loss, suffering, and spiritual distress. The disappointments and unsatisfactoriness of human life for individuals and whole societies is something that everybody recognizes.

Yet beyond the spiritual awareness of particular individuals there also runs a deep spiritual search through many contemporary social movements. Often this remains a vague longing for something that cannot be clearly named or pointed to. The vast waves of migrants, the countless struggles for more freedom and just governments in so many countries, the drive for more education and participation in all aspects of community life, the desire for more health, more comfort, more human contact, more enjoyment—these are not all simply reducible to a "materialistic consumer culture." On the contrary, they can be read as signs of a vast tidal wave of human aspirations that hides secret hopes for a painful new birth of consciousness and spirit.

The present moment in human history is so critical in our development as a species within the larger web of life that a strong spiritual focus for radical change is urgently needed. The spiritual agony of the earth and its people is perhaps greater than ever before, calling on all our sensibilities and powers of attention. Already before the middle of the twentieth century the eminent Swiss psychologist Carl Gustav Jung (1875–1961) spoke of "modern man in search of a soul," whereas Pierre Teilhard de Chardin pointed to the task of finding "a common soul" for humanity. Both writers emphasized the need for personal *and* planetary spiritual transformation. Since they first expressed these ideas, humanity has become much more aware of the interconnectedness of *all* life, of human life with the whole of nature, with the earth itself, with cosmos and planet. Contemporary ecological consciousness relates to profound spiritual insights, to new religious experiences that can enhance and expand human life and its flourishing. But human beings need to listen to the voices of the earth and develop a full earth literacy to respond to this new situation.

Understood in its widest sense, spirituality can thus relate to several larger perspectives: our sense of the global and the earth; our experience of pluralism, especially religious pluralism; the urgent need to nurture human flourishing for all people at every level of human activity. This in turn is closely linked to the flourishing of all life on earth.

SENSE OF THE GLOBAL

We all live on one and the same planet—we form one humanity, however different and divided. As humans with a responsibility for our being and actions we share a common destiny in terms of life and death. We also carry responsibility for the future of *all* life on earth. In the history of our planet it is an appropriate moment to reflect on the transformative potential of spirituality for the entire human community. In spite of the great problems of our current geopolitical situation we can perceive the outlines of what several thinkers have called a "world civilization." The consciousness of one world, of the existence of globality as a new way of connecting and thinking, is growing every day. Equally growing is the awareness of the distinctiveness of local and regional conditions and cultures, but also the painful knowledge of the tremendous lack of peace, equality, and justice among the peoples of the earth.

The word "globalization" is widely used today. Yet it is often associated with mainly negative contexts, so that it is frequently opposed and contested. The process it describes is criticized for its excesses and negative effects, whether they are those of global market capitalism, of multinational corporations, industrial militarism, or excessive consumerism. Too often globalization is implicitly identified with economics and politics, whereas the social, cultural, and spiritual aspects of the globalization process have been less reflected upon, nor have they been sufficiently developed yet.

But the "consciousness of the global," of one planet, of one world, possesses many positive features. It can point to a greater sense of belonging together, a new global sense of responsibility and ethics, which tries to address global problems through concerted human effort and consensus, created by sharing the same intentions and spirit. This positive aspect is visible in the pioneering work undertaking by many non-governmental organizations (NGOs) such as Amnesty International or Doctors Without Borders/Médecins Sans Frontières. The multiple efforts to advance the recognition of human rights through the work of some of the United Nations agencies are also global in their outreach, just like the work of the Red Cross, the Red Crescent, and the newly founded Red Lotus, all of which provide emergency help in situations of natural disaster, conflict, and war.

The adjective "global" does not carry the same meaning as when we speak about "the whole *world*," as in world literature, world history, world economy, world geography, or world religion. "Global" can sometimes be identical with "world" in this sense, but more often it indicates another perspective, a new consciousness and different awareness altogether. It captures a new sense of oneness of the world and ourselves, the intimation of possible unity wherein our many differences come to be related to similar aims and orientations. As Ewert Cousins and others have pointed out, contemporary spirituality needs to be a "*global* spirituality"—global in the sense that it is both rooted in the earth, and connected to the diversity of peoples, cultures, and faiths around the globe.

The expression "global spirituality" is relatively new and can be understood in several ways. First, spirituality is not only of personal importance, but it now has great significance for the contemporary social and cultural realities of the whole globe; it is of vital concern for the flourishing of *all* of humanity, not just that of a select group of religiously-minded people for whom spirituality happens to be of special interest. Second, global spirituality does not only relate to the present state of our globe, but it extends into the past and reaches out toward the future to feed and strengthen the human spirit on its journey through time and space. Third, spirituality is becoming global in yet another sense: it is related to our rootedness in the earth.

Because of the critical stage of the world we live in we have to pay attention to the deep need for spiritual well-being beyond the existing physical, mental, and moral needs of humankind. This was already recognized in the 1960s by the Burmese U Thant (1909–1974), the third secretary-general of the United Nations, and also by the former assistant secretary-general Robert Muller from Alsace-Lorraine in France, who reflected in the early 1980s on the place of spirituality in secular society in his inspiring book *New Genesis: Shaping a Global Spirituality*.

Until now, global development has been understood as primarily economic and social. To care for all the future needs of people and planet, questions of ethics and spirituality will also have to be addressed. Will spiritual development one day become an integral part of our efforts to ensure global developments toward peace and justice? What initiatives are currently being devoted toward developing the inner resources of human beings, their power to love, care, be compassionate and collaborative, as well as peaceful and happy, within themselves and within their communities? These are serious questions at the level of global development. If people on our planet are to flourish, these questions cannot be solved by religious institutions or individuals alone. They have to be faced by the whole of society, including countless secular institutions.

SENSE OF THE EARTH

Human flourishing cannot occur without a balanced, harmonious relationship with all of life on earth, of which humans are an integral part. Personal spirituality has often been nourished by nature. Many writers and poets, scientists, and ordinary folk have been touched by the extraordinary power and beauty of it; they have sensed some kind of presence in nature, an intimation of the Divine or Spirit, or they have experienced a deep inner unity with it. But the contemporary experience of nature, or what we now call the biosphere (a word first coined in 1875 by the Austrian geologist Eduard Suess) is very much the experience of *one planet*, of the living world as a great, vulnerable habitat that is now threatened by many disasters and by much exploitative human behavior.

The general awareness of the history of the earth, the history of life, and of the vast, but immensely precarious biodiversity of our planet is much greater today than it has ever been before in spite of earlier celebrations of the abundance, awesomeness, and beauty of nature by philosophers, poets, and mystics. Much of this altered state of consciousness is due to new scientific research in the earth sciences and life sciences, and to the influence of the global environmental movement. At a popular level, documentary nature films, TV programs, and photography have also exercised an immense influence on our consciousness of one planet. The American religio-ecological thinker Thomas Berry hauntingly speaks of "The Dream of the Earth," whereas the British scientist James Lovelock refers to this oneness as the vision of Gaia.

Already in 1972, Indira Gandhi (1917–1984), then the prime minister of India, asked at a U.N. conference on the environment, "Will the growing awareness of 'one earth' and 'one environment' guide us to the concept of 'one humanity?' Will there be a more equitable sharing of environmental costs and greater interest in the accelerated progress of the less developed world?"

We are still living on the same earth, the same globe that our forebears inhabited. But our relationship to it, and our awareness of it, have changed profoundly during successive historical periods. Our technological means of communication in terms of worldwide information, contacts, networks, and travel exceed anything ever known in previous periods of history. The quantity of these links has created a crisscross-patterned web around the entire globe, which has had a profound qualitative effect on the nature of contemporary societies. These weblike connections can be used for good or ill. They have created many new opportunities and possibilities—hopes for better health and education, for more peace and justice, for less poverty and more sustainable development. But they are accompanied by an equally increased risk potential, the danger of negative developments, the possibility of ruin and destruction through more violence, war, poverty, injustice, and ecological disasters. All these issues raise enormous ethical problems and invite mature moral decisions that need to be worked out through consensus and collaboration.

The world is truly global in ways not experienced ever before. Planet Earth is a vulnerable habitat with an extraordinary richness of life that is precarious and most precious. Our consciousness of the world includes so much more knowledge about the immense evolutionary history of the universe. We recognize our earth as a life-bearing planet within a vast cosmic setting, and our own history as human species within the larger history of life. Earth is truly our home.

A NEW ECOLOGICAL CONSCIOUSNESS

At the present time, perhaps more than ever before, our planet exercises a numinous attraction on human beings everywhere. While much of modern culture threatens the stability, beauty, and integrity of the earth, the rise of ecology, the environmental sciences, and the search for sustainable development provide a creative new vision which may make it possible to counter, perhaps even reverse, some of the destructive human interventions in nature.

The word "ecology" was first coined in the nineteenth century by the biologist Ernst Haeckel (1834–1919), a German follower of Darwin. Haeckel described ecology in 1866 as "the body of knowledge concerning the economy of nature." He defined this as "the total relations of the animal to both its inorganic and organic environment." With the subsequent growth of this field several other definitions of ecology have been proposed, but it is still most generally understood as the study of the relationship of organisms to their environment. This includes the relationship of human beings to all life on the planet.

Embracing a vision of the earth as a whole is part of a new planetary consciousness. This includes seeking wholeness for the human community, living in harmony with nature, taking seriously our responsibility for the future well-being of planet Earth, and for the future of all people. These new perspectives run through many public debates, affecting the work of politicians, educators, artists, and writers worldwide.

The transformation of humanity's relationship to the earth has two different aspects. On one hand, human beings need to develop a greater spirit of caring for the earth; on the other hand, this spirit cannot develop fully without a change in human awareness of the connection with, and dependence on, the earth and its products. Contemporary spirituality is drawing great strength from this discovery of humanity's rootedness in the earth, and the awakening of a new sense of the cosmic.

Of great importance is the contemporary theory of Gaia first developed in 1979 by James Lovelock, which explains how the evolution of the earth and life form one single dynamic system that, as an organism, regulates itself on a global scale.

"Who is Gaia? What is she?" writes Lovelock in his latest work, *The Revenge of Gaia*. "The What is the thin spherical shell of land and water between the incandescent interior of the Earth and the upper atmosphere surrounding it. The Who is the interacting tissue of living organisms, which over four billion years has come to inhabit it. The combination of the What and the Who, and the way in which each continuously affects the other, has been well named 'Gaia' . . . a metaphor for the living Earth. The Greek goddess from whom the term is derived should be proud of the use to which her name has been put." While New Age followers were thrilled by the idea of Gaia, scientists at first distanced themselves but later supported it. At an international meeting in 2001, researchers from four global research programs issued a declaration that clearly stated, "The Earth system behaves as a single, self-regulating system, comprised of physical, chemical, biological and human components. The interactions and feedbacks between the component parts are complex and exhibit multi-scale temporal and spatial variability." Gaia is changing and is now under severe threat from the damage done by humans, which puts the self-regulation on which all life depends at risk.

The ancient worship of the Earth Goddess shows that approaching the earth as a living being is a widespread custom in the history of human religiousness. The contemporary Gaia theory raises many critical questions about the dominant anthropocentric focus of Western culture and the underlying Christian teaching on which this is based. In the light of our new understanding of the mutual relationship between all organisms and their environment, and the interconnections between all levels of life, human thinking must now change from an anthropocentric to a biocentric and ecocentric focus.

But the many global challenges can only be met if the earth community, as well as local and regional communities, will take on full responsibility for the present and future well-being of the human family. This has been clearly articulated in the important Earth Charter, first promulgated in 2000, after a decadelong consultation with numerous organizations, countries, and faith groups around the world. Its preamble states, "Our environmental, economic, political, social, and spiritual challenges are interconnected, and together we can forge inclusive solutions." The current *spiritual* challenges facing the world and ourselves are particularly important, but have been given far less attention until now than the other challenges.

But what kind of spirituality can truly meet the urgent needs and new opportunities of a global world? Many people have a deep yearning for greater peace and unity in the world, but the state of contemporary world politics and economics make this ideal seem far-fetched, if not impossible to achieve. "There are too many obstacles," the pessimist will shout; "human individuals and groups are too egoistic and will only seek their own gain and advantage." One of the great stumbling blocks may be the sheer diversity of peoples, cultures, and beliefs, the pluralism of ethnicities and identities, the opposing creeds and doctrines. How to cope with all this by promoting spirituality, and an ideal of oneness?

DIVERSITY AND RELIGIOUS PLURALISM

Yann Arthus-Bertrand's book of stunning aerial photographs, *The Earth from the Air*, has sold over one and a half million copies worldwide since it was first published in 1999. This extraordinary collection of visual images from around the world provides abundant visual evidence that planet Earth is not only immensely rich in natural, but also in cultural diversity. His pictures of vastly different places from all continents reflect the myriad ways in which humans have cultivated the earth, farmed the land, dammed rivers, built dwellings, formed communities, and created settlements.

Most of us are familiar with the famous image of our bluish-green planet floating suspended in space and surrounded by blackness, first made known by the amazing photograph of "Earthrise" over the lunar horizon, taken from Apollo 8 in December 1968.

Few sights in human history have been as exhilarating as the appearance of that first earthrise, a defining moment in humanity's collective psyche that has become a celebrated icon of our global world. This image of great simplicity and beauty can be seen as a symbolic expression of our evolution toward oneness and global awareness, an image of hope and inspiration, although it conceals the great ethnic, religious, and cultural diversities among humans, and the splendid varieties of species.

The biosphere provides us with a *biological* vision of oneness— the web of life—but human history, philosophy, and religion also know of the dream of a *cultural and social* oneness of humankind. This theme is very ancient, found in numerous creation stories and myths. The vision of a common belonging, of a shared origin and destiny, is also deeply enshrined in the teachings of different world faiths. In Christianity, for example, there exists the notion of the *oikoumene*, the whole inhabited world, an idea that the early Christians took over from the Greeks and Romans. The *oikoumene* expresses a belonging together, a common identity, beyond particular individuals and groups. Other faiths possess their own images and words pointing to this greater, underlying unity of humankind patterned by the flux of history and destiny. Numerous religious teachings speak about the inclusiveness of creation and salvation for all human beings, visions that are all-embracing and universal in their intentionality. Traditionally, religions have fostered wisdom and morality, have guided individuals and groups through life, and shaped entire civilizations. Yet their noble teachings on human unity, peace, and justice have shown few outward signs of real success, since religions' loftiest ideals have rarely been fully put into practice.

Today the general awareness of the religious visions of human *unity* is not as strong as the concrete experience of the *diversity* of faiths, the baffling situation of religious diversity with its ensuing tensions, misunderstandings, resistance, and violence. The unprecedented ethnic, social, cultural, and religious pluralism of the contemporary world certainly presents tremendous challenges, but it also provides great opportunities for mutual learning, help, growth, and enrichment. Instead of resisting this diversity or merely acknowledging it, one can ask about the religious and spiritual significance of such pluralism. What does the existence of religiously significant "others" reveal to us?

Some argue that we have reached a new point in time where we can discern a shared unity and common pattern in the religious history of humankind. A number of pioneering religious thinkers of the twentieth century have spoken about this, including Mohammed Iqbal (1876–1938) in Pakistan, Sri Aurobindo (1872–1950) in India, and Pierre Teilhard de Chardin (1881–1955), who spent much of his life in China. More and more people are beginning to recognize that, as an earth community, we are just as globally interdependent in spiritual matters as we are ecologically, economically, politically, and financially interdependent.

Also growing is the awareness that one humanity on one planet possesses a global spiritual heritage that can nurture all human beings. All religions have accumulated and handed down spiritual treasures from one generation to the next, precious insights and moments of revelation that have nourished, sustained, and transformed the lives of countless people past and present. We possess so many different wells of inspiration from which we can drink to still our spiritual thirst and hunger. But to acknowledge this in practice also requires the recognition of our profound diversities and otherness, the deep wounds we have inflicted on each other. There exists not only an extraordinary pluralism between our different religious and cultural traditions, but also within each of our own communities. It takes courage and humility to acknowledge and respect this diversity by treating it as a rich spiritual resource rather than a reason for competition, opposition or, worse, attack and rejection.

To develop the positive resources of religious diversity requires a genuine de-monopolization of every single religion. This means the refusal to act in an imperialistic and triumphantly exclusive manner towards religions other than one's own or, rather, towards religious people outside one's own community, however large or small. If we are open and perceptive, we can recognize an irreplaceable spiritual heritage in each religious tradition, a specific message and distinctive identity. Each faith provides a powerful matrix for ultimate meaning which can help in the shaping of meaningful lives and, ultimately, in the creation of a truly global community. There is incompleteness in each of the religious traditions; none is static or perfect. All are continually in the process of changing and being transformed—there is room and need for further growth in all of them.

It has become fashionable today to reflect on "the other" and the "othering" of people and cultures as an alienating, discriminating process. But an encounter with the other can also be a source of surprise, enrichment, and joy. We find many insights about the other as stranger, enemy, visitor, neighbor, or guest in both the Hebrew and Christian Bible, in Buddhist and Hindu stories, in religious teachings on compassion, mercy, and kindness. At all times and in all places people have dealt with others; they have accepted or rebuked, loved or hated, oppressed or liberated others. We now know how essential our relationships to others are for a healthy human development towards maturity, and we need significant others for our own development. We truly need the other, *many* others. This includes today the need for each others' faiths and worldviews. Thus we must wrestle with the question of how to account for and deal with differences constructively rather than divisively, whether they are religious, cultural, sexual, or political differences.

At the present moment in human history and global politics, when we are desperately in need of greater cooperation and mutual understanding, there is a special urgency to ask ourselves what we can learn from each other—how we can use the multiple resources of different faiths for the good of the human community rather than its violation and destruction. This is a profoundly religious and spiritual vision that can energize individuals and groups into action to create a better world and greater well-being for more people on Earth.

FLOURISHING AND SPIRITUAL ENERGY RESOURCES

Ideas of wellness and well-being attract wide attention today, especially in relation to people's health, bodies, personal satisfaction, happiness, and contentment. The fullness and enjoyment of life that these words encompass are summed up by the wonderful idea of "flourishing." The original associations of this word can be traced back to flowers, gardens, and growth. It is therefore a very ecological concept, primarily relational and not individualistic. It can be related to the whole web of life.

The *Concise Oxford English Dictionary* connects the expression "to flourish" with other words such as "grow vigorously; thrive; prosper; be successful; be in one's prime; be active." These indicate that flourishing is a very desirable process intimately connected with what others call "the zest for life." It is a dynamism and drive, a continuing source of energy which nurtures people's attitudes, motivation, and activity. It means we are fully alive and embrace life with all its ups and downs, its sources of satisfaction as well as suffering. This very positive concept of flourishing is immensely attractive as it implies that we can go from strength to strength, even when the going may get difficult at times.

Flourishing relates well to a spirituality that is holistic, one that is more concerned with the quality of life as a whole rather than only with certain aspects of life. In order to flourish individually as a person, good relations with others have to be nurtured, and the right external conditions must pertain. People cannot flourish at times of war, strife, and dissent. The idea of human flourishing can be associated with all stages of human life—with being born, with the very gift of life itself, with the growth of youth, with the declining years of aging, and even with death. Flourishing is therefore an ideal concept to be linked with the unfolding of human life, and with the spiritual potential of every stage of life.

Humans cannot live a healthy, satisfactory life if they don't eat the right food, breathe clean air, drink clean water, and have the right education. So much poverty and starvation around the world are linked to these basic human necessities, so directly dependent on our most immediate environment. Human flourishing is not possible without other forms of flourishing, especially environmental and biological, but it also extends to economic, political, and social flourishing.

Our zest for life and the flourishing of our body, mind, and spirit are fed by many different energy resources. Most of these are considered material, but we also need mental and moral resources as well as spiritual ones. We cannot live without this zest; we cannot advance the world without it. We need to love life, live it to the full, and contribute to its growth. Teilhard de Chardin described the zest for life as "nothing less than the *energy of universal evolution*" but, at the human level, the feeding and development of this energy "is to some degree *our responsibility*."

But how can this be done? Where do we find the necessary resources for this "feeding and development" of the zest for life in the global community today, when we are faced with so many different groups and nations, with opposing political interests and powers, clashing beliefs and mutually exclusive identities? To build a common future for humanity presents a tremendous task, perhaps greater than any ever met before in the history of humankind.

To feed the zest for life and advance human flourishing around the entire world must be considered a priority for spirituality. To activate human creative energy for shaping a better world is ultimately a spiritual task that requires tremendous spiritual energy resources. The greatest challenge ahead is the conscious, collaborative organization of human energy for the greater good of all, and for the growth and fuller disclosure of spirit.

In other words, spirituality is no longer a luxury of life, of mere interest to religious minorities or mystics, but it now appears as an absolute imperative for human sanity and survival. Spirituality is essential to all human flourishing, wherever we live, whether in religious or secular surroundings. The growth of discussions about spirituality, whether in conversation, in print, or on the web, of spiritual practices, teachers, retreat houses, and numerous organizations offering a spiritual vision for today's world, is accelerating so fast that it is difficult to navigate through this maze of information with critical discernment. How to distinguish between fast food and substantial nourishment of the spirit? How to interpret so many very diverse phenomena?

We all need to learn a new language of the spirit to ensure the future flourishing of people *and* planet. New reflections on spirituality, new spiritual explorations, experiments, and practices, are found not only among the young, but across all age groups. They are linked to interreligious dialogue; human development; education, health, and gender debates; as well as to new thinking among scientists and artists. Fresh ideas on spirituality have emerged in all these areas—ideas, themes, and practical experiments that often run in parallel, though independently from each other. Sometimes these parallel streams converge; at other times they diverge or even run against each other, but they all bear witness to the extraordinary creativity and power of the human spirit.

Four

SPIRITUALITY AND INTERFAITH DIALOGUE

Encounter and dialogue are fundamental to human life. To speak and be spoken to, ask questions and receive answers, share experiences and ideas, is an integral part of being human. In this sense dialogue is as old as humanity itself, a basic ingredient of all social fabric and activities. In a more specific sense dialogue among different religious believers has developed as *interreligious* or *interfaith* dialogue. This can happen in quite a spontaneous way, in ordinary day-to-day meetings of people from different backgrounds who encounter each other at work, through travel or leisure activities, through their children or neighbors. Numerous experiences can bring people closer together to share their joys and pains, disclose some of their religious or spiritual worldviews, and reveal some of their deepest beliefs.

The contemporary awareness of diversity, whether ethnic, social, racial, or religious, is now so much greater than in the past because our world has shrunk so much; the forces of globalization have brought different societies, cultures, and religions so much closer into contact with each other. It can be confusing, even painful, to realize how profoundly different major religious and secular worldviews are, and what a myriad of different religions and spiritualities exist, whether in traditional, contemporary, or alternative forms. What is the deeper meaning of the extraordinary diversity of religious beliefs and spiritualities in the contemporary world? Only through ongoing conversations can we find the answer to this question. Since the late twentieth century interreligious dialogue has come to be more widely practiced and accepted, and that includes dialogue between different spiritualities.

THE NEED FOR DIALOGUE

There is much talk about dialogue between civilizations and cultures, but such dialogue must include dialogue between religions at the heart of cultures. It can no longer be a question whether dialogue between different religious, secular, and spiritual worldviews is possible, because it is absolutely necessary if humankind is to achieve greater peace and justice. There exists now a "dialogical imperative" to promote dialogue above all else—among cultures and civilizations, among religious and secular people, among women and men, among rich and poor—not least to avoid the growth of more violence and hatred and to redeem the shadow side of our different religious histories. Only then can all of humankind develop new ways of living together and redeem the immense failings of the past in not living up to the spiritual truths of our core religious truths and visions.

To accept and work with each other requires the often difficult acceptance of profound differences. It also means practicing attentive listening to others, healing differences, and helping each other into mutually enriching growth. Dialogue is about listening to voices of difference, discovering different experiences, different ways of knowing, thinking, feeling, and acting. The human being has an inborn intentionality for communication and relationships, but how often is this potential actualized and really put into practice? We can rejoice in the fact that the possibilities of developing helpful relationships have grown exponentially in today's world, so that we can cultivate genuine, mutually enriching dialogue if we put our mind and will to it.

True dialogue is an art that has to be learned. It has to be nurtured at the grassroots level whenever possible. But the requirements for dialogue between people of different faiths go far beyond those of ordinary day-to-day conversation and human contact. Numerically speaking, the believers of different faiths who are actively engaged in the process of dialoguing are still relatively few. But there is no doubt that interfaith dialogue has grown considerably since the late twentieth century, and steadily continues to grow.

PARTNERSHIP IN DIALOGUE

The beginning of what is sometimes called the "interfaith movement" is often dated to 1893, the year when the first World's Parliament of Religions was held in Chicago. However, there is no exclusive single origin to modern interfaith dialogue, since its ideas developed quite independently and in parallel in several places at the same time. There were early pioneers in both America and Europe, and especially among Christian missionaries working in Asia. Interfaith organizations such as the pioneering World Congress of Faiths (WCF), founded in 1936 by Sir Francis Younghusband in London, and the Temple of Understanding (TOU), created by the American Juliet Hollister in 1960, have done sterling work in interfaith dialogue for a long time. The Temple of Understanding is now a recognized non-governmental organization in consultative status with the United Nations.

Officially, interfaith dialogue gained a new momentum among Christians when Roman Catholics launched new dialogue initiatives after the Second Vatican Council (1962–65), and the World Council of Churches created its special subunit on "Dialogue with People of Living Faiths and Ideologies" in 1971. Dialogue between members of different religions was started when Christians from several denominations met Hindus, Buddhists, and Muslims, especially in the Indian subcontinent, but today it is part of the official policy of many churches. In fact, it is now supported by small groups of believers in all the major religions. Interfaith networks are found around the globe, generating a new spirit and also new forms of interfaith spiritualities. The contemporary practice of dialogue is thus an event of great religious and spiritual significance, since it is an important seedbed for the growth of new forms of spirituality.

The end of Western colonial rule in world politics had a deep impact on Christian missions around the globe. Their former position of superiority gave way to new attitudes of openness and encounter, leading to the new context of an "equal partnership in dialogue." Interfaith dialogue, as understood and promoted today, is dependent on the process of globalization and on the understanding of *secularity* as a positive value—not secularism as a pervasive, militant ideology, but secularity as the necessary space for religious and political freedom, where religious and spiritual values can be explored without threat to one's integrity, one's job, or one's life. Dialogue is possible where human rights are respected, including the right to freedom of religion or belief. The full equality and mutuality of all partners in dialogue can only be achieved in an open, fully democratic society that accords equal rights to all religions.

Many religious groups now welcome dialogue, but they can foster it only through persuasion, not coercion. It is democracy in practice, at the grassroots level, that provides the spiritually-enabling context for fostering true exchange and mutually enriching dialogue. A number of more conservative and fundamentalist groups are actively opposed to such dialogical thinking and practice. Dialogue is always an ongoing process; it involves mutual discovering, living, studying, working, and worshiping as well as debating together, so that empathy continues to grow and mutual relations are strengthened. It requires a spirit of openness and trust, without any tacit schemes of conversion. This does not mean giving up the particularities of one's own faith, but partners in dialogue may nonetheless arrive at a certain "reconception" of their faith, perceived anew through encountering another faith in another individual or group.

The experience of dialogue has been described as "passing over" from one's own faith to another, then turning back and experiencing one's faith in a new light. Interfaith dialogue can thus lead participants to the existential realization that each faith has received valuable glimpses of a larger vision. It is in dialogue that we learn to complement each other's insights and disclosures of the transcendent or Divine. It is not about competition and exclusiveness, as so often preached by fundamentalists of all traditions, but about the complementarity of different visions that grow into greater fullness when related to each other.

Connecting different visions with each other can enlarge and enrich members of different faiths, without losing their own individual identities. It means accepting and respecting pluralism without falling into relativism. Such a nuanced attitude to cultural and religious pluralism can give access to deeper understanding and sharing, so that people may become more empowered to work together for a better world.

INTERFAITH DIALOGUE AND DOUBLE BELONGING

The art of dialogue needs to be cultivated in two different ways—as *interreligious* dialogue between members of different religions, and as *intra-religious* dialogue between different members of the same faith. There is also a need for dialogue *beyond* religious boundaries, between people of different faiths and those who hold nonreligious worldviews of secular culture and modern science.

We often hear about "world citizens" who feel at home in different countries and cultures, yet remain rooted in their own. In our global world we are not only in need of such world citizens, we also need "world believers" with deep roots in one faith, yet able to relate to faiths other than their own. Such an attitude of transcending religious boundaries has been characterized as "double religious belonging." Some wonder whether this is possible at all, or argue against it from a dogmatic faith position. But double belonging does exist. A good example are the multiple bonds that Japanese people have to different religious traditions. They may practice ancient Shinto beliefs at some time in their life, when celebrating a marriage for example, but turn to Buddhist rites at the time of death. Another example are African converts who combine some of their ancestral worship, or belief in witchcraft, with allegiance to Christianity or Islam. Other examples include individuals with a Western background who feel equally drawn to Christianity, or Judaism, and Buddhism, and who follow some practices of both traditions; Hindus who, besides worshiping their own gods and goddesses, also have a deep devotion to Jesus Christ; or Jews and Christians who are strongly attracted to some aspects of New Age religion without abandoning the central tenets of their own faith.

Double religious belonging can be spiritually sustaining and helpful for one's life, and is probably on the increase. To encourage double belonging and strengthen it further, the world needs more people who are *spiritually* multi-lingual and multi-focused. This is not arguing for relativism, but for true relationality between different faith perspectives and members of different faiths. In order to nurture such dialogue, it has to be asked how far religions remain closed systems or are open to outside influences. No genuine encounter can develop between systems that remain closed to each other. Yet a mere peaceful coexistence of religions, however noble, is no longer enough today. There must be a further evolution of religions themselves, in pursuit of their highest spiritual ideals, and in response to the world's greatest needs. The different religious traditions can only develop further through closer encounter, exchange, and genuine dialogue which, in any case, does not occur between systems as such, but happens between individuals and groups willing to meet with each other.

The profound changes of contemporary culture mean that people encounter each other more than ever before, in many different places, and through many different forms of communication. It also means that all religions are now faced with similar questions and problems. By searching for viable spiritualities in the contemporary world the different world faiths, each in their own way and all together, can make a significant spiritual contribution. Through dialogue and collaboration they can help solve some of the planet's pressing problems and enable more people to live a dignified human life. By speaking to the soul and uplifting the human spirit, they can point to a greater, transcendent vision, keeping open larger horizons within the midst and beyond the ordinariness of daily life.

SPIRITUAL SIGNIFICANCE OF
THE WORLD'S FAITHS

For many religious thinkers, whether Thomas Merton, Teilhard de Chardin, the Dalai Lama, Thich Nhat Hanh, or the theologian Hans Küng, it is abundantly clear that new relations are needed between the world's religions because of the new global context in which we live. The development of new relations between members of different faiths will affect individuals and communities in new ways and transform some of their heritage from the past. In Teilhard de Chardin's view, it is ultimately a particular kind of spirituality and mysticism that matters most. Without it, humanity cannot build a satisfactory future.

Teilhard reflected a great deal on the spiritual significance of world faiths, and the important contribution they make to human development. He considered a rightly understood spirituality as the very center of religion, but criticized any religion whose spirituality is only concerned with the individual. Instead he was advocating "a religion for humanity and the earth" in which some of the best insights of traditional faiths could be combined with a newborn faith in our world today.

Indeed, we cannot do without the cumulative wealth of religious experiences and visions around the globe; they are indispensable for what we call today a "global religious consciousness." The active currents of faiths are needed for feeding and maintaining humanity's zest for life. People of faith, people of prayer and spiritual practice, people who are seekers and pilgrims on the path of life, can meet, share, and walk together respecting each other's spiritual heritage and treasures. Thus we need to be aware of and respect the very diversity of faiths, but also acknowledge and heal the misunderstandings and pain we have inflicted on each other. We need to approach this diversity in a much larger framework that recognizes the different faith traditions as interconnected and belonging together. This can inspire and affirm a humanity that wants to understand itself as one.

The great faith traditions of the world are not isolated, fortified territories of an exclusive kind that have to be fought over and defended against each other. Historically, particular religions are often linked to particular lands and people, but at their deepest and best they transcend these limitations. They are genuine homes of the spirit, homes where our whole being can be nurtured and strengthened. If we do not look at religions exclusively from the outside, but discover their deeper spiritual core and vision, we come to realize that all the spiritual traditions together present an immensely rich, global heritage that belongs to all. The religions of the world are part of the human planetary inheritance, but also so much more—a rich revelation of an inexhaustible divine ocean of love, of compassion and mercy, and of the possibility of human dignity and wholeness beyond all brokenness and wounds. We can see that the ethical codes of different faiths can help us construct a "global ethic" for conflict resolution, for the overcoming of violence, poverty, and inequality, and for learning the art of peacemaking.

Many traditional Christians, especially Christian fundamentalists, are suspicious and skeptical about dialogue. With the presence of so many Eastern religions and new religious movements in our midst, some Western people retreat into an unnecessarily narrow, defensive position, almost fearing that we might be invaded by alien creeds. This is part of the fear of otherness that may at first appear as a barrier and stumbling block to dialogue. It is therefore essential to nurture openness that will seek deeper understanding and *acceptance* of the otherness around us—which includes the otherness of spiritual paths, practices, and goals.

What spirituality might then be created by interfaith dialogue? What is the contribution of interfaith encounter and dialogue to contemporary spirituality?

INTERFAITH SPIRITUALITY

Among the numerous forms of spirituality emerging at present, the practice of interfaith dialogue has led to particularly vibrant spiritual insights. This interfaith spirituality is often neither perceived nor mentioned by those who divide spirituality sharply from religion, or look at spirituality only from inside one religious tradition. The creative dynamic and new energy that are irrupting from the worldwide encounter of religions at so many different levels are often completely ignored in contemporary debates on spirituality. It thus remains far too little recognized except by those directly involved in practicing it.

Interfaith spirituality is a very recent development, though. We have only just begun to move *toward* this new form of spirituality. At present we can only discern its direction and dynamic, rather than have a complete picture of this newly emerging spiritual path forged by dialogical encounter.

Each of the world faiths possesses a rich spiritual heritage that is being discovered with renewed interest today. We not only have better access to the rich spiritual resources of Christianity, but also to those of Buddhism and Hinduism, Judaism and Islam, Daoism and Confucianism, not to forget African spirituality, as well as that of indigenous and native peoples, and of numerous new religious movements. The recognition of this diversity leads away from Western Christian dominance and exclusiveness in the articulation of spiritual matters. A spiritually significant international interfaith meeting, and a publicly highly visible act, was the interfaith prayer meeting in Assisi in 1986, when Pope John Paul II invited religious leaders from all over the world to pray together for peace. The only regrettable aspect was the complete absence of any female religious figures, as if spirituality were still the exclusive domain of men. At local and regional levels in different parts of the world, in interfaith meetings of different groups, there exists a more equitable gender balance. Sometimes women are even more active and visible in these local gatherings than men.

Besides actually meeting together, the general availability and access to each other's religious texts and sacred writings is of prime importance in developing a new interfaith spirituality. Given our multiple means of communication, we can now study the sacred sources of many different religious and cultural traditions. But these scriptures, sutras, and commentaries are not so much studied from an insider's perspective, where sacred writings are foundational for one's beliefs and lifestyle, than they are drawn upon as globally available spiritual resources that have become accessible to outsiders as well as insiders. Thus we can approach them as precious spiritual wells from which we can all drink and quench our thirst, and which will nourish a new, more holistic spirituality.

Spiritual experiences and practices that emerge within and outside of interreligious dialogue are still comparatively rare phenomena, although an ever-growing number of people are now experiencing the vital energy of these confluent streams of different spiritual traditions. Immersed in a new venture, they are exploring a "spirituality across borders"; they are discovering new paths through a deep personal engagement not only with their own faith, but also with that of others. Sharing other people's spiritual worlds and practices can lead to new experiences, but also to new questions and uncertainties.

The Sri Lankan theologian Wesley Ariarajah considers the development of "dialogue and spirituality" one of the pressing issues of interfaith relations. He probingly asks, "Can we pray together?" In other words, can people of different faiths and none come together for interfaith worship, for the sharing of spiritual practices drawn from different faiths? Although such coming together for prayer occurred at the highest level at the Assisi meeting, for example, it is at present still hotly debated and can provide a source for controversy and difficulties at the local level.

A new spirituality nourished by interfaith dialogue has perhaps been furthest developed in the dialogue between Christians and Buddhists. A wide variety of Buddhist teachings and practices, particularly the different forms of Buddhist meditation, have deeply influenced numerous Christians, and Hinduism, too, has exercised wide attraction.

PIONEERS OF INTERFAITH SPIRITUALITY

Several twentieth-century Christians have pioneered interfaith spirituality in their own lives. There are Swami Abhishiktananda (1910–1973), a French Benedictine monk who settled in India but undertook his spiritual experiments largely in isolation, and the well-known British Benedictine Bede Griffiths (1906–1993), who spent a large part of his life in the South Indian Shantivanam Ashram. There he practiced meditation, taught and wrote on different faiths, and acted as a guru to numerous Western followers who were drawn by his writings and example to his particular version of interfaith spirituality. Best known of all is perhaps the American Trappist Thomas Merton (1915–1968), who wrote profusely on spirituality, mysticism, and interfaith matters from his hermitage in Kentucky, but died tragically on his first visit to Asia. These three well-known figures are like spiritual beacons whose brilliant light has attracted many people to explore the spiritual depths of a faith other than their own.

Abhishiktananda's original name as a French Benedictine was Dom Henri le Saux (sometimes he is still called by this name). After having been a monk in France for nearly twenty years, he left his monastery for India in order to seek renunciation and follow the path of Indian Vedanta. Like numerous Indians, he eventually became a wandering holy man, a sannyasin. He took the saffron robe of Indian renouncers, and an Indian name—Swami Abhishiktananda ("Bliss of the Anointed One"). Later he also adopted Indian nationality, and never left India again. Deeply immersed in Advaitic spirituality, he was seeking the "One without a second." He considered it his special calling to express his dedication to Christ from within the depth of Hindu spirituality, a calling lived out in "the cave of the heart," as he used to say.

Together with another French priest, Father Monchanin, he

founded the Sacchidananda Ashram in South India, on the banks of the sacred river Kavery. This name combines Hindu terms for the Absolute, conceived as *Sat* (Being), *Cit* (Consciousness), and *Ananda* (Bliss). Later renamed Shantivanam Ashram (Forest of Peace), this ashram has exercised a worldwide influence on inter-faith dialogue and spirituality, especially since it became subse-quently associated with Dom Bede Griffiths. He attracted many Western, and also some Indian, disciples to his particular vision of "the marriage of East and West" that sought to combine the spir-itual insights of Hinduism and Christianity.

One of the most influential spiritual personalities of the twen-tieth century was Thomas Merton. His voice bears a powerful wit-ness to the continuing vitality of Christian spirituality in the modern world, while he was at the same time in dialogue with voices from the East. As a young man he had been a nonbeliever who wanted to become a writer, a career he eventually followed, but in a different way than originally envisaged. He became drawn to Catholicism, converted, and soon joined the Trappist monks at Our Lady of Gethsemani Abbey in Kentucky. There he lived the traditional life of a monk, was novice master for many years, and first established his reputation as a writer with his highly successful spiritual autobiography, *The Seven Storey Mountain*, published in 1948.Through his reading he became interested in Eastern reli-gions, especially Zen Buddhism, and reflected on this experience in his spiritual writings. Seeking new ways of combining insights from different faiths, he experimented for some time with living in a hermitage on the abbey grounds. Then he sought his abbot's permission to travel to the East, and eventually went there in 1968, met with the Dalai Lama and took part in an intermonastic dialogue meeting, but then had a fatal accident in Bangkok. His deep spiritual insights and powerful impressions of Asia—Sri Lanka, India, and Thailand—are recorded in his *Asian Journal*, which forms a powerful part of his spiritual legacy that continues to influence many people around the world in their search for a more integral interfaith spirituality.

Merton's papers, photographs, and paintings are preserved at the Thomas Merton Center at Bellarmine University in Louisville, Kentucky. The International Thomas Merton Society, founded in 1987, actively encourages the further diffusion of Merton's ideas through its conferences and publications. The Merton Institute for Contemplative Living, also situated in Louisville, works independently to provide easily accessible resources for people's spiritual journey through the works of Thomas Merton, and by promoting his vision of a just and peaceful world. It is remarkable that Merton's posthumous books, published between 1969 and the present, far outnumber those that appeared during his lifetime— an indication of his ever-growing influence.

Besides these three very well-known pioneers of interfaith spirituality among Western Christians, there are quite a few other spiritual teachers who exercise considerable influence and attract a large following, whether in Christianity or other faiths. Internationally outstanding among Buddhists and non-Buddhists alike is the Dalai Lama, who shows a great openness to the spiritual message of different faiths by encouraging his followers to learn from them without giving up their own faith. Another Buddhist who exercises great influence is the Vietnamese monk Thich Nhat Hanh, whose name means "One Action." Zen master, poet, and peace activist, he has lived for the past thirty years in exile in France, and has written numerous books teaching people how to live mindfully in the present moment and achieve relationships of love and understanding. In his *Living Buddha, Living Christ* (1995) he explores the contemplative traditions of Buddhism and Christianity with deep insight and compassion. He says, "When we see someone overflowing with love and understanding, someone who is keenly aware of what is going on, we know that they are very close to the Buddha and to Jesus Christ." His commitment to social action, and his projects for helping people, especially in Vietnam, made him develop what he called "engaged Buddhism." Thomas Merton knew of Thich Nhat Hanh's work and wrote of him that he "is more my brother than many who are nearer to me in race and nationality, because he and I see things exactly the same way."

In the interfaith encounter with Islam many Western individuals are particularly attracted to Sufism, the mystical strand in Islam that consists of a number of traditional nonmonastic orders that have exercised much social as well as spiritual influence on different parts of the faith. They give much importance to the individual's "oneness with God" achieved through meditation and other spiritual practices, which include music, poetry, ritual chanting, and dance. Several modern branches of Sufism were founded in the twentieth century, and some of these settled in the West. One is the Sufi Order International, whose best-known teacher was Pir Vilayat Inayat Khan (1916–2004). Like his father, Hazrat Inayat Khan (1882–1927), who founded the order in 1910, Pir Vilayat Inayat Khan had a great openness for other faiths and encouraged his followers to go on practicing their own religion, while also exploring Sufi mysticism.

These examples show that interfaith spirituality is being explored by influential individual teachers, and a growing number of their followers. But it is also encouraged and moved forward through certain organizational developments such as the revival of the Parliament of the World's Religions, newly begun in Chicago in 1993 to celebrate the centennial of the 1893 Parliament, followed by meetings in Cape Town (1999) and Barcelona (2004). These large gatherings of 7,000 to 9,000 individuals provide a unique opportunity for the meeting of people from different faiths, cultures, and nationalities. They lead to practical collaboration in many areas, but also contribute to the further growth of interfaith spirituality.

Interfaith dialogue and spirituality also play a central part in the dynamic organization of the United Religions Initiative (URI), founded as recently as 2000. Organized locally, regionally, and globally through Cooperation Circles, it has built up an effective communications- and knowledge-sharing network through which it seeks to promote "enduring, daily interfaith cooperation to end religiously motivated violence and to create cultures of peace, justice and healing for the Earth and all living beings," as is stated in the preamble of the URI charter. This is also URI's overall purpose, which sees itself not as a new religion, but as building bridges between different religions, and seeking and offering cooperation with other interfaith efforts. Its many practical aims require a spiritual outlook and orientation, and the realization of these aims will in turn lead to a more engaged interfaith spirituality.

Such an ethos appeals to many people who seek a spirituality drawn from more than one religious tradition and transcending narrow denominational boundaries, while others feel genuinely threatened by it, since it may also lead to loss of certainty and of firmly established identities. Yet from a spiritual point of view this can be acknowledged as a good thing, since it encourages humility, searching questions, fresh insights, and new growth.

A large amount of spiritual advice has been gathered out of such interfaith experiences. This is a rather fluid body of knowledge that is informally transmitted through reading, discussion, teaching, small retreats, or gatherings. A growing number of Western Christians have explored in some depth what they can learn from the spiritualities of Eastern religions, whether those of India, China, or Japan. The writings of the Sri Lankan Jesuit Aloysius Pieris, grounded in the Christian experience of Buddhism, have exercised a wide influence, as have those of the Spanish-Indian Raimon Panikkar, who is more oriented toward Hindu spirituality. The teachings of Zen Buddhism are very attractive to many Christians, as are the spiritual practices of Tibetan Buddhism. Catholic monks and nuns, especially those from the Benedictine order, but also Cistercians and Trappists, are deeply involved with the pioneering Intermonastic Dialogue between East and West. This fosters a sharing of monastic life, with Benedictine monks and nuns staying in Japanese Zen or Tibetan monasteries in India. Likewise Japanese and Tibetan monks have come to stay in Western monasteries to share the daily life and spiritual practices of monks and nuns in the West, whether in the United States, England, Scotland, France, or Germany.

These examples indicate the richness and diversity of intercultural and interfaith encounters between East and West. A historical in-depth study of such encounters since the late nineteenth century would reveal many more women and men from different faiths who were deeply immersed in another faith.

Interfaith spirituality arises out of different forms of encounter and dialogue, whether those of a shared life, joint action, theological reflection, or religious experience. Individuals and groups engaged in interfaith spirituality share the experience of relating to something greater than themselves. They learn to create bridges across their distinct differences through the gift of love and compassion, and work together for a common purpose. Such in-depth encounter succeeds only if participants possess openness and humility, a willingness to listen, learn, and change, an element of patience and attentiveness, and genuine respect for the integrity of the other. There is a shared sense of discovery and celebration, although at times dialogue partners can also experience gulfs of misunderstanding, a deep sense of hurt and pain, a frustrating feeling of incompleteness, with only fragmentary glimpses of a greater wholeness dimly apprehended and fervently longed for.

A NEW INTERSPIRITUAL AGE

A refreshing challenge to the understanding of interfaith spirituality is provided by the Indian theologian Samuel Rayan. He describes spirituality as linked to "openness" and "response-ability." By response-ability he does not mean accountability, but rather the ability to *respond* to the many different dimensions of reality, to different things, events, and people. This includes the ability to respond to the realities of other faiths, to their spiritual horizons and insights. We have to cultivate a deep inner awareness to develop such openness. Only then can we discover the mysteries, meanings, and revelatory moments of other faiths. In all of them the power of the Spirit breaks through again and again, transforming the continuing stream of our historical brokenness and becoming.

In Rayan's view, the "more open we are, the more spiritual" we are. "The more realities to which we are open, the greater the spirituality; the greater the depths and the profounder the meanings of reality to which we are open, the more authentic the spirituality." The interfaith approach to spirituality is itself very open—open to new experiments and experiences, open to learning and listening, open to the promise of the future and to greater growth. Rayan's perspective is a very fruitful definition of spirituality, since it highlights spirituality as a dynamic process full of further potential.

Encountering people of other faiths and getting seriously engaged in interfaith dialogue opens up a magnificent opportunity to take spiritual otherness seriously. Interfaith dialogue reveals not only the pluralism of cultures and faiths, but the pluralism of spiritualities themselves. That can be a difficult but also strengthening, deeply enriching, and transforming discovery. It opens up new lands of mind and soul, and can reveal the gracious traces and touches of the Spirit in ever so many unexpected ways.

The American Catholic lay monk Brother Wayne Teasdale (1945–2004), who was initiated by Bede Griffiths in India and actively participated in interfaith dialogue for many years, spoke of a new "interspiritual age" in relation to discovering a universal spirituality in the world's religions. He promoted this idea of "interspirituality" since the 1993 Chicago Parliament of the World's Religions, and understood it as the sharing of ultimate experiences across traditions. He described interspirituality as "the assimilation of insights, values, and spiritual practices from the various religions and their application to one's own inner life and development." This is very much an encounter at the level of religious experience, especially mystical experience, which is an invaluable resource for transforming human awareness and for purifying human will and intention.

Yet it is not enough on its own, for it can be misunderstood as too exclusively focused on the individual. To develop spirituality globally, radically transforming changes have to occur at the level of the individual, but they also have to be worked out at a structural level by changing our educational, economic, political, and financial institutions. In Teilhard de Chardin's view we not only need interfaith dialogue, but also a new mysticism, above all a new mysticism of action that can transform the world. On closer examination this seems also part of the "universal communal spirituality" which Wayne Teasdale describes in his book *The Mystic Heart*. It is a spirituality that can emerge when people from different faith traditions discover the mystic heart of the world together, and share their deepest spiritual experiences and visions.

The spiritual probing of religious pluralism and the drinking from each other's spiritual wells may be today's great spiritual event, full of significance for human well-being, and for the future of humanity on earth. The further evolution of religion and spirituality can occur only if more dialogical thinking is developed in practice. If religious and spiritual leaders were less concerned with positions of power and influence, and more attentive to the spiritual well-being of their members, and if ordinary believers followed the spiritual message at the heart of their tradition, then the world might become a different place where all human beings could truly flourish. Alas, we are still a long way from realizing this vision, and much work remains to be done to develop a genuine interfaith spirituality that can inspire a harmonious personal and social life in our global world.

More and more people are beginning to recognize slowly that interfaith dialogue is the spiritual journey of our time, out of which a new spirituality will be born. Teasdale described the characteristic features of such a spirituality as contemplative, interspiritual and intermystical, socially engaged, environmentally responsible, holistic, engaged with a wide range of cultural media, cosmically open, and aiming for an integration of the spiritual journey with the natural world, and an openness to the cosmic community. This is an impressive list but, as Teasdale himself recognized, it will require institutions and structures to carry, express, and support the creation of a new interspiritual age. He mentioned the Catholic Church as one matrix of interfaith encounter, but also proposed a "universal order of sannyasa" or renunciation, and emphasized the important role of the spiritual teacher or guide. The universal order of sannyasa is understood as an interspiritual order of monastics or contemplatives open to people from all faiths or none, who are united in their desire to seek a deeper, more meaningful life. This spiritually pluralistic orientation is shared by the new Interfaith Seminary with locations in both New York and London. It has been set up to train interfaith ministers and spiritual counselors to serve the spiritual needs of people from all backgrounds, whether religious or secular.

Interfaith perspectives are growing. There is not only much talk and reflection about interfaith spirituality, interfaith pilgrims, and an interfaith seminary, but even of an interreligious ashram for monastics, founded in 2003 near Rishikesh in the Himalayas with the help of the Abhishiktananda Society. Dialogue among people of different faiths can help to open up and transform religious traditions. It can bring about a spiritual renewal. But it is important to recognize that creative dialogue about spirituality is not and cannot remain restricted to people of religious adherence. It must embrace the secular world to make a difference to all the peoples of this planet. There are signs that this already occurs with much vigor in many areas of contemporary culture. This is evident from current debates on human development, psychology, education, health, and many other aspects of the arts, humanities, and sciences. It is within these secular fields that many people now seek and find solace, inspiration, and wisdom for living.

Five

SPIRITUALITY WITHIN LIFE'S DANCE

The search for spirituality is often understood as an inner journey or personal quest. This universal theme is found in religious and mythical tales all over the world. Yet several other metaphors can be used. Spirituality has also been likened to wrestling, struggling, or even dancing. The evolution of matter and life encourages us to imagine the dynamic movement of spirituality in many new ways. We can perceive it as part of the rhythmic pattern of the cosmic dance of energy and life in the universe, and also as the dance of life within us. Our life in the world is an expression of the cosmic dance, animated by the life-giving breath of the Spirit. Thomas Merton wrote of "the joy of the cosmic dance which is always there. Indeed, we are in the midst of it and it is in the midst of us, for it beats in our very blood, whether we want it or not."

Comparing the image of a journey with that of a dance, one can think of solitary journeys, but also others undertaken with a companion or friend, or even with a larger group of people. But many journeys are made alone. And a dance can be solitary, too. Yet it is more likely that a dance occurs with two, three, or more people joining. A dance is usually accompanied by music, whose changing beats and rhythms make a dance more dynamic than an ordinary journey. While we dance, we also touch each other closely. We enjoy the sheer presence of another person, grow closer physically and emotionally, feel the sense of energy, delight, and fun that accompany the exuberance of dancing. Thus it seems an appropriate metaphor to speak about the dance of life that involves body, mind, and soul—our whole being. And life's dance is always interwoven with the dance of the Spirit.

The largest setting for life's dance is the vast web of life, the continuously ongoing process of universal becoming. We are part of the immense rhythm of being born and dying, integral to the evolutionary history of the cosmos itself. Usually we tend to see this rhythm of life rather individualistically, yet our personal life can greatly expand in meaning when it is understood as part of this larger, universal pattern.

The English writer Michael Mayne has used the dance image for spirituality in his book *Learning to Dance*. He shows with much sensitivity how spiritual analogies can be drawn from the dance of the bees to the dance of the cosmos, from nature, genetics, the arts, to human actions of love and forgiveness. He even speaks of the creative dance of language, which he sees as witnessing "to the godlikeness of the human spirit." Maria Harris, an American writer, uses the same dance analogy in her book *Dance of the Spirit*, where she explains the dynamic development of spirituality through the moving steps of a dance. She sees spirituality inclusively related to all of life, as when she writes that "initially spirituality is seeing. This means not just looking, but *seeing* what is actually there, seeing into and entering the deep places and centers of things. . . . Our spirituality begins with our cultivating the inner eye that sees everything as capable of being . . . saturated with God."

Spirituality as part of our deepest inwardness and innermost being is closely interwoven with our awareness, sensibility, and capacity for reflection. Human yearning and will are involved in fostering and nurturing it; the deepest search for human identity, self-understanding, and transcendence is at stake here. Yet the enlivening, dynamic presence and power of the Spirit are ultimately not of our own choosing. They are graciously bestowed on us as many seers, saints, and mystics have personally testified. Thus spirituality is both a tremendous task and a gracious gift.

There is the cosmic dance, and the dance of nature, but also the closely intertwined dance of the human and divine Spirit based on mutual indwelling, likeness, and loving attraction. Since the human spirit is embodied and earthed, spirituality must be grounded both in the experience of the body and in contemporary earth-consciousness. Yet spirituality is also drawing us to ever-larger worlds beyond ourselves, beyond the horizons of the known. The invitation to join the cosmic dance is deeply alluring, but it is not without risks and trials. Life's dance can be a whirlwind, and dancing with the Spirit can mean walking through an all-transforming fire.

SPIRITUALITY AND EMBODIMENT

We cannot imagine any dance without the full involvement of our body and senses, the use of physical gestures and movements of our limbs. Anyone who has ever watched the dancing Sufi dervishes from Turkey will have felt deep within themselves the sheer sense of abandonment expressed through the frenetic rhythms of their ecstatic mystical gyrations, performed for the divine Beloved. Their dancing expresses the perfect union of spirit and body, of devotion and physical action, a celebration of life that transcends death. The sacred use and spiritual meaning of dance was known among ancient peoples around the world and is still practiced in a number of non-Western cultures, especially in Asia and Africa. Several Hindu temple cults and folk religions also make extensive use of sacred dance. Best known of the temple dances is probably the South Indian *Bharat Natyam* dance, now widely practiced in secular dramatic settings. Equally famous is the Sun Dance of the hunting peoples of the Great Plains of North America, or the religious dancing of the Shakers. Even today, Hasidic Jews communicate with God through ecstatic dancing designed to create a mystical state. Congregational dancing in worship is also used by some Christian groups, but on the whole, attitudes to religious dance have been rather restrained among Christians. The Puritans, for example, were strongly opposed to the use of any dance.

The joys and pains of being human are so deeply connected with our physical existence and bodiliness that we need to reflect explicitly on the matter-body-flesh reality we indeed are. Religious thinkers have often ignored this aspect of human nature in preference to abstract, disembodied thinking that separates mind, soul, and spirit from the physical aspects of the body, especially from human sexuality. So many religious and philosophical teachings seem to imply a radical separation of the body from our sense of the self; so many ascetic practices reflect a profound dis-ease with our physical embodiment. Yet spiritual energy flows through our body and limbs. It affects our whole being in the world, since spiritual life is fundamentally relational, and that includes an intrinsic relationship between body and spirit. We are above all *embodied selves*. Some prefer to speak simply of a "bodied self" (rather than "embodied"), an expression that tries to counter the mistaken view that our mind and psyche exist within a separate corporeal container. We live as an integral unity patterned by body and selfhood which can be distinguished, but not disentangled and separated.

Religions have often disdained the physical body for its

blemishes and weaknesses, for imprisoning us and leading us astray. It is not only the Christian idea of human "fallenness" connected with the teachings of so-called original sin that comes to mind here. Derogatory views of the body can be found in most religions, especially among the teachings of ascetics, which have often been especially anti–women's bodies. This is as evident from the writings of the Christian church fathers as it is from numerous statements in the Buddhist sutras. The human body is ambiguous as an experience and sign—it is both lived and imagined. It serves as a symbol in religious and social life, for the human body is used as a metaphor for the larger social and cosmic body. We live, think, and experience *through* our bodies, and religious beliefs are *embodied* through religious practices. The body can assume very different meanings in different religious and cultural contexts, yet our embodiedness expresses simultaneously our individual particularity and our common human condition.

The twentieth century experienced a strong return to the body, a greater recognition of its existence, an affirmation of its needs and desires, its central role in all experiences of human intimacy, friendship, and love. It is through our body that we first develop a sense of a separate self and a sense of the world. It is through our body that we are located in space and time. We also understand much better today how infinitely diverse the human body is in its individual expressions, and how culturally variable the meanings given to the body are. The body is thus of central significance for human identity, self-understanding, and self-transcendence, but also for the experience of human vulnerability, frailty, and finitude. The dignity of the human body is enhanced when we connect it with the body of the earth, the whole world body, especially when this world is seen as "God's body," as the creation of a divine spirit and power.

From a past neglect of the body, contemporary society has now become obsessed with the body, with our flesh and bones, our sheer physicality, its form, image, and representation. Nowhere is this more evident than in the current emphasis on global sports that involve the relentless training and top performance of numerous bodies. There is also the tyrannical imposition of socially prescribed, physical norms of beauty, the obsession with one's body image, with regimens of diet and physical health, and the excessive bodily display in wide areas of public life. But does this mean we are liberated from an earlier disdain and rejection of the physical, that we love and appreciate the body, that we have achieved a harmonious balance between body, mind, and spirit?

On the contrary, none of these contemporary fashions guarantee a healthy attitude to the human body. In fact, many of their manifestations lack an integral, balanced attitude that honors the body as an expression of spirit. The human body is also always a gendered body, since sexuality is constitutive of our selfhood. In the changing climate of modern thought, sexuality and eroticism have played an ever-larger public role, so that people are often proud of the sexual liberation that has occurred. Sexuality as an integral human trait is important for spiritual growth, but few writers on spirituality have deeply reflected on the connection between sexuality and spirituality. How far human sexual activities translate into radical love, true intimacy, and real spiritual growth requires much further reflection. Sexual relations and eroticism, so highly praised in modern Western culture, can often mask an egoistic and self-seeking attitude. Yet sexuality too can become a path for spiritual transformation.

A healthy, balanced spirituality must be related to the diverse forms of human embodiment. Only a spiritually aware attitude can give human bodiliness its true meaning and respect, including all the dimensions of our sexuality. It is not even entirely satisfactory to speak of "embodiment," since this word could be understood as if our spirit was encased within flesh and blood, muscles and nerves, and everything else that is part of the physio-chemistry and biology of our body. Instead, the human body is an *ensouled* body, an entirely living thing, vibrating with energy and spirit. Following the philosopher Edmund Husserl, the German mystic Edith Stein (1891–1942) spoke of the "lived body" (called *Leib* in German) to distinguish it from the mere material body (*Körper* in German). It is this lived, ensouled body that is of great significance for understanding and practicing a holistic spirituality.

This ensouled body, however, still remains a profound miracle and mystery that we do not yet fully comprehend, in spite of all scientific knowledge, including the X-rays and MRI scans that can now be taken of it. In the contemporary secular world, it is perhaps only in certain forms of psychosomatic and holistic medicine, and in some movements of psychotherapy and psychology, that the mysterious link between our body, mind, and spirit is more fully acknowledged and taken into account.

A contemporary publisher's catalogue contains the statement, "At the outset of the twenty-first century people are faced with a spiritual dilemma, where neither secularism nor religion seem adequate. . . . A mature form of spirituality will be the hallmark of future years." But what is a truly mature form of spirituality? Connected with human growth and development, such a spirituality can emerge only over time; it cannot be an unchanging, static ideal that is the same for all people and remains identical throughout one's life. The anthropological approach to spirituality understands this as a complex process wherein the psychological and spiritual developments of a human person are closely interrelated. It is not surprising that much contemporary discussion on spirituality occurs more frequently in the literature on psychology, psychotherapy, gerontology, or in publications for the caring and nursing professions, than in traditional books on religion. People who work with practical problems of life—whether these are education, health, aging, birth, or death—experience the concrete spiritual needs of others in very specific circumstances, whereas traditional religious

writers tend to think of spirituality in more general, abstract terms ᵕ
without relating it to life as lived. Often the most helpful approach
to spirituality is pragmatic rather than prescriptive: how and why
spirituality works, what it does for people, how it can help them in
different contexts and at different stages in their life. Different professions place quite different emphases on spirituality in relation to
the human life cycle, as experienced by different individuals at particular moments in their lives.

SPIRITUALITY, BIRTH, AND CHILDHOOD

The foundational human experience of being born is associated
with myths, symbols, and rituals in all religions of the world.
Human birth is not merely a biological life-event, but displays a
natural sacrality, a spiritual dimension reflected in the countless
celebrations and religious observances that surround it. Many
religions also know of a symbolic second birth, often considered
the "real" birth brought about by initiation, baptism, or later conversion in adult life. The philosopher Hannah Arendt (1906–
1975) captured the miracle of being born in a newly coined word,
"natality." This points to the new beginning, opportunities,
chances, and hopes that arise with the arrival of each human
being. Birth is a new, exuberant affirmation, a sign of hope and
renewal for humanity. Birth is the necessary condition for human
action, with the potential to change the world.

In classical texts on spirituality the physical process of childbearing and giving birth is generally not a religiously specifically
valued activity. More than birth it is the activity of mothering
that is drawn on as a religious symbol. While childbirth may be a
spiritually significant experience for a mother, the spiritual awareness and development of the child has, until recently, not
attracted as much attention as the spirituality of adults. In fact,

the figure of the child occupies a relatively minor role in religious teachings and practices, although many religions know of special rites of initiation for the newborn, or for adolescents on their path to adulthood. In mythical stories we find the figure of the primordial child linked to the origin of life itself. We also know the divine child, although in comparison to all the male and female deities worshiped throughout history, this figure remains a relatively hidden one. The best-known examples are probably the infant Jesus and the Hindu God Krishna as a child. Truly exuberant and joyful devotional practices to the divine child exist, and we find them in Catholic Italy, Spain, or Mexico, or in the North Indian Hindu city of Vrindaban.

The small, newborn child embodies the mystery of beginnings, the freshness and wonder of life not yet touched by the narrow ambitions, confusions, and uncertainties of adulthood, not yet burdened with the responsibilities of consciousness or a sense of guilt. A child has a simple, even naïve view of life, a playful attitude and sense of enjoyment that many adults have lost. There is the outburst of a child's energy to learn, discover, explore, and grow—a vitality and immersion in the present that never seems to be part of adult life in the same way again, but lingers in memory as a primordial experience that can haunt grown-ups as a yearning for unity and oneness long lost but never forgotten.

It is thus not surprising that when the Oxford scholar Sir Alister Hardy (1896–1985) invited people in the 1960s to provide accounts of significant religious experiences in their lives, about 15 percent of over 4,000 respondents described experiences in their childhood that had been of lasting importance for the rest of their lives. It was the unforgettable, vivid, and authentic nature of these experiences that related to a sense of presence, to something other than the self, to a sense of unity, of love, of a caring personal deity. These early experiences were reported as retaining a lifelong authoritative quality, as something that was not wiped out by subsequent experiences. These accounts of early spiritual experiences were published as *The Original Vision: A Study of the Religious Experiences of Childhood* in 1977, relating formative experiences and memories that sustained people's spiritual awareness and development throughout their lives. This is an intensely personal, inner vision to which traditional schooling has often little to offer.

Building on Hardy's work, British scholars David Hay and Rebecca Nye undertook further research with the Children's Spirituality Project at the University of Warwick. They studied the spirituality of 300 six- and ten-year-old children, and published their findings in *The Spirit of the Child* (1998). Hay maintains that spirituality is natural to children, that there is in fact a biological basis for spiritual awareness, since it is essentially part of human evolution and not an element implanted through culture and education. He affirms the prelinguistic experiential foundation of spiritual sensibility in human beings. His work also shows that explicitly religious practice and language do not necessarily promote spirituality. Knowledge about religion acquired later through formal religious education can in fact prove to be a hindrance to the inner knowledge gained through personal experience at an earlier stage in childhood. How to provide the language and means to keep a child's innate spirituality? That is a key question for spiritual educators.

Any educator must take note of the spiritual world in which children live, their experiences, hopes, dreams, as well as pains and fears. This requires intuition and empathy, a focused listening to children's own stories, their real and imagined worlds. The vision of children can relate to the flowers, meadows, woods, and trees in nature, to different plants and animals, but also to their toys, and now for many to electronic games, to the imaginative worlds of songs, poems, stories, films—and to family members, siblings, friends. It is a world of vision and color, of diversity, expectation, great excitement, little hurts, and sometimes also deep pain, a world of laughter, tears, and fears as well as a world of trust and innocent abandon.

It may be debatable whether one can be spiritual without being religious, but there can be no doubt that education towards greater spiritual awareness is needed for all humans in order to discover their spiritual potential within themselves. Very few become accomplished in the spiritual life without learning about it from others, or being introduced to it in some way or another. The active awakening of our spiritual potential into a spiritually active approach to life is still very underdeveloped in contemporary society. We need to give far more attention to the education of the human spirit; we must learn to develop a deep inner freedom and consciousness to become spiritually more alert and alive than we are at present most of the time. Our individual development from birth to death may be likened to a progressive unfolding of the potential we carry within ourselves, but much of this we never fully actualize, and therefore our spiritual awakening and progress remain partial.

The capacity for spirituality is present in every human being, but it needs to be activated and realized. That means it has to be taught in some way, and this requires new approaches to spiritual education. We teach our children to learn to walk, to talk, to dance—to acquire all the immensely subtle and complex aspects of human culture and to master a wide variety of skills. But often enough our children are not taught how to develop spiritual awareness unless they are given the right kind of spiritual and religious education. At present this does not happen in large parts of secular society, nor does it necessarily always occur in a traditional religious environment. The spiritual potential of each human being has to be awakened, trained, and practiced, just as training is needed to develop the potential to do well in sports, make music, sing, or dance. But even then not all people make good singers or dancers. Similarly, not everybody is equally spiritually gifted.

SPIRITUALITY IN THE MIDST OF LIFE

Human spiritual development belongs to all stages of life's dance, whether childhood, adolescence, middle age, or the final stages of growing older. Spiritual disciplines and practices, once the prerogative of a spiritual elite of ascetics, monastics, and mystics, have become widely democratized and secularized, unfolding into many forms of spirituality that emerge within the course of a person's life. Ordinary, day-to-day lived spirituality thus encompasses birth and growth, one's home and neighbors, family and friends, one's work and leisure, one's joys and pains, one's dreams and disappointments. All these experiences provide material for spiritual elucidation and transformation.

Developing one's spirituality in a relational way by being connected to others can occur throughout one's whole life, but it flourishes especially in the midst of life when we develop close bonds with others through mature relationships. These include the experience of deep human love and a shared life, whether lived together in friendship, partnership, or marriage. Human relationships are so complex and diverse, and operate at so many different levels, that it is impossible to generalize about spirituality lived through relationships. Spiritual reflections on friendship and hospitality have a long history in the Christian monastic tradition, where they were highly valued. In today's secular society these values appear to be less openly acknowledged, but they are present in numerous people's efforts to welcome "the other," the stranger, the refugee, the asylum seeker, who all need to be befriended and helped. Through stretching out arms, through opening a home, through providing moral and practical help and support, human inwardness can be deepened and transformed.

The active life of most people will involve close personal relationships that need careful attention and nurture if a partnership, marriage, and family life are to flourish. In many traditional spiritualities, marriage has often been considered a lesser spiritual path, a vocation that ranked second to the celibate, ascetic life, considered the highest calling and a more direct path to God. Although Christian marriage is a sacrament, at least among Orthodox and Catholic Christians, for much of its history it was seen as a largely secular, practical affair that spiritual writers did not concern themselves with. Since the 1960s and 1970s, however, a new interest has developed in what is called marital or conjugal spirituality, a new, slowly growing field that reflects the widening out of the understanding of spirituality as involving all fields of human experience.

The nearest we come to an earlier perception of the spiritual side of marriage is in the marriage symbolism found among Christian and Jewish mystics. It is particularly in the Jewish Kabbalah that human sexual love is taken as a symbol for the love relation between the Holy One that is God, and his *Shekinah*, his indwelling presence that makes itself felt in the love between husband and wife. The togetherness of these two partners in their intimate love and connectedness is surrounded by God's own presence.

At a spiritual level the bond of mutual love and communion between two spouses is at the same time experienced as shared communion between the couple and God. The recognition of marital spirituality as a subject in its own right is evident not only in the growth of topical workshops and books, but also through the founding of the international journal *INTAMS Review*, which is uniquely devoted to marital spirituality. In the words of one of its researchers, marital spirituality refers to two aspects, "the ways of living the married life in light of the spiritual dimension, or God," and also "the ways of living the spiritual life in light of married persons' conjugal bond." This understanding is based on a Christian perspective where the experience of marriage can become an occasion for encountering grace and spiritual growth.

People from other faiths might use other theological and spiritual concepts to reflect on the spirituality of marriage, but these ideas show that marriage is now explicitly, and much more emphatically than in the past, recognized as an important occasion for the practice of everyday spirituality. In the day-to-day experience of conjugal love and fidelity people can encounter a horizon of transcendence, where the mystery of divine presence and the touch of the spirit reveal themselves in surprising ways.

Another example of an actively lived life, and everyday spirituality for such a life, is the spirituality of work. This can be understood as reflecting on the meaning of work, but it can also refer to a changed attitude towards one's work, so that it is undertaken and perceived from a deeper spiritual perspective. But what is work? It figures so centrally in all our lives, yet it can be experienced and practiced so differently. Work means activity, it means concrete tasks and goals; it can also mean a vocation to which one devotes one's whole life. Or it can simply be the practical means whereby one earns one's living—just a job, a duty, a drudgery even. Many people find deep inner fulfillment and reward in their work if it is freely chosen, and when it involves responsibility and creativity. But the large majority of human beings have to work out of sheer necessity for survival, often under oppressive, unfree, and exploitative conditions.

A spiritual approach to work invites thoughtful reflection on one's attitude and practical outlook. It can make a big difference if one's way of working becomes more detached, more contemplative, more open-minded, and yet also compassionate toward others. There is physical work, mental work, and spiritual work. At first they seem far removed from each other, and at great distance from what is sacred and holy. Yet they are all interrelated and help to maintain the world. All these activities can be blessed and transformed through deeply spiritual attitudes and intention.

Work, marriage, and the blessings and tribulations of family life belong largely to the middle part of human life. This is a time when many people are too preoccupied with their social and financial obligations, personal relationships, their work situation, ambitions, and worries to have much room for a spiritual deepening of their lives. But renewed opportunities for deeper reflection occur during the later part of life, when one becomes much more conscious of, and actively involved with, the process of aging.

SPIRITUALITY AND AGING

The experience of children belongs to one end of the lifespan, while aging belongs to the other. Children and older people have certain features in common: both are especially vulnerable and often dependent on others; both together represent the continuity and flow of life. American author Elizabeth Tisdell, who interviewed many people about spirituality, found that among the most commonly cited spiritual experiences were those related to birth, death, and near-death experiences which "speak to the great miracle of life and its never-ending circle."

Spiritual development can happen at any moment and stage of one's life. It is not necessarily always old people who are wise—some rather young people are deeply spiritual as well. But it is generally acknowledged that in the older, mature years of one's life one finds more occasions for deeper personal reflection and spiritual maturation. Many personal struggles have been resolved by then, responsibilities have been lightened. At a time when one can slow down, and is physically forced to, one can gather in life's riches and graces, and find opportunities for a deeper healing of life's wounds.

Integrity, wisdom, and transcendence are celebrated as the hallmark of a mature spirituality, as is the making of connections—which is like weaving a rich tapestry that creates deeper meaning in one's life. Such a mature spirituality can be nurtured throughout the aging process that each person undergoes.

We are living in a new historical time where growing older does not simply mean living longer than previous generations did, but also living without the prescribed, fixed social roles that were given to the elders of traditional societies. This presents us with an exciting new freedom, a challenging task to shape our lives in new ways by making use of this special time. It presents a valuable opportunity to reflect on our life, to act out its deeper meaning and purpose.

It is important to distinguish biological aging from social aging. As one grows in years, our chronological age increases; we are getting older biologically. But chronological age alone says little about a person, as we realize when we compare different individuals of the same age. Social aging, as distinct from biological aging, relates to the social stereotypes about being old that are accepted in society, the different images of being old that are applied to us, or that we apply to ourselves and to others.

What value do we assign to old age? What wisdom do we see in old people? In modern Western society old people are not valued enough for what they are, or what they can contribute to the community. Youth and the young are valued above all else in the West, whereas old people are perhaps most valued among the Chinese. Demographically, people are living much longer and reach a greater age than previous generations, and thus it is of immense social importance to reflect creatively on the opportunities and constraints of being older without falling into ageism. The process of aging is recognized as universally important around the world. One of the non-governmental organizations at the United Nations is Global Action on Aging (GAA), providing a global forum and pressure group for the concerns of seniors around the world.

It is helpful to speak about a continuous "process of aging" rather than "old age" as a definite stage that, in any case, occurred formerly at a far younger age. Aging is an ongoing organic experience, since we are all involved in the process of getting older from the moment we are born. The process of aging is integral to human life; it involves both biological and psychological aspects, and occurs on a continuum. But its different stages are evaluated very differently by different individuals. Old age has been described as a journey into simplicity, and it involves a change in our time perspective, since we grow more conscious of the time left to live.

It has been said that there is no time in the human life cycle when there exists a greater variability between different individuals than during the time of growing older. This brings with it a new responsibility, an exciting task of living life to one's full potential, as well as exploring questions of life's meaning and significance that arise from one's inner being.

The concept of "empowerment" is useful for dealing with the process of aging. When growing older, one needs to be empowered to still think and act for oneself. Growing older has sometimes been seen as a journey into submissiveness, as a period when one is involved in the process of stripping away while making sense of one's life. However, far too few people consider what is sometimes called the third period of life as an opportunity for flourishing, where aging can be seen as good news rather than only negative diminishment.

Contemporary research has produced fascinating data about people who are in their eighties and nineties, and yet are still learning new things. With regard to physiological and biological levels, studies have shown that even at this age new synaptic connections can still grow in the brain if it is sufficiently stimulated, for human brains possess what is called synaptic plasticity. It is well known that the synaptic connections in the brain will not develop properly in a newborn baby if one does not nurture her sufficiently, speak to her, and thus stimulate her. Brain matter will not develop if the brain lacks the necessary mental, psychological, and spiritual input. This is also true of older people. They can go on learning new things, and through this learning experience new synapses will continue to grow in their brain. It is therefore of the utmost importance to stimulate the brain, to enhance people's awareness to develop new thinking through new learning processes. This is a most important principle in caring for older people.

Quite a few senior people have learned extraordinary things at an advanced age. A well-known example is Grandma Moses (1860–1961), the famous American painter who, after raising numerous children and grandchildren on a farm in upstate New York, decided to learn to paint at the age of seventy, and then painted for more than thirty years. Although there are no explicitly religious subjects in her paintings, her whole work is suffused with a spiritual quality that one might call the transfiguration of the ordinary. Some musicians began to write music at a comparatively late stage, and there are successful writers who started writing very late in life. Other seniors learn a new sport, or become proficient in playing an instrument or speaking a language that they have wanted to master all their life.

Another insight relating to older people concerns the development of a "spirituality of the senses"—to cultivate the sense of seeing, speaking, hearing, listening, and touching in a new way, at a time when many people experience a gradual diminishment of their physical faculties. As we age, it is especially important to care for the health of the body as well as for mental and emotional balance. All the senses come into play, for they will be involved in the loss and diminishment that accompany aging, but they can also be drawn upon for spiritual strength and nourishment. Spiritual care and guidance can help seniors to see things differently by learning to be more attentive, by looking more deeply at their life's experiences in a wider, more understanding perspective. Seeing, especially inner seeing, is important for developing much more integral and holistic relations with oneself, one's friends and family, and one's acquaintances.

Speaking, listening, hearing, and being heard are important for all of us, but they gain a special importance in old age. On their journey toward life's end people need to be encouraged to share their life's narrative, to articulate their experiences and put them into words for themselves and others. Sharing stories, telling their joys and pains, can be a very positive, energizing experience. Speaking to each other is living communication through the word. The word embodies, nourishes, and sustains life. "In the beginning was the Word" teaches St. John's Gospel, and Christians believe that the Word is both flesh and spirit. Thus it is profoundly true that speaking the right words can embody strong spiritual nourishment. It can be soothing and healing.

Loving attention given to older people in a personal conversation often lifts up their spirit and revivifies them, so that they suddenly become more engaged and alive, to such an extent even that they appear to look younger and more like their former selves. The actual content of such a conversation may not be all that important or especially spiritual; it is the shared presence and the living connection through speaking with each other that counts. Someone concerned with pastoral care in homes for the aged once said that, if it were possible, the best care would be to have enough people available to speak regularly, and for long periods of time, with all the seniors in a home. And some people whose facility for speaking has diminished may enjoy writing instead or simply sharing a loved one's presence in silence.

Another very important sense for maintaining living connections is touching, whether simply touching any part of the body, shaking hands, or giving an embrace. The personal warmth expressed through such a gesture is life-affirming and invigorating. It is this affirmation and warmth, even physical warmth, that we all, but the elderly especially, need and find life-giving, thereby communicating something of the invisible dynamic of the spirit.

Developing spirituality can also be described as creating an oasis for the soul. This links the nurturing of spirituality to a sense of place by grounding ourselves in a particular "spirit spot," both in our actual environment and within ourselves, by cultivating attentiveness and new ways of seeing. Many seniors may find such a spot in their garden, especially when they go on enjoying gardening. If they have no garden of their own, they may deeply appreciate visiting a public garden, park, or other place of natural beauty. This can create a sense of wonder and spiritual joy, which deeply refreshes their spirit. We can thus truly "re-create" ourselves. For many people this happens through particular forms of recreation, but also often through the experience of the natural world, or through different forms of art, or sports, that draw us out of ourselves into another dimension.

The time of aging into maturity can thus be a time of great opportunity—truly a time of grace where one can work on spiritually deepening one's life. The expression "growing older" is a wise one, for we are still growing, although in a different way from when we were young. Perhaps more than ever before, that time in life provides the opportunity for contemplation and meditation, for nurturing wisdom and fostering spiritual development.

The former pastoral director and senior chaplain of the British MHA Care Group (known earlier as Methodist Homes for the Aged), who has been regularly involved with the International Conference on Ageing, Spirituality and Well-being organized since 2000, lists as some of the most significant spiritual needs of people, including older people, the following: first, "the need to receive and give *love*"; second, "the need to sustain *hope*: something to look forward to day by day and in relation to longer term purposes, plans and dreams"; third, "the need for something or someone to believe in—*faith/trust*"; fourth, "the need for *creativity*: to develop skills and talents to make something of the raw material of the world and of one's life"; and fifth, "the need for at least a reasonable degree of *peace*. This peace is one not just of circumstance (which can never be guaranteed) but of heart and mind."

If these spiritual needs can be met, the process of aging can be a very positive experience. There can still occur spiritual development at a time when physical and mental powers decline. If we have faith, we can discern the hidden dance of the Spirit across the landscape of our lives, and feel the helping hand of God in our hearts—a dance with a rhythm and pattern not of our own making or choosing, yet a dance to which each of us contributes some beats and patterns of our own. Growing older can be a great season for human flourishing, especially when we remain open to the animating Spirit within and around us.

The world religions possess a vast store of rites and beliefs relating to the human life cycle. These are spiritually instructive and uplifting. Particularly striking are the links between the search for liberation and the different stages of life taught by Hinduism since ancient times, from the life stage of the young student to that of the householder, followed by the stage of the forest-dweller to that of the complete renunciate, exclusively devoted to the search for ultimate reality that is Brahman. Each stage of the Hindu life cycle has its particular spiritual orientation and duties. Although recommendable from the psychological perspective of human development, this schematic pattern of spiritual life also has its definite limitations, especially as it is a scheme that originally belonged only to the male members of the upper castes. (It provides an excellent example of spirituality in the past that was often the elite pursuit of a religious and social minority.) This is no longer enough if we yearn for the spiritual transformation of the whole world. The development of a holistic, balanced spirituality for life is needed for *all* people since individual *and* social flourishing cannot happen without it.

SPIRITUALITY, DEATH, AND DYING

A spirituality for life that relates to all steps of life's dance must include reflections on the experience of death and dying. It is a profound paradox that death is an undeniable fact of life, of all life across space and time. Biological death is a universal human occurrence, but how this is experienced and responded to varies enormously between different people and cultures. Beliefs and rituals concerned with death are found in all religions; there even exist theories that humans specifically invented religion to overcome death. The comparative study of religious teachings on death shows that human beings have rarely accepted death as an inevitable condition of life. They have created countless myths that claim death is the result of some primal accident or mistake, the trickery of a god, the breaking of a taboo, or a transgressive act by one of their ancestors. The biblical account of the disobedience of Adam and Eve, followed by their expulsion from paradise, is only one such myth, but one that has deeply influenced Western culture and left a permanent imprint on many attitudes and beliefs.

Death is a profoundly personal experience, even when people die together in large numbers. But death is also a profoundly social experience that cuts deep lines into the lives of human groups and communities. Human beings have always been deeply concerned with the meaning of death and raised many unanswerable questions about it: Why do people have to die? What happens after death? Do the dead continue to exist in an altered state of life? And if so, how does this happen?

We need to distinguish between death as an event that completes human life, and the process of dying that we undergo slowly, culminating in this event whose after-effects weigh on others differently, and perhaps more, than on the person who has died. The meaning of death has greatly changed over the centuries, even within the same culture. In Europe, for example, the attitudes toward death and representations of death have shifted enormously during the last thousand years.

There now exist powerful secular arguments against any belief in life after death that have even come to be accepted by some Christian believers. In the past, belief in an afterlife has often been understood as personal survival, but this can be interpreted as a rather egocentric desire, wanting to perpetuate one's personal existence. Christian understanding of "life after death" has come to mean not so much a place as the experience of the presence of God, the enjoyment of the fullness of life, described as the "beatific vision" experienced in communion with others. Dante's *Divine Comedy* speaks about this most poetically and imaginatively, drawing on the religious imagery of the Christian Middle Ages. Contemporary scientific culture refers more easily to human genes and DNA, which have become another way of reimagining the continued presence of the dead among the living. At the same time some scientists are probing the accounts of near-death experiences for possible evidence regarding some form of human survival after death.

These and other investigations reflect the interest in studying death, or so-called death studies, which have grown considerably over the last forty years. Death studies and death education are now found in schools, colleges, and universities. In our secular, over-medicalized, and impersonal society, death is often a singularly lonely, individual experience. Death does not only mean personal suffering and loss, but has much wider ramifications for family members and larger social groups who need help and counseling for dealing with the process of dying. The changing attitudes about death and dying have produced new reflections on the spiritual meaning of the process of dying and the experience of death.

The mourning, funeral, and memorial rites following the death of a person respond to the psychological and social needs of the living, helping them to cope with their loss and grieving. Religions have given us more than this, however, by teaching numerous ways of preparing for death, facing it calmly, with serene dignity, with a sense of peace and hope, and by providing rituals that help the dying person with the transition from life to death. Roman Catholicism knows the sacrament of extreme unction or anointing for the dying, when a priest comes to anoint, bless, and pray with a person approaching death. Tibetans draw on the *Book of the Dead* that is recited to a dying person to facilitate a smooth transition and rebirth into the next life.

Death has been called a terrible gift, the shadow of human existence. Yet it can also be seen as an experience of liberation, even exaltation, and a new opening. Death can be assigned meaning as a stage of further growth, of ultimate transformation and metamorphosis, a critical threshold and peak of life. For this it is important to prepare for a good death, and to accept dying as another face of life. If the process of aging can be experienced as a spiritual journey, so can death. A consciously developed spirituality for dying will include the awareness that our life span is limited, and that we are facing death throughout life. The pull of death always gnaws at us through accidents, disease, and other diminishments, but when we learn to face death with full awareness, we can discover new wonder, wisdom, and gratitude for what life has given us, whether we believe in life after death or not, whether we hope for enlightenment, liberation, the fullness of God, rebirth, or simply accept the natural cycle of life and death through which we blend into the energies of the universe.

Accompanying the dying, and increasingly the terminally ill and very elderly through their gradual process of decline, by giving counsel, solace, support, or simply company, is a lofty spiritual ministry. In Western society in the past, much of this was carried out by the Christian churches. They still give much help, but in today's secular society the modern hospice movement has also become very important in fulfilling some of the spiritual counsel needed for the dying.

The first modern hospice was St. Christopher's in London, founded in 1967 by Dame Cicely Saunders (1918–2005), who once mentioned in a radio interview that her attitude to the ill had been inspired by Teilhard de Chardin's writing on the spiritual energy of suffering. Although St. Christopher's began as a Christian foundation, it took in patients of any belief or none, and this came to be accepted throughout the hospice movement. It is based on the principles of caring for the sick, researching into pain control, teaching doctors and nurses how to cope with terminal disease, and how to combine spiritual with medical care. "We have to concern ourselves with the quality of life as well as its length," Dame Cicely once said. She saw dying not as something to be feared, but as a spiritual event that can bring meaning to people's lives, and also provide an opportunity for reconciliation. Since her first foundation, the hospice movement has grown worldwide. It now includes hospices for terminally ill and dying children, who also need intensive care, including spiritual care. The International Association for Hospice and Palliative Care has given the movement a global profile and influence, and among its many concerns are spiritual issues and the recognition of spiritual needs in people who are dying, whether old or young.

Within life's dance are many stages and occasions when the Spirit moves imperceptibly, though at times most forcefully, across the expressions and gestures of human lives. The dance is a symbol of being alive, yet it continues to be created anew again and again, never complete. As Michael Mayne sums it up in his comments on *The Dance*, the famous large-scale paintings by Henri Matisse: "The dance will never be perfected, for perfection is always just out of reach. Indeed, the dance is more exhausting than it looks, for there are tears at the heart of things, and much heartbreak along the way."

Six

SPIRITUALITY, EDUCATION, AND HEALTH

Health and education are two of the possessions that human beings value most highly and wish to enjoy throughout their lives. They are essential for human well-being but cannot be taken for granted. For some people it requires great efforts to attain them, while others seem to be blessed in abundance with these precious, largely immaterial goods. Are education and health an essential condition, a process, a task, or the result of human choices and initiatives? Or are they all of these aspects combined?

Both health and education are dependent on countless social, cultural, and economic factors. Both involve high stakes, investments, and risks that feature prominently in national and international politics. And we have to ask, how far is their presence linked to the spiritual dimension of life? How far can we increase the beneficial influence of education and health for individuals and society by approaching them from a spiritual perspective?

Health issues represent some of the most important considerations of our society. How to achieve health, and how to maintain it? Or how to regain health after experiencing illness and disease?

How to find healing from sickness and suffering? These questions are not new but perennial. Although differently experienced today, they have occupied human minds through the ages. This is evident from the wealth of resources on healing and indigenous medicines known to different religions and cultures. The figure of the healer, the shaman and medicine man, is an ancient one. So are the religiously rooted practices of healing related to life-cycle events such as birth, illness, and death. Others deal with spirit possession, the healing of mind and body, or the use of herbs or simple surgery, as found in traditional African, Chinese, Tibetan, or Indian medicine.

What is different today is the immense increase in medical knowledge and power, and the greatly lengthened life span, which encourages us all to desire a long and healthy life and an altogether better quality of life. Yet paradoxically, as we live so much longer than in the past, we are also likely to suffer many more years of ill health. For this reason the search for healing has gained enormous momentum in contemporary society. Modern scientific medicine has made stunning progress, but its most discerning practitioners are willing to acknowledge that in spite of all its sophistication, allopathic medicine often lacks the basic healing strengths of older, nonscientific, traditional medical systems. Modern doctors are often not trained to help patients in coping and making sense of their illness. Religious and spiritual perspectives can therefore make a significant contribution to healing and health, as is now increasingly being recognized, even in secular contexts.

Education, whether formal or informal, is one of the most important factors in the development of individuals and in the transformation of the world. It contributes to the personal growth and maturing of human beings and affects their mind, body, and spirit. There is always room for more spiritual growth of a person, for the transformation of consciousness and soul, but there is also the possibility of a further spiritual evolution of the whole human race. The process of education occurs in many different ways and contexts; ideally, it should include reflections on the fundamental questions of human existence. It will then open up larger intellectual and emotional dimensions that reveal the importance of spirituality in human experience and development.

A GLOBAL VISION OF EDUCATION

The education landscape around the world, whether one looks at schools, colleges, universities, or vocational education, is extraordinarily diverse and multifaceted today. Its contours and movements have global dimensions, its activities a global impact and effect. Often highly finance-driven, there is much to be criticized and in need of radical change in this educational world. It is important, though, that educators share an awareness of the spiritual dimension of education. Only then can they promote a profoundly humanistic vision of the intrinsic value and dignity of each human person, a vision of human flourishing that depends on the creation of mutually supportive human communities. The recent trend toward ever more quantitative, utilitarian, and narrowly vocational training in many educational institutions has taken much of the creative potential out of both teaching and learning. Yet all learning must include spaces for the passionate use of the imagination, for genuine creativity, originality, and community building, since the fostering of relationships is at the heart of all genuine education that has a spiritual dimension at its core.

Beyond this more general, implicit spiritual dimension of the whole educational process, much work is happening with regard to an explicitly named "spiritual education." This is understood as part of the learning process in school, and it specifically addresses the education of the human spirit. It involves the fostering of a sense of peace, wonder, joy, hope, love, sensitivity, and creativity, as well as the nurturing of a deeper sense of identity, community, and belonging.

In the early 1980s, Robert Muller, the former assistant secretary-general of the United Nations and later chancellor of Costa Rica's Peace University, wrote about the urgent need for more global education. Such an education "must transcend material, scientific and intellectual achievements and reach deliberately into the moral and spiritual spheres." Muller argues that, after extending the power of our hands with incredible machines, our eyes with telescopes and microscopes, our ears with telephones, radio, and sonar, our brains with computers and automation, we must now also extend our hearts, our feelings, our love, and our soul "to the entire human family, to the planet, to the stars, to the universe, to eternity and to God."

Like other visionary pioneers, Muller perceives the intricate, dense network of worldwide interdependencies, including spiritual ones. These closely interlink different societies around the globe that were until recently living in relative isolation from each other. Muller articulates very clearly the urgent need for global education, which he assesses from a religious perspective where the human being "must perceive his right, miraculous place in the splendor of God's creation." Thus he concludes his essay with a strong appeal: "We must manage our globe so as to permit the endless stream of humans admitted to the miracle of life to fulfil their lives physically, mentally, morally and spiritually as has never been possible before in our entire evolution. Global education must prepare our children for the coming of an interdependent, safe, prosperous, friendly, loving, happy planetary age as has been heralded by all great prophets. The real, the great period of human fulfilment on planet Earth is only now about to begin."

This is a large spiritual vision that embraces the education of the whole human race! Few possess such breathtaking powers of the imagination as Robert Muller. His reflections are grounded in more than thirty years of practical work with United Nations agencies around the world. Yet since he first dreamed of shaping a "global spirituality" through the use of education more than two decades ago, many more trends have unfolded, pointing in the same direction. New ideas have emerged in educational discussions that parallel some of Muller's own thinking, ideas that concern the spiritual education of children as well as the lifelong learning and spiritual growth of adults.

SPIRITUAL EDUCATION AND CHILDREN

Contemporary interest in spirituality often appears to be more pronounced among educators and health-care professionals than among religious thinkers. The better understanding of human development, of the growth of personality and identity as complex psycho-dynamic processes that include a spiritual dimension, makes this perhaps inevitable. It is generally accepted that the growth of the human person, and the educational nurturing of such growth, is a complex, long-drawn-out process influenced by many formative experiences and ideas. Although the understanding of spirituality remains controversial, it can certainly be related to a search for the meaning of human life. As such it has a place in education. Approaches from a dynamic perspective of growth and transformation also explain why spirituality cannot primarily be identified with the transmission of content, such as specific beliefs, doctrines, and practices, or with that of past spiritual ideals. On the contrary, within an educational context it is understood that spirituality has much more to do with nurturing particular processes and attitudes within human beings in relation to themselves, to others, the world, and the divine Spirit.

Spiritual educators and psychologists wrestle with the intellectual and spiritual issues involved in these processes. Yet in spite of all the writings of psychologists, psychotherapists, and health professionals regarding the importance of spirituality, the subject of children's spirituality remained for a long time a relatively neglected topic. Research into children's own accounts of their experiences brought to light the richness and diversity of children's spiritual insights and visions. A wonderful documentation of this generally unknown wealth of spirituality is found in the lively conversations and colorful drawings of children from different religious and cultural backgrounds gathered by the Harvard psychiatrist Robert Coles in his book *The Spiritual Life of Children* (1992).

Over a period of thirty years Coles interviewed children about their spirituality and found that it strongly connected with questions about life and death, but also with questions relating to the environment and the earth. He vividly describes "the child as pilgrim" and speaks about "young spirituality," commenting perceptively that much attention is paid to the special problems of children with disabilities, or those who have experienced the stresses of war, forced migration, homelessness, racial or religious persecution, but not to children's spiritual needs, which must equally be addressed: "None of these ways of thinking about children need to be exclusive, of course. The child's 'house has many mansions'—including a spiritual life that grows, changes, responds constantly to the other lives that, in their sum, make up the individual we call by a name and know by a story that is all his, all hers."

British educators have debated for years how to develop the spiritual education that is a legal requirement in Britain. This debate has by now grown so much nationally and internationally that spiritual education is considered a discrete academic area of study. New specialist books and articles reflect this growth, as does the existence of the regular International Conference on Children's Spirituality, the *International Journal of Children's Spirituality*, founded in 1996, and the North American charity ChildSpirit Institute, a network of families, researchers, teachers, health-care providers, community and religious leaders, dedicated to understanding and nurturing the spirituality of children and adults. These developments show that spiritual education is finding a language and voice of its own. It is addressing contemporary society, while also radically challenging some of its current values.

A few years ago a British research initiative, funded by the American John Templeton Foundation, tried to investigate how to articulate what spiritual development is and how it can be fostered and measured in schools. This research used a broad, inclusive interpretation of spiritual development. It stated that spiritual development relates to that aspect of inner life through which pupils acquire insights into their personal existence that are of enduring worth. It is characterized by reflection, the attribution of meaning to experience, valuing a nonmaterial dimension to life, and intimations of an enduring reality. For this research, "spiritual" was not synonymous with "religious," and all areas of the curriculum may contribute to a pupil's spiritual development.

Here the spiritual is taken to be wider than the religious. Yet there always remains a certain tension, since different educators do not necessarily agree on this definition. There are those who take an open, widely inclusive view of spirituality as something humanistic, mainly secular, and fundamental to human existence, whereas others adopt a more exclusive stance by linking spirituality more directly to a specific faith tradition, especially to a belief in God. In educational debates spirituality is now associated with a wide range of characteristics—from wonder, search for self-knowledge and meaning, creativity, relationships, to the experience of transcendence, and to explicitly religious convictions that relate to beliefs in some ultimate reality that is transindividual and suprapersonal.

The teaching of spirituality thus remains a controversial issue. The literature on the spiritual education of children, especially in schools, is growing fast. In Britain it is discussed together with the intellectual, moral, social, and cultural education of children.

There exists particular concern with the education of "the whole child," and that must include spiritual education, however understood. In Rebecca Nye's view, the heart of children's spirituality consists in their "relational consciousness" which is reflected in "an unusual level of *consciousness* or perceptiveness," and in conversation "expressed in a context of how the child related to things, other people, him/herself, and God."

For the adult educator, the question is how to encourage the growth of children's innate spiritual sense, how to expand their awareness, their deep sense of mystery, their original trust in the ultimate goodness of the world and life. The story of a first-grade class is told where the teacher tried to still the noisy activity of small children at play by making them sit down on the floor, inviting them to look quietly at the light of a candle in the middle of the room—a focus for their vision and the gathering-in of their thoughts. The children liked that so much that, a week later, they eagerly asked, "Please, when can we do that candle thing again?" They had obviously enjoyed that beautiful moment of quiet, a space for coming to themselves in stillness, so precious yet so rare in our world of constant movement and activity.

SPIRITUALITY AND LIFELONG LEARNING

To develop spiritual inwardness and be attentive to one's inner voice and vision is not something only children have to learn, but adults as well.

Human beings learn throughout life. From cradle to grave people have to cope with new circumstances, be open to new encounters and relationships, and adapt to the unexpected. Thus the process of learning is often an informal one, as when we speak about a steep learning curve. Yet there also exist countless formal programs of lifelong learning in different institutes, colleges, and university education departments around the world. Previously this was often referred to as adult education.

In some institutions "lifelong learning" is just another name for learning during the third stage of life. But lifelong learning also carries a more inclusive sense by referring to an ongoing process of learning during all the years of adulthood, rather than just schooling during childhood and youth. Lifelong learning programs enable people beyond school and college age to acquire new skills, broaden their interests, cultivate hobbies, or simply enjoy themselves through learning something new. Although spirituality is still a highly contested concept that some people remain uncomfortable with, it has increasingly gained greater legitimacy in lifelong learning as a dimension of human consciousness and reflective practice. It can be integrated into our ways of knowing, being, and making sense of the world. Thus adult learning, therapy, counseling, guidance, and spirituality can be connected in many different ways. In Britain the Economic and Social Science Research Council has sponsored research on "Spirituality as a Dimension of Lifelong Learning," and interest in this relatively new development is growing fast in North America and Europe.

Spiritual education as part of a formal program thus no longer belongs only to the learning stages of childhood and youth, but is becoming an explicit part of the lifelong learning of adults in their mature middle years and also later stages of life. A fundamental aspect of spirituality is about "meaning making," about making sense of one's life and relationships, and accepting them with gratitude. Spiritual development involves a process of growth and transformation that is both individual and social. Some people may still reject the language of spirituality, but may nevertheless espouse what one might call spiritual values through commitment in their lives to care and concern for others, or to such values as social justice, work for racial and gender equality, or for peace making in their communities. The American adult educator

Elizabeth Tisdell strongly argues that we need to break the widespread silence about spirituality in adult and higher education, explore the connection between spirituality and culture, and consider the role of spiritual experience in developing a positive cultural identity. Her book *Exploring Spirituality and Culture in Adult and Higher Education* closely examines the convergences and divergences between spirituality, religion, and culture. She makes it quite clear that exploring spirituality is not about pushing a religious agenda. It is helpful to ponder her seven assumptions about the nature of spirituality: "(1) Spirituality and religion are not the same, but for many people are interrelated; (2) spirituality is an awareness and honoring of wholeness and the interconnectedness of all things through the mystery of what many refer to as the Lifeforce, God, higher power, higher self, cosmic energy, Buddha nature, or Great Spirit; (3) spirituality is fundamentally about meaning making; (4) spirituality is always present (though often unacknowledged) in the learning environment; (5) spiritual development constitutes moving toward greater authenticity or to a more authentic self; (6) spirituality is about how people construct knowledge through largely unconscious and symbolic processes, often made more concrete in art forms such as music, image, symbol, and ritual, all of which are manifested culturally; (7) spiritual experiences most often happen by surprise."

This is a list not everybody may agree with, but it reflects the multiple associations made with the large area of spirituality rather well. Some of these are discussed in other chapters; in the present context of education it is particularly significant that spirituality is recognized as always being somehow present in the learning environment, without necessarily being acknowledged. Learning theories, whether for children or adults, need to be based on a spiritually grounded pedagogy to transform the world and ourselves.

To awaken spiritual awareness and develop spiritual sensitivity is something that needs to be done for all people. So far, the awakening of spirituality, whether in adults, teenagers, or children, is still a relatively unexplored field. A wide public debate is needed on how to initiate an open-minded sharing of spiritual insight and understanding across the globe. We all need to learn more about the spiritual nature of humans and the oneness of life. A whole cluster of ideas has emerged around the central focus of spiritual education. Initiatives are needed to develop programs relating to spiritual education for all age groups, from primary to higher education, both for students and faculty.

If the global resources of wisdom are to be shared across the earth community for the enhancement of all life on earth, a global network of spiritual education is needed if it is to have an impact on our ways of life. This task goes beyond the teaching of any single religious tradition or that of secular spirituality alone, but has to be taken up by contemporary culture as a whole. We need spirituality for the old and young, spirituality in homes, schools, and colleges, at work and in the marketplace, in economics and politics, and not just in education or in places of worship. We need to relate spirituality to the whole of life, so that we can foster a tangible sense of the spiritual and a sense of moral solidarity within one single earth community.

SPIRITUALITY AND HEALTH

When we think of health, numerous ideas immediately come to mind, especially the idea of well-being—human flourishing—and the expectation of living a good, happy life. This is an ancient, universal notion to which philosophers and religious thinkers have given much thought. Traditional Western understanding of the good life is much influenced by the ancient Greek notion of *eudaimonia*, often translated as happiness or well-being, although it means literally "having a good guardian spirit." The concept of *eudaimonia* points to the goal of living an objectively desirable life, thought to be the supreme human good. Greek philosophers discussed in great detail what constitutes the good life. Their emphasis on objective criteria that can be agreed upon by all as characteristics of the good life is distinct from the modern approach that understands happiness primarily as a subjectively satisfactory life. These two perspectives show that well-being and health in their widest sense include both objective and subjective criteria, external and internal conditions. Biological, psychological, and spiritual factors as well as other conditions have a decisive influence on human flourishing.

The relationship between religion, spirituality, and human well-being in terms of both physical and mental health, and in connection with human development during different stages of life, is now a leading-edge research area in the United States, with a growing influence in many other parts of the world. This interest in the connections between religion and health first became more prominent in the 1980s, and subsequently it was refocused on spirituality and health, or sometimes religion/spirituality and health, since spirituality was understood as a broader, more inclusive and personal concept than institutionalized religion with its organized system of beliefs and practices.

The many studies that have been undertaken by now supply growing evidence for the positive relationship between a religious or spiritual outlook on life, better mental and physical health, and health-promoting behavior. Although this view is not without its critics, more and more research is being carried out in this field.

A steadily growing number of websites on spirituality and health relate to new research projects, journals, research centers and institutes, such as the Center for the Study of Religion/Spirituality and Health at Duke University, or the Institute for Spirituality and Health at George Washington University, or wider networks and organizations like the International Center for the Integration of Health and Spirituality, affiliated with the University of Florida. The John Templeton Foundation provides financial support for research programs on science, health, and spirituality, and so does its affiliated organization, the Metanexus Institute of Religion and Science in Philadelphia.

Also relevant is mind/body medicine as practiced by the Benson-Henry Institute at Massachusetts General Hospital. This is closely connected with the work of Dr. Herbert Benson of Harvard Medical School, who has devoted his life to the development of this complementary form of medicine that makes use of self-care rather than conventional drugs and surgery for healing people's ailments. Mind/body medicine draws on the natural healing capacities of body and mind, especially in the case of stress-related complaints. Fundamental to it is the use of what Benson calls "the relaxation response," an ancient technique of simply following one's breath, in and out, while avoiding distracting thought. The relaxation response requires slowing down, doing one activity at a time, and becoming fully aware of both one's activity and one's inner experience of it. Thus one can become empowered to take care and control of one's life, and thereby regain and maintain one's health. This mind/body healing approach has an implicit spiritual dimension to it, not least in its use of breathing techniques. These are not unlike Buddhist meditation practices that concentrate on breathing and give central attention to mindfulness.

Concern for human well-being in the most comprehensive sense includes physical and spiritual well-being. Since religions have always provided some explanation for human suffering and offered counsel to overcome human frailness, hurt, pain, and wrongdoing, the notion of healing sickness in both a spiritual and physical sense has always played an important role in the religious and cultural traditions of the world. It is no accident that Western concepts of health care and healing are originally derived from

Christian teachings and practices, and are deeply rooted in Christianity. After Christianity became a state religion in the Roman Empire, the Council of Nicaea (325 CE) urged Christians to provide for the poor, widows, the sick, and strangers, and ordered the construction of a hospital in every cathedral town. One of the first hospitals in the Western world was built in Constantinople in the late fourth century CE. The first nurses were members of Christian religious orders, and in the twentieth century the first modern hospice was developed by a practicing Christian.

Many believers give witness to God's or the Spirit's healing power in their lives. They understand that health and wholeness belong together, but extend beyond the individual toward society. There is much need to bring healing to a sick society by addressing the wider social, moral, economic and environmental causes of ill health in the world today.

Thus there remains a strong connection between faith and healing, however understood. The best-known example of this is perhaps Christian Science, founded in the late nineteenth century by the New Englander Mary Baker Eddy (1821–1910). After recovering from an illness, she worked out a new understanding of Christianity as divine healing, expressed in her book *Science and Health with a Key to the Scriptures* (1875). She institutionalized her teaching in the Church of Christ, Scientist, founded in 1879 in Boston. It now consists of some 3,000 independent congregations in fifty countries. There are no priests, but there are Christian Science practitioners who devote themselves full time to the ministry of spiritual healing. The Mother Church in Boston has gathered a significant body of testimonies of such healing over the years. It has been suggested that this commitment to spiritual healing of an entire church for more than a century was a significant factor in the renewed interest in Christian healing among many denominations during the 1960s and 1970s.

When modern medicine began to develop after the Enlightenment, it increasingly became separated from earlier religious influences. With the rise of modern scientific medicine during the late nineteenth century, this separation between religion and medicine became complete. But the churches and other religious groups remain concerned with alleviating suffering and offering healing through diverse means, whether through prayer, laying on of hands, anointing, healing services, or a special healing ministry and counseling. Contemporary healers may often still be religious specialists, such as hospital chaplains, or they may come from diverse religious backgrounds, or combine some therapeutic and religious training. Patients who are looking for solace and healing often find that medical professionals cannot always help them in making sense of their illness, since modern doctors are mostly not trained in this role. David Kinsley, in his book *Health, Healing and Religion*, mentions the helpful act of writing a journal about one's illness as an inner healing process. He calls this a pathography, an act of writing that describes the experience of a particular disease while providing an opportunity to reflect on its meaning, as some cancer patients have done. In his view such writing almost never simply records the illness experience but becomes part of the healing process in the sense of helping a patient to find meaning in a situation of extreme suffering, loss, and distress. This certainly is a deeply spiritual approach, an extraordinarily meaningful, creative act that far transcends the potential of any medical cure.

Given the open-ended and often vague definitions of spirituality, it is difficult to know with certainty whether a strong spiritual attitude to life, and the regular pursuit of spiritual practices, make a definite difference to a person's overall health and longevity or not. The research undertaken so far presents many heterogeneous findings, showing that it is very difficult to develop precise ways of measuring different outcomes of spirituality. Thus, in terms of concrete health or healing results, we have to remain cautious about how to assess the impact of prayer, meditation, worship, pilgrimage, and the cultivation of benevolent emotions such as peacefulness, compassion, love, and other spiritual characteristics. It is generally known, though, that positive emotions and attitudes, as well as a social engagement and commitment to others, are important for the overall condition of a person's well-being and can speed up the process of healing.

It seems therefore logical to pursue investigations that might establish closer correlations between religion, spirituality, and human flourishing in the widest sense. Many researchers in medicine, psychology, psychiatry, neuroscience, and other disciplines are now engaged in the scientific exploration of such potential links. This represents a new, groundbreaking advance in what can be defined as "the science of spirituality." The scientific study of spirituality from a health perspective involves strong transdisciplinary approaches that are quite different from traditional religious and philosophical reflections on spirituality.

This is an exciting new development. It may eventually lead to new findings that could have a tremendous impact on individual and social transformation. New research results would provide an additional impetus for working out more clearly articulated goals for different forms of spiritual education, relating to the personal and social aspects of every stage of human life.

A most important aspect in the area of health and spirituality concerns the huge influence of ideas from psychology, psychoanalysis, and psychotherapy, beginning with leading figures such as Freud and Jung, followed by many others. Important for the modern understanding of the self in search of growth, transformation, and wholeness, certain forms of psychotherapy have come to embody a particular spiritual quest, and have themselves developed into examples of what is now called secular spirituality.

PSYCHOTHERAPY AS SPIRITUAL JOURNEY

Since spirituality is about self and community in relation to tran-scendence—whether conceived as ultimate ground, immanent spirit, or some form of the Divine—traditional religions have much to say about the development of spiritual life. But many people in the postmodern Western world are bereft of this knowl-edge, since they have moved far away from religious institutions and beliefs. When in pain, grief, or distress, many no longer seek help from a traditional religious figure, priest, or spiritual coun-selor. They go to see a therapist instead, someone who will have been trained in one or several of the different schools of psychol-ogy, psychoanalysis, and psychotherapy.

Until quite recently there reigned a considerable "spiritual skepticism" in scientific psychology and psychoanalysis, as they were then predominantly shaped by Freudian views based on instinctual biology. One striking exception to this is Jungian an-alytic psychology, which has always emphasized the spiritual as-pect of the self, the numinous and archetypal within the psyche. Jung himself used the term "psychotherapeutic spirituality" and considered therapy a kind of spiritual journey. Yet he has been criticized for maintaining the isolation of a spiritually based psy-chology from its secular scientific counterpart. This isolation was due to the artificial division of mental life through Jung's recourse to theories about the collective unconscious and archetypes. It is thought that the long delay in incorporating spirituality into mainstream psychology may have been caused by the rift between Freud and Jung in the early days of psychoanalysis.

Because of the work of many analysts and therapists since then, the interest in the spiritual dimension of psychology, psychiatry, and psychotherapy has grown tremendously. Some practitioners find it immensely helpful to attend to the spiritual dimension of their patients, whether experienced as a dark night of the soul or as transforming illumination of the spirit. A whole new field of "spiritual psychotherapy" has emerged, covering spiritual approaches to counseling, mental illness, family therapy, and other issues.

The psychotherapist Victor Schermer argues in his book *Spirit and Psyche* that a spiritually based psychology provides a new paradigm for psychology, psychoanalysis, and psychotherapy. He speaks of a "psychospiritual self," and maintains that important empirical evidence exists to show that spirituality is linked to human development. Three areas support this view: first, research on infants that shows that their development occurs within a living-systems, relational perspective; second, the expanding research on higher states of consciousness, from dreaming states to the slowed brainwaves of meditators, to differentiated left/right brain functions and other experiments; and third, studies on the increased capacity for perception, healing, altruism, concentration, and other characteristics which are developed through spiritual practices.

Spiritual relationships and transformations certainly go beyond therapeutic experiences, but many revealing parallels and convergences exist between the two. Schermer is right when he points out that many spiritual practices and concepts have analogs in psychotherapy: "The structural differences between a house of worship and a therapy office, or between various liturgical and therapeutic 'texts,' obscure deep similarities that stem from the fact that psychotherapy and religion have many convergent sources in history and human need. How can a Jew reciting the Torah, a Muslim bowing to Mecca, a Christian taking the Eucharist, or a Buddhist sitting in zazen—all forms of devotion— be compared to a therapist in an urban office building, with no obvious object or task of devotion, and with a minimum of ceremony? Yet, if we examine the deeper structure of such practices, parallels become apparent. Prayer, spiritual poverty and simplicity, affirmations of faith, and birth, confirmation, and death rites, for example, all occur spontaneously within psychotherapy."

Yet it is also true that the highest spiritual ideals, the search for a pure heart, for holiness and spiritual perfection, for forgiveness and reconciliation, for the love of God and fellow human beings, supersede therapeutic practice without necessarily negating it. The great impact and immense prestige of psychotherapy, especially in North America, is probably an important contributory factor in the resurgence of so much interest in personal spiritual direction.

Contemporary psychotherapy reveals numerous links to spirituality. It can also work as a secular form of spirituality, and as such it exercises a wide appeal. Yet we must remind ourselves that the significance, attraction, and influence of spirituality are much larger than an exclusively psychological focus can reveal. If spirituality can emerge from any experience and is interwoven with every aspect of human life, then it must also exist within numerous other contexts of contemporary culture—a culture so often characterized as having lost a sustaining spiritual vision.

Moreover, a secular spiritual approach is found in many other fields than psychology and psychotherapy. Contemporary secular spiritualities include different forms of New Age spirituality, holistic health practices, certain expressions of feminist spirituality, ecological spirituality, social justice struggles, and other forms of personal and social commitment.

The immense richness and varieties of spirituality come clearly into view when approached from the different perspectives of the human life cycle, education, health, psychotherapy, and other expressions of secular culture. This approach allows for a more nuanced, richer picture than when spirituality is merely discussed in general terms, or only from a traditional religious perspective. Another differentiating aspect is that of spirituality and gender, which will be explored next.

Seven

SPIRITUALITY AND GENDER

Spirituality is often discussed in such general terms that no attention is given to either women or gender. If spiritual practice and understanding relate to all of life, then one of the most significant markers of human life is gender, and the difference it makes to spirituality. But gender perspectives remain often hidden and unacknowledged in writings on spirituality. Gender is not simply a word that stands for "women," though. It concerns both women and men, bears on their relations with each other, and affects the power and influence they hold over each other. Yet as in most other areas of life, men have usually defined what counts as spirituality, who can practice and teach it, who holds spiritual authority, and what the spiritual life is all about. And this has had a deep impact on the spiritual lives of women.

MEN, WOMEN, AND SPIRITUALITY

Our understanding of God, of ultimate reality in whatever form, and of ourselves as persons, is deeply interconnected. And we are always embodied selves patterned by different genders. Thus male and female approaches to spirituality have been profoundly influenced by their respective embodiments through which the life of the Spirit flows and expresses itself. Contemporary awareness of gender differences has given new expression to spiritual life and the flourishing of new spiritualities among women.

In Western theology God has often been described as the "wholly Other," but today we hear far more about "the other" as another person from a different culture, country, or religion. Yet there is also a strong gender dimension to otherness, for women have been "the other" par excellence in much of human history and culture. Sexually different from and other than men, women have in the past been mostly defined by men, often without a right to their own voice or to an independent role. Religions have frequently assigned women to a position of inferiority and subjugation. Within a Christian context, it is only in the modern period that the biblical teaching about both man and woman being created in the image of God, each representing the *imago dei*, has been interpreted in a truly egalitarian sense that affirms equality and partnership. This important teaching, linked to the recognition of the full humanity of women, had a considerable influence on the emergence of the first wave of the women's movement in the mid-nineteenth century.

Traditionally, spirituality has been the official prerogative of human males. It was primarily among men that spiritual disciplines were developed, taught, written down, and passed from one generation to the next. While women did have their own spiritual practices and devotions, they were usually of a more domestic, private, and folk nature rather than being part of official religion. The search for spiritual perfection and holiness was often closely related to men's contempt for their own bodies, but also for the bodies of women and the body of the world. In most societies and religions, women occupied an inferior social position and were

kept dependent on men. Women were largely valued in their primary social role as wife and mother, for which they were as much
praised as denigrated. Traditional spirituality often separated men
from women, from each other, and from wider society.

Although ultimately gender-transcendent, spiritual ideals are
far from gender-neutral. They are shaped by deeply embedded
patriarchal structures and androcentric (male-centered) thought
that has affected all traditional spiritual practices and teachings.
On first encounter, much spiritual advice appears to be quite neutral. It sounds as if it were simply addressed to all spiritual seekers,
whoever they are. Spiritual counsels thus often seem to refer to
apparently neutral, asexual beings of no specific gender. But on
closer examination such advice frequently turns out to be anti-
body, anti-woman, and anti-world.

In the past, spiritual practice was mainly developed by particular social and religious elites, such as ascetics, monastics, yogis,
pirs, gurus, holy men, and occasionally also holy women, who possessed the necessary leisure and ability for pursuing paths of spiritual excellence and attainment. Most models of holiness were
male models based on men's experience. The global history of
renunciation and religious asceticism remains still to be written,
but we already know enough to recognize that asceticism is
responsible for a great deal of misogyny found in the teachings of
many of the world's religions.

Past spirituality—and many present-day spiritualities, for that
matter—is deeply dualistic. It divides the world of women, work,
body, and matter from that of the spirit. The contemporary
re-visioning and renewal of spirituality, by contrast, seeks holiness
through *wholeness*. By connecting and integrating all experiences
of human life, traditional attitudes to gender, work, the environment, and many other aspects of personal and social experience are now being radically transformed.

Nowhere is this more evident than among contemporary

women, in the diverse forms of feminism, and in the creative reimaging that has occurred in the women's spirituality movement. Here the three trajectories of a search for personal, social, and planetary transformation come together in an exciting new way. They converge and give birth to new experience and new spiritual vision. Women's spirituality combines the search for an embodied self, a balanced sense of subjectivity, with a new awareness of the power of the spirit. This finds expression in a new sense of self, a new sense of community, and a new relationship to the whole environment of all living beings on earth.

Alongside the worldwide growth in "women's spirituality," especially "feminist spirituality," another important development concerns native spiritual traditions and the spiritual heritage of indigenous peoples and cultures. These different movements share an inherent reverence for life and nature, especially the belief in the sacredness of the earth. This is also an important element in the new "ecofeminist spirituality."

WOMEN'S SPIRITUALITY IN HISTORICAL PERSPECTIVE

Contemporary women's interest in spirituality has truly prophetic and radical features. This is evident among women of different faiths as well as women in the secular realm. The new spirituality among women is sometimes described as "womanspirit" movement, or as spiritual and metaphysical feminism. This first emerged during the second phase of the women's movement in the twentieth century. Some feminist activists with strong political commitments reject this interest in spirituality as a soft option, an opting out, so to speak, from active campaigns for social change. Others consider spirituality a necessity beyond political and social activism, since in the long run only an ultimately spiritual orientation can sustain practical advocacy and personal engagement.

The whole modern women's movement has been described as a spiritual revolution. In fact, it can be argued that contemporary feminism as a social and political movement possesses an implicit spiritual dimension, even when this remains veiled or is explicitly denied. The feminist search for liberation, equality, peace, justice, and the full humanity of women can be understood as not only linked to social, political, and economic goals, but to spiritual ones as well. Besides this implicit spiritual orientation, the development of women's spirituality took off in a major, explicit way in the last decades of the twentieth century.

But women's interest in spirituality goes back much further, to the first phase of the modern women's movement in the nineteenth century. Women then not only toiled to change their social, legal, and political position, but strove to develop the spiritual dimension of their lives and take a more active part in the religions to which they belonged. Religious motivation and spiritual aims played an important part in the lives of many early women campaigners for social and legal reforms. This is evident from the biographies of such well-known figures as Mary Wolstonecraft, Florence Nightingale, Elizabeth Cady Stanton, and Matilda Jocelyn Gage. Historians of the modern women's movement have only recently begun to pay closer attention to the religious elements and spiritual ideals that shaped the thinking and actions of these and other women reformers.

Another interesting example is provided by the first modern interfaith event, the celebrated 1893 World's Parliament of Religions in Chicago. Often mentioned in interfaith dialogue circles today, the considerable presence of women participants and their contribution to this event is far less often acknowledged. It was mainly Jewish women and Christian women from the liberal Protestant traditions (but not from among Catholics) who took part in this first ecumenical assembly of faiths in modern history. Significant women leaders were involved in the organization of the parliament, and spoke at its opening and closing ceremonies. Nineteen of the plenary addresses were given by women, or 10 percent of the total. Many more women were active in numerous committees and parallel events, so that the parliament was rightly claimed as a breakthrough for women in religion. Their hopes were high in forecasting the equal participation of women in religious offices and institutions. Sadly, this remains a goal not yet reached in our own time, more than a hundred years later.

The Reverend Antoinette Brown Blackwell, a Unitarian minister, was the first Christian woman to have been ordained, in 1853. Her life is a particularly fascinating case of a woman's dedication to religion and spirituality. She carried out her ministry for many years, combining it with marriage and the upbringing of six daughters. At the World's Parliament of Religions in 1893, she could look back on forty years' work as a Christian minister. Reflecting on this extraordinary experience, Blackwell spoke on "Woman and the Pulpit," a speech in which she mentioned "the opposition still felt by very excellent persons to the presence and the wise, helpful teaching of capable women in the Christian pulpit." Yet she also felt that the arguments against women preaching had long been answered, and "that the sex of the worker is not a bar to good work." She strongly argued that the world needs "more women in the pulpit," and that women will become "indispensable to the religious evolution of the human race."

This was not merely wishful thinking but a prophetic vision that has taken on more concrete form since. Blackwell included statistical information in her lecture, stating that over two hundred Christian women had been ordained by 1893. Later, in 1921, when Antoinette Brown Blackwell died, it was calculated that there were more than three thousand Christian women ministers in the United States, belonging to the Free Churches. It took many more years before more established churches would ordain women. Presently it is mainly the Roman Catholic Church and the Orthodox Church that refuse to accept fully ordained women ministers in their midst. Yet in both churches women carry out numerous spiritual tasks, whether as women religious (nuns and sisters) or as laywomen. They act as chaplains in hospitals, prisons, and educational institutions, and perform much pastoral work in parishes and church organizations.

Today women across a wide variety of denominations inside and outside the churches and in different religions across the globe call into question many traditional forms of spirituality. They reject past spiritual ideals of submission and obedience that hold little attraction for them. Instead, they seek alternative patterns of a new, more embodied and immanent spirituality, more attuned to their own experience, more actively engaged and concerned with contemporary social and personal problems. They also draw on women of past ages who, in spite of numerous obstacles, struggled to follow their own spiritual quest within the religious and cultural constraints of their time.

Recent research has discovered rich resources of female imagery and symbolism in the world's religions, such as the wealth of goddess imagery in ancient Mediterranean cultures or in Hinduism, the presence of female figures of wisdom from the ancient *Sophia* in the Hebrew Bible and Christian Old Testament to the personification of *Prajna* (Wisdom) in Asian Buddhism, or the gracious, infinitely compassionate figure of the female bodhisattva *Kuan Yin*, worshiped as "she who hears the cries of the world" in much of East Asia. The conscious appropriation and imaginative reflection on this rich symbolic heritage can be spiritually very affirming for contemporary women.

Another source of affirmation and strength can be found in the countless women saints and mystics of the past. Their experiences and life stories, their spiritual search, struggle, and achievements can greatly appeal to both women and men. Strong inspiration can be drawn from innumerable "women of spirit" that have existed and continue to exist in different religions, from ancient cultures to the Middle Ages and the modern period. To mention just a few Western examples, there are Hildegard of Bingen, Julian of Norwich, Teresa of Avila, or the Beguines. Nearer our own time we have Simone Weil, Edith Stein, Mother Teresa, or the less well-known Orthodox Mother Maria Skobtsova. Among Eastern women of spirit are Akka Mahadevi and Mira Bai in medieval Hinduism, Sarada Devi and Anandamayi Ma in modern Hinduism, and the early Buddhist nuns who sang about their search for spiritual liberation and enlightenment in the *Therigatha* or "Songs of the Sisters." We have the spiritual biographies of Korean or Japanese Buddhist nuns, and in early Islam the great woman mystic Rabia, followed by other women Sufis.

Women of different faiths are now discovering their spiritual foremothers, so long neglected in the past. We can read a book like *Sacred Texts By and About Women*, learn about Jewish women's spirituality, or that of women in Buddhism, Hinduism, Islam, Sikhism, in Chinese, Japanese and many other religions. For Christian women it was an affirmative experience to be given greater visibility and recognition when the World Council of Churches called in 1988 for a "Decade of the Churches in Solidarity with Women." Much reflective work, practical action, spiritual energy and empowerment came out of this initiative. It inspired women and men around the world, and it would be very desirable if other religions would follow this example. They could all give more space and recognition to women through another decade of action and reflection by publicly calling for a "Decade of Religions in Solidarity with Women." Alas, this has remained an unfulfilled dream so far.

FEMINIST SPIRITUALITY

The goals of modern feminism and the perennial human quest for spirituality seem at first to have little in common, at least not when each is understood in a narrow, exclusive way. When both are approached from a wider, more inclusive perspective, then all sorts of connections are discovered. "Feminist spirituality" in its widest sense means the spiritual quest and creativity of contemporary women, whether pursued in more traditionally religious or nontraditional, secular ways. In a more specific sense, "feminist spirituality" refers to a new spiritual movement that has arisen out of second-wave feminism, and exists outside traditional religious boundaries and institutions. Feminist spirituality is the reclaiming by women of the reality and power designated by "spirit," but it is also a reclaiming of female power, of women's partaking in the Divine, and their right to participate in shaping the realm of spirit by fully participating in religion and culture.

Feminist spirituality is rooted in women's experience and oriented toward bonding among women. It believes in the inherent goodness of matter, body, and the world, thrives on ecological sensitivity, and reimages the Divine. It has created new rituals and liturgies, drawn from Wicca and folk traditions celebrating especially life and nature cycles, but it is also based on the imaginative reinterpretation of traditional religious rites and texts.

Contemporary women's spirituality is a tapestry of many strands. Prominent among them is women's discovery of their own self and agency, the experience of networking and sharing, the new awareness of empowerment from within to work collaboratively for personal, social, and political changes. There is the creative reimaging and renaming of the sacred, a growth in sensitivity to the interdependent connectedness and sacredness of all forms of life, and to a special earth-human relationship. Many of these themes are reflected in contemporary women's culture that, through poetry and fiction, through songs, music, film, art, and theater, explores different aspects of women's spiritual quest. This includes their experience of loss and pain, oppression and freedom, intimacy and mutuality with others, and the multiple connections between sexuality and spirituality.

Women's spiritual quest and their discovery of self is vividly described in the works of contemporary writers such as Margaret Atwood, Doris Lessing, Adrienne Rich, and Ntozake Shange. Carol Christ mapped the stages of this discovery as a series of steps moving from initiation to awakening, then to insight, transformation, and wholeness. Groundbreaking, and of immense influence among women in the United States and elsewhere, was Carol Christ's and Judith Plaskow's publication *Womanspirit Rising: A Feminist Reader in Religion* in the late 1970s, followed ten years later by another collection, *Weaving the Visions: New Patterns in Feminist Spirituality*. Equally influential was Charlene Spretnak's edited work on *The Politics of Women's Spirituality*, which contains essays by many founding mothers of feminist spirituality. These clearly show that women's search for wholeness and integration requires a radical transformation of traditional patriarchal attitudes to gender, sexuality, work, and society. In other words, the profoundly empowering spirituality of women has important political implications for their life in society as well as their participation in religious life if they continue to belong to a specific faith community. Women's spirituality groups, whether inside or outside specific faith communities, have created new symbols, prayers, songs, and feasts, and they also use special blessings, silence, and meditation.

Where can women find the necessary spiritual resources to meet their specific spiritual needs today? Many, but not all, can come from women's own experience, their inner power and strength, but also their suffering, pain, and oppression—and their sense of empowerment and achievement, of new dignity and respect, of connectedness with others, of a newly found mutuality and trust. Women of faith will find many resources in their own religious traditions that can inspire and nurture their spiritual life, even though much will require adaptation and new interpretation.

A surprising source of enrichment is the discovery of the great spiritual heritage of women across the different religions of the world. So many spiritual "foremothers" exist, so many female saints and mystics through the ages can provide inspiring examples for women and men today. Yet we are also painfully aware that most religions have validated women's lives more in terms of domestic observances and family duties rather than encouraged women's search for religious enlightenment and spiritual perfection. Thus we may rightly ask, how far have women really possessed a spiritual space of their own? How far were they able to pursue the same spiritual disciplines as men?

Throughout history, particular women have struggled, often against great odds, to pursue a spiritual path contrary to the wishes of their families, friends, and religious authorities. Ample examples of women following extraordinary paths of spiritual devotion and attainment can be found in the histories of Jain, Buddhist, and Christian nuns. Women had to struggle to create their own religious communities, and their gender always provoked male resistance to women's claim to autonomy, independent power, and spiritual authority. Thus women's activities remained in most cases constrained and controlled by male religious hierarchies, and this is still the case today. Perhaps nowhere is this struggle more evident than in the richly documented history of Christian nuns and sisters, in whose cloisters and convents lived countless women scholars, mystics, artists, activists, healers, and teachers over many centuries. This is a most precious heritage for women today. Whether Christian or not, all women can be truly proud of this as they can be of the spiritual achievements of women in Buddhism, Hinduism, Islam, and the other faiths.

Taking yet another perspective, the rich female imagery and symbolism in different world faiths, though often profoundly ambivalent, also provide numerous spiritual resources for women. We can ask of all of them, where do we find symbols and images of a feminine Divine, of female figures of wisdom, and of the Spirit? Reading religious texts from a specifically female gender perspective can lead to surprising new insights into the human experience of the Divine, whether in gendered patterns of mystical experience, sometimes with marked differences between men and women, or in the intimate presence of the Spirit within our bodies and in the natural world.

Discussions about the possibility and necessity of a feminine Divine, accompanied by a new reevaluation of the body and maternal experience, have a central place in contemporary philosophical and theological thought. Among Christian and Jewish feminist theological writers, the greatest effort has gone into reimagining the Divine by developing more inclusive metaphors for God that are not uniquely male. Central to this is the recognition of the power of the Goddess and the rediscovery of many very ancient goddess traditions around the world. Yet however powerful such traditions are, they do not necessarily exercise a positive influence on the status of women in society.

GODDESS SPIRITUALITY

The most significant feature of contemporary feminist spirituality is probably the (re)discovery and contemporary worship of the Goddess in Western societies. For this reason feminist spirituality is sometimes simply equated with "goddess spirituality." Although these two forms of spirituality overlap considerably, they are not simply identical. Some women reject all anthropomorphic approaches that link the representation of the Divine to female or male forms, but prefer instead an androgynous or monistic understanding of ultimate reality.

Current goddess spirituality draws on both traditional and nontraditional religious sources, and it has produced many new religious rituals and practices. The Great Goddess, manifest in myriad historical and cultural forms, is seen as immanent rather than transcendent, and is strongly connected with body and earth. Thus she can be experienced within ourselves, within other human beings, within nature. One of the most powerful symbols of the Goddess is the moon, which is linked to women's bodily cycles of monthly bleeding, of fertility, and giving birth.

Systematic reflections on the Goddess are now called *thealogy* after Naomi Goldenberg, who first suggested this expression in order to distinguish it from traditional Jewish and Christian *theology*, so much concerned with God-talk in male terms. The rediscovery of the Goddess has produced a vibrant Goddess thealogy. This uses female images and metaphors largely drawn from goddesses of the ancient Mediterranean world, but much less so from goddesses of other cultures and religions, whether African, Asian, Central or South American.

For example, Hinduism is one of the historically richest traditions regarding female perceptions of the Divine; it probably possesses the most vibrant living goddess worship in the contemporary world. Yet very few Indian goddesses figure in Western thealogy and feminist spiritual practice. Moreover, the relationship between female symbolism of the Divine and the real lives of women is very ambivalent. Many religions that worship goddesses do not necessarily affirm women's actual lives, as is evident in numerous countries around the world.

The greatest contribution of thealogy probably consists in the reaffirmation of female sacrality by seeing the life-giving powers of women's bodies linked to divine creative activity. This has led to a new "spiritual feminism" which has contributed to contemporary transformations of religious practice.

The (re)discovery of the Goddess is also linked to women's reclamation of witchcraft and the practice of Wicca, originally meaning "wisdom." Wicca is a Goddess-centered religion that forms part of the wider Goddess-worshiping community. It is organized in covens that can consist of both women and men. Followers of Wicca have created their own rituals, dances, and chants. One of the most influential practitioners and teachers of feminist witchcraft is the American Starhawk, sometimes described as the high priestess of the modern witchcraft movement. Her original background was Jewish, and her earlier name was Miriam Simos. Starhawk's ideas have been widely diffused through her writings, lectures, workshops, and covens, which have created distinct communities, especially the Reclaiming Collective in and around San Francisco. Her book *The Spiral Dance* is a classic of feminist spirituality, containing many exercises, invocations, chants, blessings, and spells.

Other forms of renaming ultimate reality include Rosemary Ruether's suggestion to describe the Divine as "God/dess," whereas Carol Christ has more recently adopted the expression "Goddess/God." These are not terms that can be easily used in worship. They are attempts to be more inclusive, to enable women to claim all that is true of what has been traditionally said about Goddess and God, while at the same time rejecting the patriarchal and exclusive aspects of that tradition. Another way of doing this is represented by calling the Divine "Holy Wisdom," which can be taken as both female and male.

Contemporary feminist spirituality is widely influenced by psychological writings about the Goddess, primarily based on Jungian thought. Much use is made of Jung's archetypal theory about the feminine and masculine that coexist within every human being.

However, Jung's ideas about the harmonious complementarity of the feminine and masculine, of *anima* and *animus* in each person, unfortunately often reinforce traditional sexual archetypes and gender hierarchies. Even in an androgynous approach to humans and the Divine the male still seems to be given priority over the female.

Changes in religious practice also include the adoption of gender-inclusive language in religious readings and prayers, and institutional changes which give women access to official religious positions. Women's new opportunities in the field of religion and spirituality include their taking up traditional paths of renunciation in Hinduism, or the reclaiming of full ordination for Buddhist nuns in Sri Lanka and other Theravada countries. But it will still require considerable effort and time before the full equality of women and men is achieved in all religions, or before women's new spirituality groups are fully accepted in secular society.

ECOFEMINIST SPIRITUALITY

One of the most exciting developments in spiritual feminism is the growth of "ecofeminist spirituality." Similar to feminist spirituality in many ways, it focuses more explicitly on ecological issues. It also puts a far stronger emphasis on women's connection with the earth and all forms of life. Ecofeminist spirituality grew out of ecofeminism, a word first coined in 1974 to describe a new movement based on the close connection between ecology and feminism. One of the principal ecofeminist insights consists in the belief that the oppressive exploitations of women and nature are closely related, and are both equally destructive to the wholeness of life and to peace on earth.

From an ecofeminist perspective, there exists a disconnection between our selves, the earth, and the Divine—a deep split that must be healed. Women can make an essential contribution to this earth healing, for earth and women are linked through their birthing activities, through weaving the fabric of life in continuous renewal, creating a multi-stranded web of which we are all part. This is a very creation-centered spirituality where nature itself is experienced as hierophany, revealing the presence and beauty of spirit. The world is seen as the body of God/dess, or simply as Gaia, and therefore we must revere the earth.

Ecofeminism thus has a strong orientation towards the sacred. It seeks the revisioning of traditional religions through the development of new ecofeminist spiritualities but also draws on alternative religions and spiritualities as well as on the spirituality of the land, found among indigenous and native peoples. Significant themes of ecofeminist spirituality are the connections between the bodies of women and the earth, the alignment with the seasons of nature, the dynamism and energy of life, and the interconnectedness of the web of life. This spirituality aims at an alternative culture that is more peace loving and nonhierarchical, breaking down the boundaries between nature and culture.

Like ecofeminism itself, ecofeminist spirituality is a movement involved in global activism. It is committed to global planetary and social change. These cannot happen without a spiritual change nor without the indispensable, essential contribution of women from all parts of the world. *Women Healing Earth*, to cite the title of one of Rosemary Ruether's books, is an integral part of the activism of many women's groups in the so-called Third World. However, it is not only in the two-thirds of the developing world but in all countries of the globe that women and their spirituality are necessary to promote sustainable development, ecological integrity, and a just and peaceful world.

Following the feminist reinterpretation of traditional religions, and the rise of feminist, ecofeminist, and goddess spiritualities, there now also exists a growing movement of new male reinterpretations of religion and spirituality. This is similarly concerned

with issues of embodiment, sexuality, the deconstruction of traditional masculine roles and images, and new approaches to the
Divine. However, these are grounded in the specific experience of
men rather than women. New forms of masculine spirituality
reclaim the male body as a positive element in male religious identity. This line of thinking was pioneered by the American theologian James B. Nelson in his book *The Intimate Connection: Male
Sexuality, Masculine Spirituality*, and has since been taken up by
other writers and different men's groups. So far, the much younger
male spirituality movement has remained a largely Western phenomenon, whereas the women's spirituality movement and the
feminist critique of traditional religion have spread around the
globe, and include many women from non-Western religions.

GENDER AND SPIRIT

Many traditional stereotypes still subtly influence people's attitudes
in thinking about spirituality. Most pervasive are the customary
associations with masculinity and femininity that are still deeply
rooted in Western culture. Masculinity is often perceived as being
linked to reason, transcendence, and divinity, whereas femininity
is associated with body, immanence, and humanity. Such stereo-
typical associations provide some, though not all, explanations
why women were often deemed unable to reach the exalted, transcendent heights of the spirit. This is not only true in Christianity
and Judaism, but also in most other religions. The widespread perception that women are inferior to men, characteristic of so many
religious teachings, has meant for a long time that women were
excluded from the realms of spiritual authority and from the spiritual hierarchies of established religious institutions.

   For women's equal participation in spiritual life, especially in
spiritual teaching and direction, it is essential that they be fully

trained and acquire the same intellectual and spiritual attainments as men. This was already recognized at the 1893 Chicago World's Parliament of Religions. One of the women speakers at the parliament interpreted the women's movement of that time as due to divine providence, but acknowledged that "we are still measurably ignorant of the nature of woman in women, of her real capacities, inclinations, and powers, nor shall we know these until women are free to express them in accordance with their own ideas, and not as hitherto, in accordance with man's ideas of them."

These words were then mainly addressed to Western men and women from a predominantly Christian and Jewish background. It is remarkable how, since this event just over a century ago, highly trained Christian women ministers, Jewish women rabbis, women theology professors, and religion scholars have played their part in shaping contemporary religion and spirituality in the West. It is fascinating to see how an ever-growing number of Jewish and Christian women have become trained in the languages and interpretation of their sacred scriptures, and in the history of their faith community. Thus many women are now eminently qualified to teach about their faith traditions up to the highest academic level. Similar developments can also be observed among women in Hinduism, Buddhism, Islam, Sikhism, and other religions in Asia, Africa, and elsewhere in the world. Not many Western people are aware that we are at present witnessing a silent revolution in the way women are fast acquiring both scholarly and spiritual competences, thereby gaining an authority that is sometimes only acknowledged with reluctance. Contemporary female Muslims, Buddhists, and Hindus, and women from many other faiths, who have acquired a critical feminist awareness and possess an activist inclination to work for change in their communities, all show what was already expressed indirectly in the speeches made at the 1893 World's Parliament of Religion: for women to gain equal access to the realm of the spirit, and to exercise authority in spiritual matters, traditionally divisive gender patterns have to be transcended. This requires a huge effort, for it is vital that women gain full access to literacy and education at all levels. In general, literacy means the ability to read and write, but it can also be understood as "spiritual literacy"—the competence to understand and interpret religious thought, to be able to interpret the sacred scriptures and traditions of a faith, to offer spiritual advice with discernment, authority, and wisdom. More and more women in Judaism, Christianity, Buddhism, Hinduism, and Islam are now acquiring such spiritual literacy. They study the heritage of their faith, seek access to professional training and positions in their religious institutions, and become teachers and religious leaders whose spiritual authority is recognized and respected.

This worldwide phenomenon is a new contemporary development. For the first time in human history a growing number of women from different religious and secular backgrounds are articulating their own spiritual experiences, reflections, and quests not simply as individuals, but as a *group* of virtually global size. This radically new process will have a profound impact on the future of religion and spirituality, and on that of the human species as a whole. Not only Western women, or women from a Jewish or Christian background, are actively engaged in the reinterpretation of their religious and cultural heritage, but women from very different religious and secular contexts around the whole globe are fully involved in the transformation of their tradition.

The creative tensions that exist in the field of spirituality and gender, and the new spiritual ideas, rituals, and practices that are emerging out of the women's (and men's) movement in religion, bear witness to much zest, energy, and fresh creativity. They can be read as signs of the spirit in contemporary culture, pointing toward profound transformations, and perhaps new beginnings.

Individual religions are differently affected by contemporary feminist thought and practice, and respond to them in different ways. There is little doubt that women of faith, and women deeply involved with transformative spiritual practice, are in dialogue with each other. This is interreligious dialogue in a new key, since women have developed a global network of contacts with each other. Such contacts among women worldwide are steadily growing and being strengthened, in spite of many criticisms, backlashes, personal difficulties, and disappointments. They include many new experiments in undertaking dialogue with hands, head, and heart—a more holistic way of experiencing dialogical encounter through practical, intellectual, and artistic activities. These involve new attempts at conflict resolution, peace making, finding ecologically balanced ways of living, and new expressions of spiritual practices.

Contemporary thinking has moved on from an exclusively feminist and woman-centered approach to a more inclusive re-visioning of gender relations which will have a radical impact on spiritual practice. We must not forget that we are still only in the early stages of this process. Global visions of the mutual enhancement of faith and feminism provide much ground for promise, and hope for the future. If we seek to ensure not merely the survival of the human species on planet Earth, but human flourishing for all peoples in East and West, South and North—a flourishing that is closely dependent on the advancement of greater peace and justice around the globe—then it is imperative that women's spiritual commitment and dedication play a full part in this process.

Eight

SPIRITUALITY, NATURE, AND SCIENCE

The 2005 World Exposition held in Aichi, Japan, was devoted to the theme "Nature's Wisdom." It emphasized the close links between humanity and nature while exploring the possibilities of how we can live in harmony with nature in the twenty-first century. Between March and September 2005 over 22 million people visited this Expo, far exceeding the 15 million projected by the planners. This huge response reflected the great international appeal of "Nature's Wisdom." As the Expo publicity stated, "Nature—the source of all life—has provided humankind with sustenance from the very beginning. . . . A vast network of knowledge and wisdom has evolved from this basic relationship between humans and nature. Nature's wisdom, her mysteries, her awe-inspiring beauty and power, have been unlocked by inquiring minds and scientific processes. Humans have become masters of this knowledge and have developed incredible technologies to harness energy and other resources. In an increasingly over-crowded world it is sometimes hard to focus beyond everyday life and onto the long-term effects of our technological progress. Concrete jungles bear no resemblance to the beauty of the forest. Surely then, we must be reminded of the true wisdom found in a sustainable relationship with nature."

The theme "Nature's Wisdom" emphasizes the urgent global concern for the environment, but also an ancient, enduring spiritual attitude of humans toward nature. It is notable that this theme was chosen for an Expo in Japan, since Japanese culture is so deeply marked by reverence toward nature's sacredness—nature is the abode of the *kami*, or nature spirits. Japanese people delight in the exquisite beauty of nature, whose recurrent renewal is embodied in so many beliefs, rituals, and festivals. Whether one thinks of the harmonious colors and shapes of Zen monastery gardens, the joyful celebrations of the cherry blossom festival in spring, the awesome majesty of Mount Fuji, or the popularity of mountain shrines and pilgrimages, one realizes the luminous beauty and attraction of nature and senses its deep spiritual significance.

Expressed in myriad different ways, spiritual attitudes to nature are found in all human societies and cultures. During the last two hundred years such attitudes have been profoundly changed through the influence of modern science and technology, at first in the Western world, and now around the globe. The German sociologist Max Weber (1864–1920) spoke of "the disenchantment of the world," a pregnant expression that captures the modern estrangement from nature through the rise of industrialized society and the growth of secularization. Yet at the same time new spiritual ideas and attitudes have developed through the emergence of science itself, through the immensely detailed knowledge we now possess of the very fabric of nature—of the exuberant forms of life, their intricate patterns of evolutionary growth and development, the dynamic processes that underlie and interlink them all. These provide humans with new resources for the spiritual contemplation of nature.

ATTITUDES TO NATURE

But what is nature? And where to find nature in the overdeveloped, highly urbanized and industrialized world of the West?

The very idea of nature has a long, complex history. Sometimes nature is highly idealized and romanticized, for example in literature or art. Many people are deeply influenced by the Romantic poets like Wordsworth or Blake, or by the transcendentalists like Thoreau, Emerson, or Whitman. When nature is imagined as a paradise-like garden, as the Elysian fields, or a peaceful pastoral scene, the idea of an unspoiled natural environment of virginal quality appears like a dream that conjures up deep longings in the human heart. Such longings also come into play when nature is visually represented in the form of a woman, as often happens, so that the idea of female and natural beauty are fused together. Moreover, nature is experienced as a place of great beauty and stillness, of awesome grandeur and quiet contemplation, a place of rest and recreation, of gathering in and simply being. This is something deeply desirable to humans. But untouched places of nature hardly exist anywhere in a pristine state.

We are attracted to nature not only because of its beauty and the exuberance of its forms, but also because we perceive nature as pure, unsullied wilderness untouched by human intervention. This is of course a romantic projection onto nature. The ideal image of "pure nature" is particularly associated with existing spaces of wilderness, whether high mountains, virgin forests, large deserts, or arctic regions of the globe. Much of contemporary ecotourism caters to this desire of visiting the world's great natural spiritual spaces that, perhaps more than anywhere else, reveal to us something of the unity of nature and spirit.

John Muir (1838–1914), America's most famous naturalist and conservationist, was a lover of the wild. For him the wilderness of Yosemite Valley and the Sierra became a place of pilgrimage. There he found spiritual replenishing like nowhere else. He experienced a deep unity with nature, and wrote in his *Wilderness Essays*, "You bathe in the spirit beams . . . you lose consciousness of your own separate existence, you blend with the landscape, and become part and parcel of nature." The wilderness became home for him—the mountains were not only fountains of timber and irrigating rivers, but fountains of life.

Yet the heritage of wilderness also contains a darker side, since untamed nature has often been understood as opposed to human civilization. As many myths and fairy stories vividly tell, living too close to nature can turn a person into a savage, even a beast, living without morality and restraint and shunning human company. The conquest and cultivation of nature was often considered by colonists and pioneers, especially in North America, as "taming the wilds." It was a short way from there to the domination and exploitation of nature.

Nature—whether understood as landscape, seascape, animals, or plants—untouched by human hands is increasingly difficult to find, however. Most of nature can no longer be separated from the influence of human beings, even when they live in urban settlements far away from the wild. Human culture has profoundly transformed and, some would say, irrevocably damaged nature. Thus the conditions of its existence have been irreversibly changed through processes that have been going on for millennia, but have incredibly accelerated over the last few decades. Yet from a more inclusive perspective, humans themselves are an integral part of nature. As such, they urgently need to redefine themselves *and* their understanding of nature in a more holistic way.

Spiritual attitudes to nature are at present much influenced by the considerable interest in Celtic spirituality. The idea of the Celts as an ancient, spiritually gifted people was first articulated during the Celtic revival in Europe, especially in nineteenth-century Ireland. It then expanded to a distinctive way of being Celtic linked to the peoples of Ireland, Wales, Scotland, and Brittany. The roots of modern Celtic spirituality lie in contemporary popular culture, with New Age religion embracing Goddess worship and shamanism on one hand, and the search for a more holistic, ecologically sensitive and inclusive Christianity on the other.

Celtic Christianity is highly attractive to many contemporaries, since it responds to a number of current spiritual needs. With its sense of the sacredness of nature it is perceived as being close to the world rather than withdrawn from it, environmentally friendly, celebrating the goodness of God's creation, nonhierarchical, nonsexist, and exceptionally creative in the brilliant imagery of its art, prayers, and music. Widely known and admired are the vivid Gospel illustrations of the Book of Kells (ninth century CE, now at Trinity College, Dublin) and the Lindisfarne Gospels (seventh to eighth centuries CE, at the British Library, London) with their intricate, interweaving designs from the natural world and their brilliant colors. The calligraphy and illuminations of these famous Gospel books belong to the supreme art treasures of the human race. One of the most significant ways in which people first become interested in Celtic spirituality is through such Celtic art and artifacts, which are wide-ranging and span 2,500 years.

Besides the role of scripture as a focus of Celtic spirituality, we know of public and private prayers, devotion to angels and saints, the life of Celtic monks, the strong sense of justice and hospitality, and the existence of the *anam chara*, the "soul friend" of Celtic monasticism who provides an early example of spiritual direction that could be given by either men or women.

A place of special importance in contemporary international Christian Celtic spirituality is the island of Iona on the western side of Scotland with its medieval abbey, rebuilt during the twentieth century. Centered on the ecumenical Iona Community, founded in 1938 by George MacLeod (1895–1991), a Church of

Scotland minister, the island became well known when the current Celtic movement took off in the 1980s. It is linked to an ancient sense of place and deep belonging, and through MacLeod's imaginative approaches to the revival of Celtic spirituality, Iona is now seen by many as the world center of Celtic Christianity.

THE NATURE OF NATURE

The Western concept of nature is rooted in ancient Greek thought. It not only consists of the idea of an impersonal, external environment confronting and surrounding human beings, but also includes the concept of an *anima mundi*, the existence of a world soul, and the ensoulment of the world. With the deepening of the modern technological crisis, the specter of diminishing energy resources, the increasing loss of animal and plant species, and the looming threat of ecological disaster, human beings have to ask themselves with great urgency: What is the nature of nature? What is the nature of the human being? And what is the relationship between these two? These questions are not merely "natural" questions that can be answered in a matter-of-fact way, but they belong to some of the most fundamental inquiries humans can and must ask. They are connected to deep philosophical perspectives and decisive spiritual choices that shape our understanding of the world and of ourselves.

Religious and philosophical traditions around the globe possess a profusion of myths and stories that poetically describe the creation of the world and of humans, explaining the diversity of forms and exuberance of life as one grand, interdependent tapestry of beings. Such creation stories and cosmogonies of old reflect the profound insight that human beings belong to a moral and cosmic order that extends far beyond humankind. During modernity, many people have lost this integral vision, but it presents us with a deep spiritual intuition that needs to be reappropriated and become an essential part of a new ecological consciousness.

During the nineteenth century the spiritual aspects of nature were much reflected upon by European philosophers in their so-called *Naturphilosophie* (philosophy of nature). They looked at nature as a whole, and taught a deep affinity between nature and human beings, so that humans could feel at home in the world. This mysterious attraction to nature was also prevalent among early modern scientists such as Johannes Kepler (1571–1630), Galileo Galilei (1564–1642), and Isaac Newton (1643–1727). They combined a deeply religious attitude and reverence for nature with stringent scientific inquiry. In addition to their rigorous use of mathematics in formulating the laws of nature with utmost precision, they also still drew on religious reasoning and arguments in some of their works, unlike most scientists today.

Early and medieval Christian theology praised nature's benevolence as governed by a loving creator. Christian thinkers approached nature as another "book," second only to that of scripture. Reading it revealed to them something about God, and this attitude was still prominent among some of the early modern scientists, who hoped to learn more about God by studying nature and by discovering the laws that governed it. But this perspective of inquiry was soon abandoned, especially under the influence of evolutionary theory from the mid-nineteenth century onwards. Nature now came to be seen as characterized above all by the struggle for existence, a realm where the survival of the fittest and self-assertion counted for more than self-sacrifice and the self-abandonment of love for the well-being of others. This disenchantment with nature is summed up in Tennyson's often quoted description of nature as "red in tooth and claw." Thus the nineteenth-century separation of the natural sciences from religion and theology led to a profound estrangement from nature in the West. New scientific theories encouraged the view that nature is more hostile than benign, an environment where humans do not feel at home.

Yet even for ancient and medieval thinkers it can never have been a straightforward move from thinking about the natural world to gaining an insight into God and Spirit. The experience of nature has always been profoundly ambivalent for humans. Nature continues to provide human beings with essential, vital support and nourishment that they cannot do without, but it is also linked with brute, savage powers, evident in the animal world or in the powerful natural forces of fire, floods, tempests, and earthquakes. We still experience their destructiveness today in spite of the immense growth of scientific knowledge about the natural world and the technological ability to control many aspects of it. One only needs to be reminded of the tragedies created by the tsunami disaster in Asia, Hurricane Katrina in the United States, earthquakes in Pakistan and China, floods in Bangladesh and Europe. They have wrecked and destroyed so many lives and done much damage to the environment.

What spiritual attitude toward nature remains open to us when faced with the magnitude of these destructive natural events and the immense human suffering associated with them? Faced with such calamity we merely seem to be reduced to humility, silence, and passive surrender. Yet compassion calls on us to help reconstruct the lives of our neighbors and overcome the vicissitudes of nature, made so much worse through human failings and lack of forethought.

Such powerful outbursts of nature teach us clearly that even with all the scientific data and technological know-how available, the immense energies of earth remain ultimately out of human control. The meaning of nature is by no means self-evident. The mystery of the universe is never made unequivocally clear, not even to those who study its phenomena most intimately. The evaluation of factual scientific data is open to widely varying interpretations;

their significance must always be established through human assessment and choice that remain open to further questioning. Nowhere is this more evident than in the acrimonious debates about the meaning of evolution, carried on between different evolutionary biologists themselves, and also between scientists and theologians. These lively controversies are reflected in what is taught in science classes in schools around the world.

Is evolution occurring at random? Or has it a purpose and direction due to a divine creator or superior intelligence? Some scientists acknowledge the presence of an infinite, eternal energy in the cosmos, whereas others will deny it. But is this energy identical with the presence of the Spirit, or the existence of God, as understood by traditional religion? Nature, though now a far more open book than our ancestors could ever have imagined, still contains many undeciphered pages. Therefore scientists, theologians, and religious thinkers continue to argue about the nature of matter, consciousness, and spirit.

SPIRIT AND MATTER

Ever since the French philosopher René Descartes (1596–1650) sharply separated mind from matter, a dualistic worldview has been prominent among Western philosophers and scientists. But there are others who perceive a deep unity underlying the human quest into matter and spirit, pursued in different ways by science and religion. A more holistic understanding of mind and matter is now on the rise, especially through a new understanding of evolution and new attitudes to nature that have developed through the growth of the environmental movement. A more integral approach to spirit and matter has always been evident in traditional thought, in Chinese science, in the science and civilization of Islam, and in that of India, whose intellectual and religious thought is so deeply marked by the search for unity. Unlike in the West, this religious outlook is also widely supported by modern Indian scientists.

One of the pioneers of experimental science in India, the physicist and plant physiologist Sir Jagadish Chandra Bose (1858–1937), was "amazed to find boundary lines vanishing and points of contact emerge between the realms of the Living and the Nonliving." He searched for a wider synthesis between the different sciences against what he described as the excessive specialization of scientists in the West. In his view India is "peculiarly fitted to realize the idea of unity, and to see in the phenomenal world an orderly universe." By concentrating his attention on the boundaries between the physical and biological sciences, he hoped eventually to demonstrate the underlying unity of all things by the discovery of the One in the many, and thereby to understand a little more of the message that his ancestors, the great seers, had proclaimed on the banks of the Ganges thirty centuries ago. Bose wrote in one of his speeches, "In my scientific research . . . an unconscious theological bias was also present. . . . It is forgotten that He, who surrounded us with this ever-evolving mystery of creation, the ineffable wonder that lies hidden in the microcosm of the dust particle, enclosing within the intricacies of its atomic form all the mystery of the cosmos, had also implanted in us the desire to question and understand."

An English scientist much concerned with the relationship between matter and spirit was the Oxford zoologist Sir Alister Hardy (1896–1985). He was deeply interested in the spiritual nature of the human being, which he saw as part of the natural world. Besides his zoological research he was involved in studying religious and spiritual experiences empirically, inviting people to describe such experiences by writing them down. One of the questions he asked was, "Have you ever felt a presence or power, whether you call it God or not, which is different from your everyday self?" People's responses have shown that such a presence or power was often strongly experienced in nature, a presence not necessarily called God, but what the eminent German scholar of religion Rudolf Otto (1869–1937) described as a "numinous experience." Similarly, the Anglican theologian Austin Farrer (1904–1968) wrote that "matter is one of God's languages; that it is indeed the bearer of spirit; that we can come to understand, if only we would learn to open our eyes and ears. . . ."

Another scientist who widely opened his eyes and soul toward the natural world and its history of evolution was Pierre Teilhard de Chardin. He sang the praises of the spiritual power of matter with extraordinary passion and sensitivity. His deeply unifying, mystical vision of cosmos and nature has been rightly described as a "Hymn to the Universe." Matter was for him the matrix of spirit. Firmly grounded in the natural sciences of the first half of the twentieth century, especially geology and palaeontology, the science of human origins, he considered the immense research efforts of humanity as ultimately leading to the adoration of something greater than ourselves, in spite of the shadow sides and new ethical problems raised by science. His deepest desire was to see the ultimate essence of things, to find their heart, and to probe into the mystery of life, its origin and goal.

Teilhard described the creative power of matter evolving into energy, life, and thought as linked to a spiritual center, a soul of the world. He spoke of it as a living, pulsating heart, animated by the fiery energies of love and compassion. The human heart is really living flesh. Widely used metaphorically in religion and literature, the image of the heart has long served as a powerful symbol for the engaged, feeling center of the human being. The heart as a concentration of living, breathing matter came to symbolize for Teilhard the very core of spirit. Thus he could write, "At the heart of matter a world-heart, the heart of a God."

NATURE AS DIVINE MILIEU

The divine Spirit radiates from the depths of blazing matter. Teilhard was often magically entranced by the beauty of nature. At times it overwhelmed him. Yet he criticized the lack of a cosmic sense in the Christian mystics, and maintained that Christian spirituality needed a strong "blood transfusion from matter," so as not to lose its vigor and become lost in the clouds. His understanding of spirit in matter was neither monistic nor pantheistic, but is best characterized as "pan-en-theism," where *all* of nature and reality is held in God, where the Spirit suffuses everything.

It troubled him immensely that while science has revealed to us the immensity and unity of the world, the implications of this new understanding of the universe, the earth, and the whole of life have not yet been fully incorporated into contemporary religious thought and spirituality. The closely interdependent, dynamic interaction between matter and spirit was experienced by him as a "divine milieu," a new expression which figures as the title of his major work on spirituality. Two different meanings come together in the French word *milieu*: it can mean a center point where all realities come together and converge, but it can also refer to a surrounding environment, a complete ambience, like the air we breathe or the atmosphere in which we live. Everybody needs beauty as well as bread, places to play in and pray in, where nature may heal, and give strength to body and soul alike. The presence of the divine Spirit is this mysterious "milieu" that radiates throughout the universe and penetrates everything within it and gathers everything into a center.

Human beings are immersed in this divine milieu, which can invade them and transform their whole being. Teilhard spoke of it also as a "mystical milieu," a "divine ocean," in which human beings may become divinized. As he explains at length in *The*

Divine Milieu, all realities, all experiences, all our activities and passivities, all our joys, labors, and sufferings have this potential for divinization, for being set on fire through the outpourings of divine love. As a Christian believer he interpreted the whole evolution of matter, life, and spirit within the cosmos as an immense process of progressive spiritualization that ultimately converges onto and culminates in what he calls the Omega point. This is the final goal of evolution, the plenitude of life in God.

Although other scientists, philosophers, mystics, and theologians will interpret the relationship between matter and spirit differently, there can be little doubt that Teilhard de Chardin provides an eminent example of a contemporary scientist and religious believer who drew on seminal ideas in modern science as powerful spiritual resources for living. Not only did scientific ideas fire his imagination and passion as a researcher, they also provided him with vital nourishment for his spirituality.

SPIRITUAL RESOURCES OF SCIENCE

The great public authority accorded to science within the dominant secular culture of Western society makes people of faith inquire into the spiritual significance of modern science. Many scientists agree on the awesome character of science and praise the creative power of the scientific imagination, but will not necessarily draw spiritual conclusions from this. On the contrary, they may even take a strongly antireligious stance—a well-known example are the vehement attacks on religion by the British evolutionary scientist Richard Dawkins, professor of the public understanding of science at the University of Oxford, a passionate advocate of atheism who speaks about "the God delusion" in human beings. Yet other scientists have developed a deep spiritual reverence and even speak of the wisdom of nature.

How do contemporary science and spirituality relate to each other? The historian of science David Knight, former president of the British Society for the History of Science, thinks that they have a "volatile connection." While science will not automatically boost spirituality, both of these two important realms of human experience nevertheless mutually enhance and complement each other: "But while experience indicates that no scientific method or discovery can establish the existence, wisdom and benevolence of God for a doubter, one or other of them can surely refine (or perhaps upset) the ideas of a believer. Thus our science can tell us what is sensible or plausible to believe, and what isn't, allowing us to discriminate between what is important in our faith, and what is mere accretion or baggage. . . . Science need not be cold-hearted: there is room for imagination and enthusiasm."

Writing from the perspective of Buddhism, the Dalai Lama suggests the convergence of science and spirituality in his book *The Universe in a Single Atom*. He tries to show how these two important sources of knowledge and well-being can both serve our world. In his plea to bring our spirituality to bear upon the course of science and the direction of technology, he writes, "In essence, science and spirituality, though differing in their approaches, share the same end, which is the betterment of humanity. At its best, science is motivated by a quest for understanding to help lead us to greater flourishing and happiness. In Buddhist language, this kind of science can be described as wisdom grounded in and tempered by compassion. Similarly, spirituality is a human journey into our internal resources, with the aim of understanding who we are in the deepest sense and of discovering how to live according to the highest possible idea. This too is the union of wisdom and compassion." The Dalai Lama is devoting much effort to the closer understanding between science, religion, and spirituality, and has set up the Mind and Life Institute in Boulder, Colorado, where regular dialogues between Buddhists and different scientists are taking place. According to the mission statement on its website, this institute is devoted to creating a powerful collaboration and research partnerships between modern science and Buddhism, "two of the world's most fruitful traditions for understanding the nature of reality and promoting human well-being."

How one answers the question about the relationship between science and spirituality depends to a large extent on how the relationship between science and religion is perceived. Both fields are so large and consist of so many phenomena that it is sometimes difficult to agree on what is being talked about. Both are areas that are central to human experience; both take up vast amounts of human energy and resources. Yet science and religion are difficult to define. Both have positive and negative images associated with them. The American scholars Ian Barbour and John F. Haught, who have written a great deal on the science-religion debate, perceive a development from attitudes of conflict to contact and conversation between these two areas of human existence, so that eventually a convergence and even synthesis might occur. They both agree that it would be of great benefit to the human community if the new scientific worldview, especially the understanding of natural history and the stunning evolution of life, could be integrated with the enduring wisdom and spiritual quest that form an essential part of humanity's religious and cultural traditions.

Perhaps no one has reflected more on the spiritual implications of the new cosmology and biology, of the history of the universe, matter, life, and spirit, than the American ecological thinker Thomas Berry, who describes himself as a "geologian" (a mixture between a theologian and a geologist perhaps). Deeply influenced by Teilhard de Chardin, Berry has moved far beyond him in his stirring reflections on the grandeur of the evolving universe. Its ongoing emergence presents humans with the greatest occasion and challenge to expand the understanding of the

Divine. In Berry's words we now have a new story of the universe. In his book *The Dream of the Earth* he praises "this marvelous display of beauty in such unending profusion" found on Earth: "In its human expression the universe and the entire range of earthly and heavenly phenomena celebrate themselves and the ultimate mystery of their existence in a special mode of exaltation."

It comes almost as a surprise when he talks about the empirical modes of knowing pursued by science over the past three centuries in explicitly religious terms, considering the modern scientific endeavor as "among the most sustained meditations of the universe carried out by any cultural tradition. Truly the Yoga of the West. If our science has gone through its difficulties, it has cured itself out of its own resources. Science has given us a new revelatory experience. It is now giving us a new intimacy with the earth."

To describe modern science as the "Yoga of the West" is an amazing statement. Many Western scientists may be uncomfortable with it, but this startling assertion truly celebrates the spiritual potential of scientific thought. On one hand Berry criticizes modern science for its lack of spiritual perception and its instrumental attitude vis-à-vis nature; on the other hand he sees scientific knowledge as a new kind of revelation of decisive importance at our present stage of history. But he also criticizes Western religion whose sense of the divine is so widely derived from verbal sources, mostly from biblical scriptures, that "we seldom notice how extensively we have lost contact with the revelation of the divine in nature." For Berry the scientific account of the universe, which is also mythic in providing us with a new story called "the epic of evolution," "is the greatest religious, moral, and spiritual event that has taken place in these centuries. It is the supreme humanistic and spiritual as well as the supreme scientific event." But we are still living "in between stories" at present, since no unifying paradigm has yet emerged that "brings together the scientific secular world with the religious believing world or with the humanist cultural world."

Berry's powerful spiritual vision points the way to a new kind of religiousness and spirituality. His work provides strong evidence of how the study of the epic of evolution—the history of planet Earth and the emergence of its living forms, including the human—can lead to a deep sense of wonder, a mystical awareness of oneness, which links up with earlier mystical experiences, yet also contains something profoundly new.

The Washington University biologist Ursula Goodenough has presented her spiritual vision in *The Sacred Depths of Nature*. In response to the ultimate questions raised by the universe, she movingly articulates "a covenant with Mystery" and expresses profound gratitude for being part of the immense web of life. The American cosmologist Brian Swimme has reflected on *The Hidden Heart of the Cosmos*, an expression reminiscent of Teilhard de Chardin, seeing a divine "heart of the world." Swimme thinks that contemporary science is now entering its "wisdom phase," a position that, again, points to the manifold spiritual resources that science can provide. These examples show how the sense of presence and oneness with nature, of which nature mystics, visionaries, and poets spoke in earlier ages, is now experienced in quite a new way within the creative context provided by the immense knowledge of modern science.

Holmes Rolston III from Colorado State University argues that contrary to the superficial impression that science might chase away the holy, we now discover that nature is mysteriously animated and inspirited. Among the many phenomena that science studies, two in particular require explanation for him—"first, the nature that is full of wonder and, second, the wondering persons, these spirits that have resulted from, and now behold, this wonder-full nature." In Rolston's view, the secular quest of science makes its own demands on and for spirituality. He exemplifies this by looking at spirituality from the perspectives of contemporary astronomical, microphysical, biomolecular, evolutionary, and ecological knowledge. Each of these scientific approaches may at first challenge traditional religious sensitivities, especially when based on fixed dogmatic positions. But the stunning discoveries of these sciences also call some secular empirical stances into question. They point to new openings and possibilities that far transcend traditional empirical assumptions. Yet knowing "the secret of life biochemically may still leave the evolution of life a secret," and there lurks the question of "whether the scientific account still leaves room for a spiritual response to the phenomenon of life."

Life slowly emerging over millennia out of the pregnant Earth leads to the deepening of sentience, and the rise of thought. Thus over time, Rolston writes, "the matter that first took on life eventually took on spirit, and we ourselves are the proof of that." Humans must recognize "a marvelous endowment of matter with a propensity toward life (and, in due course, toward spirit)." Accordingly, "Responsible, creative beings arising from a creative process, arising to wonder where they are and who they are—that is matter ending in a spiritual quest." Rolston quotes a scientist working in biology as saying, "Virtually all biologists are religious, in the deeper sense of this word, even though it may be a religion without revelation. . . . The unknown and maybe unknowable instils in us a sense of humility and awe." It is perhaps more appropriate to call this a profoundly spiritual rather than a religious attitude, developed through a lifelong study of the evolution of life.

By studying nature, scientists may discover a surprising goodness and grace; they may be drawn to a spiritual understanding of the world that they themselves hardly expected at first. There is no doubt that contemporary forms of spirituality can find rich resources in science to nourish the spirit. In general, however, people still gain access to spirituality more easily through the arts than the sciences. Whether visual, performing, or literary, the arts are often seen as both an expression of, and gateway to, the spirit.

Nine

SPIRITUALITY, THE ARTS, AND THE PLANET

For people with an artistic bent, especially for practicing artists, the natural world has always provided rich pastures for the creative imagination. This is as true today as it has always been, but contemporary artistic practices also reflect many new ways of interpreting nature, of catching glimpses of the eternal through fast-fleeting media, whether in color, sound, images, lines, or shapes. Nature and art have always been closely connected for human beings; in many instances this link has also forged deeply spiritual bonds in people's minds and souls. Today this has been heightened in a very special way through a newly evolved, highly sensitive ecological consciousness born out of the recognition of both the preciousness and precariousness of our natural environment.

The environmental movement is of comparatively recent origin, but it has transformed the relationship of humans to the earth. It has created a new awareness of one planet in an immense universe, a sense of corporate human responsibility for the future well-being of this planet. New attitudes to nature have evolved, drawing great strength from the discovery of our rootedness in the earth and the awakening of a new sense of the cosmic.

THE ARTS AS GATEWAY TO THE SPIRIT

Seen from the long view of history, all creative arts have deep religious roots. Religious devotees often express their devotional surrender, adoration, and celebration through the arts, through music, dance, and chants—or through generous offerings that permit the building of shrines, temples, synagogues, churches, mosques, and other places of worship. Numerous artistic forms of great beauty are not only associated with sacred architecture, but with religious ritual, sacred music, dance, theater, painting, sculpture, and literature. One only has to think of the paintings and sculptures in Hindu and Buddhist temples, the architecture and art of synagogues and cathedrals, the chanting of Tibetan monks, the music of the Sufis, or the ragas sung in Sikh gurdwaras. How exquisite are the intricate patterns of Islamic calligraphy, the miniatures of Biblical and Qur'anic manuscripts, the haunting beauty of great and small mosques, the gracious forms of Chinese and Japanese pagodas, or that of local prayer shrines in East and West.

Myriad examples exist in world art that give compelling expression to spiritual beauty and mystery, reflecting the numinous quality of people's spirituality through the ages. Traditional religious places such as monasteries, convents, and retreat centers, usually set in beautiful natural surroundings, can help to foster spiritual development through the arts associated with them. But the spiritual appeal of the arts is not limited to sacred art. How often have we been spiritually touched by the intense beauty of some music, or the colors of a painting, the lyricism of poetry, even when the subject is quite secular. In the past, great art has often been religious art, or has been expressed through religious symbols, whether one thinks of the paintings of Michelangelo or Rouault, the music of Bach or Handel, the poetry of Dante or Blake. In contemporary secular society, the number of artists who emphasize the spiritual in their work is relatively small by comparison with the hundreds of thousands of practicing artists. Most spiritual art of the late twentieth century has probably been created outside religion, whereas so-called religious art seems often closer to kitsch than a genuine expression of the spiritual.

A remarkable exception are the works of the American sculptor Frederick Hart (1943–1999), who went completely against the grain of the contemporary art world by creating representational and figurative art, not unlike the vivid sculptures of Rodin. Renowned for his "Creation" panels at the Washington National Cathedral and for his Vietnam Veterans' Memorial sculpture, Hart has been praised for giving form to spirit, for creating art that truly uplifts the human spirit and strongly affirms life. His heads, faces, and figures embody an extraordinary dynamic energy and beauty; his innovative sculptures cast in clear acrylic resin seem to be bathed in an unearthly light that radiates an almost mystical quality and conveys a deep spirituality.

After numerous interviews to study the creative spirituality of contemporary North American artists, Robert Wuthnow has described "art as spiritual practice." He argues that it is "only a slight exaggeration to say that artists have increasingly become the spiritual leaders of our time," since it is especially artists who reflect deeply on personal and spiritual concerns. This is true of many popular art productions, as is evident in the lyrics and songs of widely known pop stars in contemporary music. Today, many people turn to artists of the various media for spiritual inspiration, even spiritual direction.

Wuthnow was interested in finding out how contemporary artists link their art and creativity to spirituality. Although only a few artists may be closely connected with traditional religious institutions, many have made their own eclectic selection of spiritual and therapeutic practices such as meditation, chanting, going on pilgrimage, or consulting a spiritual master, guru, or counselor.

While spirituality is especially concerned with transcendence, wholeness, and ultimacy, it also carries other connotations. According to Wuthnow, spirituality is often used "to suggest realms of personal experience or being that cannot be easily communicated to others . . . Many people seem to believe that the essence of spirituality lacks definition. Yet artists are often able to describe their understandings and experiences of spirituality with eloquence."

While Wuthnow sees the spiritual work of artists as relating more to personal than social issues, some artists are clearly also social activists who espouse current social and political causes. But many artists try to effect social change more by influencing individuals through their art than getting involved in large social movements. Much of their spiritual work is linked to the evocation of the mystery of life, which invariably includes an awareness of life's uncertainty and of the presence of evil. But on the whole a certain optimism seems to prevail among artists that life makes sense and is ultimately good. In Wuthnow's final analysis, "these writers, musicians, sculptors, and painters are less concerned with identifying aspects of the social world about which to be optimistic or pessimistic than they are in providing small experiences of transcendence that in themselves become reasons for hope. It is the creative process itself that momentarily transcends time, offering an awareness that something other than the ordinary can exist and, through that existence, reinvigorate the flawed aspirations of ordinary people."

It is inspiring to hear about such hopefulness coming from especially creative moments expressed in works of art. They embody the spirituality of the artist and, in turn, they become a channel for others to develop their creative spirituality by catching glimpses of transcendence through the artist's work. This close creative relationship between the inspiration of artists, works of art, and other people contemplating and enjoying these artistic creations, provides a vibrant example of the dynamic process of spirituality moving in and through people like invisible waves of the spirit.

SPIRITUALITY, THE ARTS, AND NATURE

The spiritual dimension in art is creatively drawn upon in art therapy and other techniques to effect healing and promote well-being in people. Some of this work is reflected in the activities of the Society for the Arts in Healthcare in the United States, and similar organizations in other countries. Evelyn Underhill spoke of the mystic as "creative artist"; according to her, "mystics are closer to the musician than to any other type of artist, though they avail themselves when they wish of material drawn from all the arts." She continued, "In his suggestive and allusive language the mystical artist often approaches the methods of music. When he does this, his statements do not give information. They operate a kind of enchantment which dilates the consciousness of the hearer to a point at which it is able to apprehend new aspects of the world."

According to Underhill, there exists also "another kind of mystic, naturally inclined to visualization, who tends to translate his supersensual experience into concrete, pictorial images; into terms of color and of form. He uses, in fact, the methods of the painter, the descriptive writer, sometimes of the dramatist, rather than those of the musician or the lyric poet." In a prophetic manner Underhill anticipated the growth of "a wholly new order of experience" appearing within humanity through the teachings of the higher religions and philosophies, closely connected with the phenomena of inspiration and artistic creation. She spoke of "the corporate spiritual consciousness" emerging preeminently among mystics and seers, but also "in painters, musicians, philosophers, and the adepts of physical science." Each of these "builds up from material beyond the grasp of other souls, a world within which those other souls can live and dream: a world, moreover, which exhibits in new proportions and endows with new meanings the common world of daily life."

Already in the mid-twentieth century the French writer André Malraux suggested that modern art galleries are today's cathedrals. The sacral nature of these exhibition spaces is recognized by modern artists who either exploit this resonance or revolt against it by deliberately producing such strange works of "art" that many viewers, who still expect more traditional artistic forms, feel a revulsion.

The process of looking for "otherworldliness" and for sublime, even mystical, features in art began in the eighteenth century when Romantic painters endowed scenes of nature—rivers and rocks, mountains and water, forlorn places of the wild—with an almost religious character. The connection between nature and spirituality has inspired many artistic works in the past, and still does so today. Some contemporary artists deeply sense the fragility of our natural environment, and express this in their environmentally inspired installations and structures. Traditionally, both nature and art have been closely associated with beauty, but this has become profoundly problematic today. In traditional Western philosophical discussions, beauty was considered to be found par excellence in natural phenomena, whether mountains or rivers, a landscape, a flower, a tree, the sky, the starry heaven at night, or the richness of the plant and animal kingdom. The philosopher Immanuel Kant (1724–1804), for example, thought that objects are beautiful only to the extent that they conform to the beauty of nature. The sheer profusion and variety of forms and color found in myriad phenomena of nature can give intense delight by appealing to all our senses. This very sensuous allurement can in turn open a door to spiritual awakening and experience. William Blake (1757–1827), artist, mystic, and poet, expressed this experience by speaking of the "doors of perception," and by calling the five senses "the inlet of spirit" in his *Songs of Innocence and Experience*.

In contrast to this alluring appeal of nature, so many phenomena of contemporary culture seem to manifest what has been described as a much noted "exile" of beauty. This often points also to an absence of spirit, a loss and failure in understanding the true nature of ourselves. It can also signal an abuse of our natural environment, a forgetfulness of our spiritual calling to a fuller humanity. This needs to be realized within ourselves as persons, and within the whole human community. As John Muir expressed it, "Everybody needs beauty as well as bread, places to play in and pray in, where nature may heal and give strength to body and soul alike."

Is this only a passing, poetic sentiment? Or can beauty return to our senses and spirit through a new relationship with nature, a new covenant with the planet? Is this possibility emerging now within the environmental movement through the growth of "ecospirituality"? Such a spirituality embraces the whole of the earth, seeks the wholeness of the human community, and works for a more balanced life of peace and justice in harmony with nature. It encompasses the planet and its people, and celebrates the wonder of life.

The ecological dimension of spirituality, closely related to nature, science, and the arts, provides an especially significant gateway to spirituality that opens up amazing avenues to spirit for the human senses and soul.

ECOLOGICAL SPIRITUALITY

In many archaic, primal, and indigenous religions Earth has long been worshiped as the mother of all life, to which all human beings bear a most intimate and inalienable relationship that each individual has to honor and continue. An example of this veneration of the earth is found in a statement from the Navajo Nation: "This earth you stand on is your mother, whether you are red, white, black, brown, yellow, or blue. We must unite and help one another save our precious mother, for without Mother Earth to take care and protect us we are a dead race."

A deeply reverential attitude toward the sacredness of the earth has inspired contemporary Christians and many others to celebrate and praise the whole of creation by developing a new "creation spirituality." This movement has been much influenced by the writings of Matthew Fox, especially his *Original Blessing*. Fox argues that the human race requires a new religious paradigm, which is found in creation spirituality. To promote this, he established the University of Creation Spirituality in Oakland, California, in 1996, which was renamed Wisdom University in 2005.

In addition to creation spirituality a new "ecological spirituality" has emerged. This implies an explicit cultivation of a new responsibility for the fate of the planet, an attitude that seeks to respond with integrity and profound concern to the critical ecological situation of the world.

The American writer Carolyn Merchant speaks about "spiritual ecology" rather than "ecological spirituality" as one of several kinds of ecology. The main project of such a spiritual ecology is to effect a transformation of values that in turn will lead to action that heals the planet. Whatever religion or form of spirituality one practices, it is possible to find a connection to the earth, and to the political work that needs to be done to change the present way of managing the natural resources of the planet. Some religions are more radical than others in this respect, and some people envision a more radical political transformation than others.

While reflections on ecology have a deep impact on all forms of contemporary spirituality, they also bring about the revival of ancient religious beliefs and practices and the growth of new religious movements. There is now much talk about a new "ecotheology," and an "ecospirituality" that is more bound up with the development of the earth in the light of contemporary ecological concerns than is creation spirituality. Ecofeminism belongs among these attempts to develop a stronger ecological spirituality where the concerns of the women's movement come together with those of the ecological movement. Ecological issues are also central to the agenda of the World Council of Churches' (WCC) ongoing process of theological reflection on "Justice, Peace and the Integrity of Creation" (JPIC), first begun in 1983 and carried out in partnership with 350 WCC membership churches worldwide.

Through these new developments religion and ecology have come together in a new way. Their collaboration can in turn help to re-vision spirituality ecologically. The growth of the environmental movement with its sense of responsibility for the preservation of life on the planet, and for the equitable development of the world that does not destroy the environment for future generations, is of great social, political, and spiritual importance in facing some of the most pressing and challenging concerns today.

The key issue is global sustainability, which may be impossible to achieve. After having grown from two billion to six billion people during the twentieth century, humans are destroying the life-support system of the planet at an alarming rate. The global population explosion is fast leading to a devouring of the earth's resources that is on a direct collision course with sustainable development. The specter of global warming with its catastrophic consequences, and the fast-growing extinction of many species, is now haunting the world. All secular and religious resources are needed to change the course of human action, but this is an *Inconvenient Truth*, to quote the title of Al Gore's critical documentary film on global warming.

Faced with the global ecological crisis, many religious people ask themselves how ecology and religion relate to each other. What resources do different religions possess for healing not only human suffering, but also the suffering of nature and planet Earth? Contemporary ecological spirituality has emerged as an acute response to our environmental crisis, but many ecological questions were already implicitly addressed in several religions at an earlier stage, for example in native, Asian, and early Christian beliefs. These need to be drawn out more and have to be further developed to help us deal with contemporary environmental issues. The study of traditional religious attitudes to nature is of great importance here, although it can also reveal the face of human arrogance and spiritual pride when we discover that human beings have often approached nature primarily for their own selfish use and exploitation.

The North American scholar David Kinsley has examined a variety of religious attitudes to nature in *Ecology and Religion*, a book devoted to "ecological spirituality in cross-cultural perspective." He maintains that the "so-called mastery view" of humans toward nature, of which especially Christianity is often accused, is actually not found in the Bible. The desacralized view of nature, accompanied by ruthless exploitation, stems in his opinion much more from modernity when "forests came to be seen as timber for dwellings, mountains became quarries for rock or gravel, rivers became a source of water power, plants were no longer the flowers of the hedgerows or the lilies of the field. They were a resource as food or medicine."

Interest in religious attitudes to nature and in connections between religion and ecology has grown considerably over the last few years. There now exists an International Society for the Study of Religion, Nature, and Culture, established in 2005, at the time when a new reference work, *The Encyclopedia of Religion and Nature*, was published. Prior to that, the American scholars Mary Evelyn Tucker and John Grim had been instrumental in setting up the international Forum on Religion and Ecology (FORE), associated with the Harvard University Center for the Environment. This arose out of a major conference series on "Religions of the World and Ecology," held between 1996 and 1998 at the Center for the Study of World Religions at Harvard Divinity School. Over 800 scholars of world religions met with scientists, environmentalists, and grassroots leaders to examine the varied ways in which human-Earth relations have been conceived in the world's religious traditions. They came to the conclusion that no one religious tradition has a privileged ecological perspective, but that a diversity of perspectives is most helpful. (The conferences resulted in a ten-volume series of books on various religious traditions with regard to their ecological perspectives.)

Religious responses to environmental issues are essential, and very necessary, but they are not sufficient on their own. Ecological challenges and tasks call for interdisciplinary cooperation between scientists, economists, educators, and religious people.

For Tucker and Grim, religions have not gone far enough, though, in their attitudes to the environment. They ask the question, "If religions are willing to stand by and witness the withering of the earth, has not something of their religious sensibilities become deadened, or at best severely reduced? Why have religions been so late in responding to environmental issues, and what are the obstacles to their full participation?" Yet together with many other people they also realize that religions can make seminal contributions to the rethinking of the current environmental impasse. After developing ethics for dealing with homicide, suicide, and genocide, religions are now challenged to respond with new thinking about biocide and ecocide. As religious people from different faiths are exploring questions of environmental ethics, and collaborate through interreligious dialogue, a new alliance between religion and ecology is emerging around the planet. "The common ground is the earth itself, along with a shared sense among the world's religions of the interdependence of all life. This shared sensibility and the extent of the environmental crisis pre-sent themselves as a moment of enormous opportunity for co-operation around a common cause—the activation of flourishing human-earth relations."

We can certainly find many seeds and resources in the teachings of the world faiths from which to develop an ecological spirituality and ethics, but none of the faiths possesses as yet a fully developed, truly ecological spirituality. What is needed is much more interfaith dialogue on these matters, much more critical sifting and radical re-visioning, and a profound transformation of traditional worldviews. Christians often cite the stewardship of creation as a response to contemporary ecological problems, but as John F. Haught has noted, the stewardship approach is apologetic "because it defends the integrity of biblical religion and traditional theology without requiring their transformation." It thus fails to really challenge traditional Christian theology, where the universe was created as a backdrop for the drama of human salvation, an essentially still hierarchical view that can never engender the necessary radical transformation to end human exploitation of the nonhuman.

A planetary, ecological vision also undergirds the principles of the Earth Charter. It was developed through an international consultation process and approved at UNESCO headquarters in Paris in March 2000, and has by now been translated into over thirty languages. The Earth Charter states the fundamental principles for building a just, sustainable, and peaceful global society in the twenty-first century. It draws its inspiration from, among others, the wisdom of the world's great religions and philosophical traditions. Several religious organizations were part of its consultation process, and some religious groups have already issued statements in response to the Earth Charter. Its call for action underlines the need for "sustainability education," and "the importance of moral and spiritual education for sustainable living." The Earth Charter invites people to "recognize that peace is the wholeness created by right relationships with oneself, other persons, other cultures, other life, Earth, and the larger whole of which all are a part." This is a profoundly spiritual statement which draws on religious and secular resources to meet the greatest challenge humankind has ever met: to create a new peace culture on Earth.

Thomas Berry has pointed out that Christians often show an amazing insensitivity to ecological issues. And yet these issues are the most urgent ones confronting humanity today. In Berry's view, "the renewal of religion in the future will depend on our appreciation of the natural world as the locus for the meeting of the divine and the human. The universe itself is the primary divine revelation. The splendor and the beauty of the natural world in all its variety must be preserved if any worthy idea of the divine is to survive in the human community." To renew Earth as "a bio-spiritual planet," the human community needs to draw creatively on all available spiritual disciplines, use all educational resources and energies, in an effort to cross the traditional boundaries between different religions, spiritualities, and cultures.

Thinking of ecological spirituality also means that spirituality is understood in an evolutionary sense. Spirituality itself develops and unfolds so as to articulate the human condition in a way that is commensurate with a particular time and age. Contrary to an earlier instrumental attitude that explored and exploited nature, the ecological attitude approaches the natural world as our home, as a sanctuary which needs to be treated with responsibility, care, and reverence. As the Earth Charter so beautifully states, "The protection of Earth's vitality, diversity, and beauty is a sacred trust."

Reflecting on "The Greening of Religion," Mary Evelyn Tucker and John Grim come to the conclusion that religions are starting to find their voices regarding the environment. "The monotheistic traditions of Judaism, Christianity, and Islam are formulating original eco-theologies and eco-justice practices regarding stewardship and care for creation. Hinduism and Jainism in South Asia, and Buddhism in both Asia and the West, have undertaken projects of ecological restoration. Indigenous peoples bring to the discussion alternative ways of knowing and engaging the natural world. All of those religious traditions are moving forward to find the language, symbols, rituals, and ethics for encouraging protection of bioregions and species." This is truly a new moment for the world's religions, since they have a vital role to play in developing a more comprehensive global ethics and ecological spirituality among their followers. The flourishing of people and the planet, of the entire Earth community, may well depend on these practical and spiritual efforts of moving life to a new stage.

A PLANETARY SPIRITUALITY FOR THE EARTH COMMUNITY

We marvel at the universe. The grandeur of its scale, the pure exuberance of its forms, the richness of its potential all challenge our religious sensibilities. For us humans it is above all Earth that calls forth our awe, wonder, and loving attention. Looking at our planet from the largest possible perspective, that of space, American astronaut Edgar Mitchell expressed his entrancement when seeing earthrise from the moon: "Suddenly from behind the rim of the moon, in long, slow-motion moments of immense majesty, there emerges a sparkling blue and white jewel, a delicate sky-blue sphere laced with slowly swirling veils of white, rising gradually like a small pearl in a thick sea of black mystery. It takes more than a moment to fully realize this is Earth . . . home." He even called this view of our planet "a glimpse of divinity."

Is this claiming too much? Earth and nature are not divine. Yet their wonders can lead us to the sphere of Spirit. Is this happening to people today? Perhaps it would be truer to say that humans are more often alienated from their planet than attracted by it, perhaps comparable to the way earlier generations often felt alienated from God. This is not a recent development, though. In Thomas Berry's view, we have been for centuries autistic in relation to the earth. Berry considers a truly ecological attitude as radically different from the currently dominant industrial attitude to the natural world. We need to cease our industrial assault on the planet and renew "our human participation in the grand liturgy of the universe." Like other ecologists, Berry stresses the need for a radical turnaround from the reigning paradigm of anthropocentrism to an inclusive biocentrism that takes into account the needs of all life forms, not only the need and greed of human beings.

The American ethicist Lois K. Daly sees today's environmentalists, engaged in ecological activism to promote a radical paradigm shift in human attitudes to the environment and the earth, as rooted in secular forms of spirituality. This new kind of spirituality may ultimately prove more threatening to contemporary social and political powers than religious forms of spirituality, or religiously inspired environmental movements, that can be more easily marginalized, controlled, or ignored. People find spiritual resources in nature that feed their activism and make them challenge the dominant social, political, and economic powers. Environmental activists recognize that the balance of nature is an indispensable factor for the survival of humans on the planet and for the creation of a flourishing Earth community. Humans have a moral responsibility for preserving the natural spaces of the planet that must be honored as sacred, as they were so often in the past. This does not mean a return to archaic attitudes toward nature, based on a false eco-romanticism, for which ecological spirituality has been criticized. On the contrary, it asks for the emergence of a new kind of awareness about the profound and most intimate relationship that exists between spirit, nature, and humanity.

How can we develop not only a global, but a planetary spirituality that can nurture the spirit of one Earth community?

Thomas Berry, much shaped by his deep knowledge of American native traditions, Eastern religions, and the work of Teilhard de Chardin, speaks about this task in his seminal book *The Great Work: Our Way into the Future*. This great work, which needs to involve all people, is "to create a mutually enhancing mode of human dwelling on the planet Earth." Human beings need to rediscover the spiritual sense of the universe and "to reinvent the human."

These are strong words indeed. Berry is convinced that to create a genuine Earth community and develop the new vision required for building a viable human future for all people on the planet, it is necessary to restructure global politics, governance, education, and financial arrangements. These tasks are impossible to achieve if humankind does not creatively draw on the available resources of what Berry calls the "four wisdoms" to guide us into the future. These are the wisdom of indigenous peoples which extends from far back in the Palaeolithic period and survives into the present, where 200 million indigenous peoples still live throughout the world; the wisdom of women, also very ancient, but now reasserting itself in new form, transforming Western and other civilizations; the wisdom of the classical philosophical and religious traditions of the world; and the new wisdom tradition of science, which is still in its beginning phase, but is advancing with amazing speed and success.

For Berry, these four wisdom resources represent an immense inheritance and promise to nurture the future of humanity and the planet, since all four "agree in the intimacy of humans with the natural world in a single community of existence." His holistic, prophetic approaches to the great community of life combine the central insights of religious and secular forms of spirituality. This is an integral vision that can nurture and sustain the newly emerging, growing Earth community, strengthen its resolve to bring about profound transformations, and foster the flourishing of all people and the planet. It is a vision that has attracted many others, since it calls for a truly planetary spirituality that helps to connect, revere, and nurture every element in the immense cosmic web of life.

Ten

SPIRITUALITIES
FOR LIFE

All human beings desire a good life, a life that is happy, full of joy and contentment, a life truly worth living and celebrating. If only more people could enjoy such a life! But human existence seems more often marked by suffering, failure, and brokenness than by an exuberant celebration of the fullness of life. Whatever human achievements and failures, life in the deepest sense remains ultimately a gift of the Spirit, mysteriously and graciously bestowed on people and the planet. It is the realization of this ultimate mystery that wholesome, integral forms of spirituality must make possible and embrace. Only then can humans seek and find fullness of life, "life abundant" as the New Testament calls it, that full and *real* life for which humanity was made, according to Evelyn Underhill.

When taking the pulse of contemporary culture it becomes clear that the prophetic vision of inner and outer transformation for greater good, for a more peaceful and loving world, reverberates in a thousand ways in the multiform experiences and expressions of religious *and* secular spiritualities. In the end, spiritual life is a life that cultivates wisdom, compassion, and love for the sake of other people's lives and one's own.

It has been said that Western society has now taken such an affirmative "turn to life," from honoring different ways of life to affirming one's individual lifestyle, that life itself has assumed the religious meaning formerly assigned to God. Thus we are observing the cult of a "new religion of life," much critiqued and strongly resisted by conservative and hierarchical religious institutions. Although the contemporary fascination with life may at times appear obsessive, it seems mistaken to interpret this as a new religion or quasi-religion, as some have done. The polarization between God and life is as artificial and unhelpful as that between religion and spirituality. In theistic understanding God is always a God of life, a living God who bestows life and sustains it, cares for the whole of life—the life of the earth, the life of nature, and all human life, past, present, and future.

Life in the widest sense is what humans experience and live for. But what is a truly *human* life? All life needs tending, nurturing, caring for, and human life especially requires physical, mental, and moral care for body, mind, spirit, and soul. That means human life needs spirituality like the body needs breath and blood to flourish.

The ascetic, exclusive elite spiritualities of the past have often been life-denying and life-harming. But the contemporary spirit of the secular world can be equally or even more destructive of life. The economic, social, and military elites of many contemporary societies seem to be dealing more in death and destruction than in life. Countless human lives are maimed and destroyed, and so are the lives of plants and animals. We have now reached such a critical threshold in the history of humanity, and in the history of the earth, that we must take decisive steps to adopt spiritualities that support and strengthen life in its precarious, fragile growth. We need to ensure that ever more people not only envision, but also embody a wholesome human life full of dignity and value, with all the energy, maturity, and reflective awareness this entails. To develop such spiritualities will involve much effort, even struggle, to overcome forces of ignorance, indifference, and strong resistance.

SPIRITUALITY AS STRUGGLE FOR LIFE

The spiritual dimension of wrestling with and for life is well articulated in an expression used by Christian Hispanic women in the United States who describe themselves as *mujerista* theologians. They speak of spirituality as *struggle* for life, and also as "a cry for life." Among Latin American women and minority women in the United States a spirituality for life helps especially women to overcome domestic, military, and other forms of violence. But the use of these thought-provoking expressions can be extended by linking spirituality to all experiences of life.

Understanding spirituality as a struggle for life points to the power of transformation which spirituality can and must exercise within human life. It can act as a force of survival, but also as a power for change. This expression also hints at the truth that spirituality often develops through experiences of suffering and pain. It arises out of struggling with the material conditions of one's existence, but also through wrestling with one's innermost self, and with the greater power of the Spirit.

Moreover, spirituality as a struggle for life can be quite literally understood as the immense effort, labor, and pain to bring life into the world, as women have always done. It also means to attend to the growth of this new life, to nurture it with love and care, make it grow into fullness and maturity. For so many poor, hard-working women, spirituality is the struggle to live and survive against all odds, to make ends meet, to produce the food needed for so many mouths, to calm down fights and quarrels in their families and communities.

Yet the spiritual search is more than the struggle to survive; it includes also the tremendous effort to live a fuller, more abundant, more meaningful human life. The Anglican priest and doctor Martin Israel spoke in 1974 of the search for identity through the spiritual as a "summons to life." He wrote, "The summons to life leads us from a self-centred existence to the encounter with God. But it is we who have to discover the spiritual path."

Spirituality can also be understood as the breath and blessing of life, the very "bread of life." Since women around the world are so much involved with the preparation of food, this comparison is appropriate. Developing one's own spirituality is like stirring, mixing, kneading the dough of our daily life experiences into spiritual food that is truly nourishing and strengthening, a food that is spiritual in the sense of putting us in touch with, and being the sustenance of, the whole world and each other.

These examples show that spirituality can be understood as an existential engagement, an attitude that acts as a transformative agent on the experiences of daily living, so that humans can make sense and give them meaning. Spirituality is thus like a leaven which makes our life with its sufferings and pains, its countless activities and diminishments, rise anew—and transforms it. This is a real alchemy of transformation, a process that can give sustenance and new strength as well as new freedom and identity.

SOCIAL DIMENSIONS OF SPIRITUALITY

Our world is frequently seen as bereft of Spirit. The deepest values and springs of meaning seem to be buried under so much shallow superficiality of entertainment and consumption. The flight of many individuals into inwardness, without much connection to the life of the outer world, is a reaction to the excessive despiritualization of contemporary society. But if spirituality is primarily understood as occurring at the level of interiority, it soon becomes an escapist form of spirituality. The Russian religious and political philosopher Nikolai Berdyaev (1874–1948) called this a "bourgeois spirituality." He considered the rigid division between spiritual and social life as completely erroneous, since he saw these two areas of human experience as intimately connected. In fact, he argued that the revival of inwardness might well prove to be a revolutionary act in relation to the objectified world, a revolt against its determinism, for it may lead to a spiritual permeation of the world in order to inspire and transfigure it. Already in the 1930s he pointed out that a new spirituality is required in order to deal with one of the most fundamental problems of human societies, that of work and labor.

Many decades later we have not yet found a solution to these problems at either a global or national level. Yet spirituality has now come out of the cloister, out of religious institutions, into the world at large. Reading the spiritual classics, seeking spiritual guidance, and following a spiritual discipline is no longer enough. These may be necessary, but they are not sufficient for the transformative spirituality the world needs, one shaped by wisdom, compassion, and love that seek greater equity and balance between people's spiritual and material needs. Spirituality cannot remain the privilege of a few, of the religious and educated elite. It needs to permeate social life at all levels. This requires a broader development of spiritual awareness and sensibility among all people and all groups of society. The call for the transformative work of the spirit in contemporary culture—what is sometimes described as the "spiritual imperative"—requires a creative, dynamic response. We need to feed people's zest for life, a zest for the full growth and development of life, for the further unfolding of life's possibilities, its exploration of new ways. Only a transformative, life-affirming, action-oriented spirituality can respond to the hopes and agonies of our suffering world. Only a spirituality that is fully alive can celebrate the flourishing of all life, of the entire Earth community, and of human-Earth relations. This calls for an end of human exploitation of the nonhuman and of nature and, in Thomas Berry's words, the renewal of the Earth as a biospiritual planet.

The Irish theologian and missionary Donal Dorr speaks about "time for a change" and argues that an integral spirituality can counteract the damaging effects of globalization by drawing us to the benefits of this global process. Globalization is currently dominated by economics, multinational corporations, and financial institutions, but it extends also to cultural, political, and religious aspects. Spirituality can provide the new energy that is needed to motivate people to work out the necessary strategies for change at all levels of society, from the local to the regional, to the global. This sounds odd at first since most people tend to think spontaneously of "spirituality as a soothing nourishment for the human spirit rather than a source of fiery energy driving people to change the structures of society." Yet one of the many ingredients that make up an integral spirituality is the struggle for justice and peace in the world, in South, North, East, and West.

Dorr draws on the Brazilian educationalist Paulo Freire's idea of a "generative theme" which touches people's deep feelings, whether anger, pain, or enthusiasm, to stir them into action in a way that ideas alone can never do. According to Dorr, spirituality is precisely such a "generative theme" in the contemporary world to motivate people to work for change. This includes the empowerment of people to strive for the many necessary changes in religious institutions and practices, but also in all other activities of society. In Dorr's view, the only spirituality that can adequately counter the damaging effects of globalization is one which is truly integral and can respond to the spiritual and moral aspirations of working people at three distinct levels. "These are: (1) the need for personal peace, integrity, and meaning in life; (2) the desire for respect, harmony, co-operation, and participation in management and decision-making in the workplace; and (3) the need to ensure that the business as a whole is making a positive contribution to the wider world—or at least that it is not involved in exploitation of people or of the environment." Spirituality can thus be connected with local and global action, with civic concerns and global citizenship, with the activity of organizations, business, politics, with social and political change, with every facet of social life around the planet.

Many new initiatives exist to promote a clearer understanding of spirituality within a larger social context. For example, the Metanexus Institute in Philadelphia, funded by the Templeton Foundation, is engaged in an interdisciplinary Spiritual Capital Research Program. The term "spiritual capital," coined in analogy to "social capital," sounds at first rather economistic and misleading. But its adopted working definition clarifies that this promising new research field is concerned with the "effects of spiritual and religious practices, beliefs, networks and institutions that have a measurable impact on individuals, communities and societies." The more we find out about these effects, the more efforts can be developed to promote personal and social well-being in all areas of human life.

Another interesting example comes from the International Conference on Organisational Spirituality (ICOS) that has been meeting annually since 2002 at the University of Surrey, England. One of the stated aims of this conference is "to build bridges between the personal world of individual spirituality and the spiritual aspects of work, society, and culture." The conference themes have included "Living Spirit in Self and Society," "Spirituality in Organisations," and "Living Spirit in Leadership." This initiative does not come from a religious institution, but from the School of Management that also runs a postgraduate certificate program in spiritual development and facilitation.

Developing the social aspects of spirituality within a secular context need not be a sell-out of what spirituality is about. On the contrary, rightly understood, the nurturing of spiritual insights, motivation, and orientation can contribute to the transformation of people, the workplace, and global society. While spirituality begins at home, with the individual person and a small network of relationships, it must ultimately extend to the entire world.

In the past, the personal aspects of spirituality were often more developed than any other, although spirituality, practiced in whatever form, has always had social repercussions and implications. Individuals belonged to larger groups, far more so than is the case today when there is much more room for individualism and diversity, but such membership was more narrowly defined by clearly marked boundaries, and functioned very differently from our societies today.

Traditional spirituality was usually nurtured in small groups, either in religious communities or through religious institutions to which one belonged by birth or initiation. The personal and social dimensions of spirituality have therefore never been mutually exclusive, but were usually closely related and interdependent. Thus the social aspect has always played an important part in all religious traditions, but in a very different way from what we understand by social life and the nature of society in our global context today. Traditional spiritual ideals have exercised a wide influence in shaping the rhythm of life in villages, towns, nations, and even entire civilizations. Examples are Indian civilization, or that of Islam, or medieval Christianity. However, contemporary postindustrial society, with its advanced scientific and technological developments, and its global network of interdependencies in all areas of human activity, is creating far more complex social dimensions than could ever have been dreamed of in the past. Because of this new, more complex and dynamic understanding of human social life, the social dimensions of spirituality have come much more to the fore, presenting us with new questions and new opportunities to develop spiritualities not only for personal, but also for profound social transformation. Within a modern secular context there exists an urgent need to develop the social dimensions of spirituality, a process that has only begun but needs to be more clearly articulated and much further advanced.

GLOBAL RESPONSIBILITY, ETHIC, AND MEDITATION

People involved in interfaith dialogue often think that the solutions to contemporary global problems are found in religious actions and practices, and through the collaboration of people of faith. While these make an important and necessary contribution, they are not sufficient for the creation of a truly global spirituality, since the religions themselves need to undergo radical transformation.

In the current context of religious, ethnic, and cultural pluralism, much affected by the ongoing processes of globalization, the different world religions are faced with similar challenges of modernity. These can be met only by initiating thoroughgoing reforms and by fostering a genuine openness to new developments. Yet in many cases quite the opposite occurs. A nostalgic return to the "fundamentals" of a faith leads to the rise of very conservative and traditional stances, some of which find expression in militant fundamentalism. Such returns to "tradition" are often accompanied by narrow, restrictive spiritualities that do not foster, but hinder human growth. They make dialogue and collaboration with others outside one's faith impossible. What the world needs instead are transformative approaches, new visions to build a better future, a world more at peace with itself, more accepting of the diversity of its people, cultures, and religions. For spiritual values to become effective in global society, the world also needs highly skilled translators across the religious boundaries of different societies and cultures, just as language translators work to overcome linguistic barriers. Such translation is required for the content, ideals, and practices of spirituality, while the term "spirituality" itself has come in for much redefinition and reshaping.

All sorts of new expressions have been suggested, from simply "new spirituality" to "integral spirituality," "global spirituality," "creation spirituality," "ecological spirituality," and many others. They all express an intense desire of finding an alternative to what there was before, in the institutional religious traditions of the past. The various terms refer to different forms of spirituality— some secular, some religious, some a little of both—that overlap and share many similar characteristics, yet also possess a distinct flavor of their own.

Reflections on our need for spirituality, the diversity of spiritualities, and for a new participatory spirituality abound. They are an expression of the deep spiritual hunger and thirst of our world. There exists so much human and planetary suffering that, in the words of the American theologian Paul Knitter, people of faith need to become aware of their global responsibility. They can meet in dialogue through "compassionate connectedness" and common action rather than only through shared ritual, prayer, meditation, or mysticism. To phrase this differently, we not only need a global ethic and global meditation, but also global action to change the world together. Humans are not only responsible for attention to their own selfhood, or for what happens to their immediate neighbors, but as a morally and spiritually evolving species we carry a common responsibility for all people on the globe. This applies to both the secular and the religious realm.

So far, interfaith encounter has produced a number of suggestions in relation to our global situation. Most prominent among these is the outline for the development of a global ethic. The common search for greater consensus, and for a shared basis for concerted action, produced in 1993 the Declaration Toward a

Global Ethic issued by the Parliament of the World's Religions, a widely publicized document that has raised worldwide interest and debate. This declaration, originally drafted by the German theologian Hans Küng, was much debated before and during the parliament meeting in Chicago, and after lengthy discussions it was adopted by the religious leaders at the parliament. Whatever controversy the declaration subsequently occasioned, its promulgation shows clearly that no new global order can emerge without a new global ethic. This can only be worked out together by people of different faiths and beliefs. It requires a conversion of the heart and a transformation of consciousness.

The suggested ethical guidelines presented in this global declaration are linked to four overriding commitments to: (1) a culture of nonviolence and respect for life; (2) a culture of solidarity and a just economic order; (3) a culture of tolerance and a life of truthfulness; (4) a culture of equal rights and partnership between men and women. This is certainly an excellent starting point for more widespread practical collaboration among people of different faiths and none, and it also provides a blueprint for educating the young.

Besides the development of a global ethic, which requires further input from many secular sources, there exists also a growing interest in global meditation. Not only in the sense that different religious groups around the world—Buddhists, Hindus, Jains, or Christians, for example—cultivate meditation practices, but in addition there are also new, convergent forms of meditation developing. William Johnston, an Irish Jesuit who has spent most of his life teaching in Japan, proposes global meditation as an aid for small interfaith groups to learn working together for peace. He is much influenced by his contact with Buddhism, especially different forms of Zen practices. Other Christians are inspired by the World Community for Christian Meditation, pioneered by the work of the English Benedictine John Main (1926–1982). This global movement, with headquarters in London, is now led by the

Benedictine Laurence Freeman. It has spawned a wide network of meditation groups around the world.

A different organization is the Spirit in Education Movement (SEM), launched by the well-known Buddhist activist Sulak Sivaraksa in Thailand and neighboring countries of South East Asia. Part of the growing international network of engaged Buddhists, this movement, founded in 1995 for the training of grassroots leadership, offers a spiritually based, ecological, and holistic alternative to mainstream education for the poorer sections of society. Teaching of leadership skills and sustainable agriculture is combined with meditation and social action, conflict resolution, ecology and justice concerns.

Another Buddhist example is the "Buddhism for the human realm" or "Humanistic Buddhism" developed by Foguangshan, an influential reform movement in Taiwan, which has a strong social service orientation for helping the needy and changing society for the better.

Yet another, quite different case of a creative global approach to spirituality comes from the Edinburgh International Centre for World Spiritualities (EICWS). This Scottish charity, founded in 2000, works with the world's spiritual and faith traditions through a number of educational initiatives, conferences, publications, and other activities. They all encourage the discerning use of spirituality, and include different spiritual practices. The organizers have intentionally not defined spirituality, but work with the diversity and experiential richness of spiritualities. They stress this rich diversity of different forms of spirituality by speaking of "interspirituality" and "intraspirituality" within and between different groups and traditions in all their areas of work. They explicitly state that "spirituality, and interspirituality and intraspirituality, have significant contributions to make to the crucial issues in contemporary culture and society. These include governance, leadership, education, health and well-being, arts and culture, science and medicine, the environment and sustainability, the media, work, community and service. Spirituality has a critical capacity to awaken qualities which are in critical demand, and to transform situations which are in critical distress. Spirituality can also help avoid such situations from arising."

The existence of so many different trends and movements is a proof of the vibrant search for, and growing awareness of, the immense importance of the spiritual dimension in contemporary personal and social life around the globe. Ever more people are becoming conscious of the need for a spirituality that is commensurate with the deepest aspirations of our world.

THE ZEST FOR LIFE AND THE POWER OF LOVE

To develop a more harmonious global society, strengthen local communities, and nourish our own lives, we need to love life, live it to the full, and contribute to its growth. This is impossible without a zest for life. We cannot advance the world and the life's flourishing without it.

But how can this be done? And where do we find the necessary resources for this feeding and development of the zest for life in the global community today? Individuals and societies are faced with so many different groups and nations, with opposing political interests and powers, clashing beliefs and mutually exclusive identities, that it is difficult to take on this responsibility. To develop the necessary sensibility and discernment for building a common future for humanity out of our global diversity presents a tremendous task. It cannot be accomplished without giving spiritual values their due place. Teilhard de Chardin referred to the creation of global society as the task of "building the earth," but this may be too external and positivistic a description. Given the biological, organic texture of life as well as the current interest in the new field of emergence in science, it may be more appropriate to speak of "growing" rather than "building" the future. The verb "growing" better expresses the emergent, dynamic nature of creating and working for the future of humanity—a process which is not entirely within human control, but contains elements of novelty, chance, and uncertainty.

The reference to growing links up with the vision of the American theologian, educator, and civil rights leader Howard Thurman (1900–1981) who encourages people in his *Meditations of the Heart* to look to "the growing edge"; "all around us worlds are dying and new worlds are being born." The growing edge "is the extra breath from the exhausted lung, the one more thing to try when all else has failed, the upward reach of life when weariness closes in upon all endeavor. This is the basis of hope in moments of despair, the incentive to carry on when times are out of joint. . . . The birth of a child—life's most dramatic answer to death—this is the growing edge incarnate. Look well to the growing edge!"

This "growing edge" seems a more appropriate metaphor for moving life, society, and the world forward than the more instrumental "cutting edge" that people usually speak of. It is a more organic, potentially richer way of thinking that relates more creatively to our contemporary ecological sensibilities.

Donal Dorr sees the current practical and spiritual efforts around the globe as divided between the attitudes of the people from the North, who stress above all the need for peace and ecology, and those from the South, who demand justice for the development of their societies. Both sides need to broaden their perspectives to achieve a more integral spirituality for the benefit of the different communities and the earth. According to Dorr, the meaning of spirituality "includes almost any activity we engage in or any of our attitudes or commitments or feelings." Thus spirituality relates to "the unfolding of the deeper dimensions of everything." The word "unfolding" expresses the fact "that the deeper significance is already present in a latent way, though it may not be articulated clearly." Dorr is very aware that spirituality integrates elements of the religious and nonreligious when he distinguishes between "spirituality as a religious tradition" into which people may be formed or molded, and spirituality as "a set of personal attitudes and commitments" which can embrace a wide variety of secular activities and orientations.

To promote the welfare of all people, ensure their flourishing and that of the entire Earth community, secular, religious, and spiritual aspirations have to come together. To transform our planet from one of dissension and disorder, from war, violence and strife, into one of peaceful coexistence avoiding ecological disaster, does mean a change of heads and hearts. It will require a tremendous effort, much coordination, collaboration, and genuine openness to dialogue across every ethnic, religious, cultural, and political divide. All these call for demanding spiritual work, whether carried out in secular or religious contexts, or in a mixture of both, since the spiritual is always shaped by the material.

It is remarkable to observe how many similar creative ideas about spirituality and spiritual energy resources are emerging in parallel in different individuals and groups around the globe, without direct links or contact with each other. Contemporary ideas in the sciences and arts, in religion and psychology, in human development and social thinking, provide many examples of this convergent movement toward similarly conceived ideals and aspirations for the human community. One striking instance is the completely independent, but very similar thinking of both Pierre Teilhard de Chardin and the Russian-American sociologist Pitirim A. Sorokin (1889–1968) about the absolutely necessary, transformative power of love for the development of a planetary human community. Both consider altruistic love as the highest human energy resource for the transformation of human society.

Both also agree that humans at present know less about "love energy" than about light, heat, electricity, and other forms of physical energy, so that the transformative power of love must be studied in all its different dimensions, whether cosmic, physical, biological, psychological, social, religious, or ethical. Teilhard de Chardin's ideas on love energy, relating to one's family, friends, nation, religion, humanity, and the whole universe, are scattered throughout his work, whereas Sorokin's are gathered in his amazing, magisterial study on *The Ways and Power of Love* (1954).

Sorokin, who was founding professor of sociology at Harvard University, speaks of love as one of the highest energies known but, like Teilhard, he thinks that the production and distribution of love has until now been given little systematic thought in practically all societies. This shows an astounding lack of organized effort on the part of humanity that now threatens its very future. Throughout human history the family has been one of the most efficient agencies in producing altruistic love, and so have small religious communities. But altruistic love must now be extended beyond these small groups to "the human 'world market.'" Sorokin paints a bold picture of the transformative power of love, and the systematic possibility of developing, accumulating, and storing its energy for the benefit of individuals and communities. The great geniuses, heroes, or apostles of love throughout history are like "great power stations producing love for generations of human beings." But their example alone is not enough. What is needed now is an increase of love production by ordinary people and groups, in fact by the whole culture, so that "love, radiated by culture and by social institutions, would form a permanent atmosphere that would pervade all human beings from the cradle to the grave."

Is this a utopian dream, or is it possible to work for such change? Who are these "eminent apostles of love" practicing an ethics of supreme love that provides an inspiring example for us all? Sorokin lists figures "from Buddha and Jesus up to Gandhi and

Schweitzer," but also Al Hallaj, the "great Muslim altruist and mystic," Teresa of Avila, Simone Weil, Dorothy Day (the founder of the Catholic Worker Movement), Francis of Assisi, Sri Ramakrishna, Swami Vivekananda, and many other reformers, saints, and mystics.

These are powerful examples that light up our world and can inspire countless others. In discussing the "techniques of altruistic transformation of persons and groups," Pitirim Sorokin argues for the extension of love over the whole of humankind, a vision also implicit in Teilhard de Chardin's outline of the noosphere and the divine milieu. Teilhard famously said that the day will come when humanity will harness the energies of love after harnessing the energies of space, winds, water, and gravity—and on that day humans, for the second time, will have discovered fire. Sorokin concludes his study of the power of love with the following statement: "By the mysterious forces of destiny mankind is confronted with a stern dilemma: either to continue its predatory policies of individual and tribal selfishness that lead it to its inevitable doom, or to embark upon the policies of universal solidarity that brings humanity to the aspired for heaven on earth. It is up to everyone of us which of the two roads we prefer to choose."

Is this quest for "heaven on earth" a nostalgic dream arising from deep memory traces of a long forgotten experience of primeval joy and innocence, so often associated with the paradise story of religious faith? The world presented to us daily on our television screens seems so much more like hell than heaven that any thinking person must doubt whether the human community really possesses the necessary will, the power, the energy, the love, and the living link with the Spirit to change this world into one more balanced, more supportive of human life and that of the entire planet. Is there hope in humanity's dire hour of need?

A VISION OF HOPE AND FLOURISHING

People everywhere dream of a different world than the one we live in. They hope, work, and pray for a better world, a more just and peaceful world freed from wars and tensions, where all human beings can live in harmony with each other and with nature. At present we have a world more torn apart than ever before. Yet it is also a world that deeply longs to be one and whole.

Spirituality has to transcend the personal realm and enter more fully into public life. The social dimensions of spirituality have to be more consciously attended to in small communities, and in different religious institutions, but that alone is not enough. Today spirituality is greatly needed in the larger public arena and must take on planetary dimensions. Spirituality within particular faith traditions, and within an interfaith context, is important but no longer sufficient. Spirituality has to reverberate throughout secular culture. Only then can human beings transform a world lacking in spirit into one that will grow more spirit-centered. What is needed to achieve this?

A global spiritual awakening has to occur on a much larger scale than exists at present. For this we need more spiritual education at all levels. Only then can we achieve wide "spiritual literacy," a literacy that goes far beyond learning to read and write, beyond the acquisition of professional training and skills. It also goes beyond emotional and ethical literacy to a much deeper dimension of insight and wisdom that grows from the heart and fosters compassion and love. These are the deepest energy resources humans possess, and the global community is still far from drawing on the transformative power of these resources in all situations of need.

To explore the different forms of spirituality in the contemporary world, whether secular, humanistic, scientific or artistic, and explore their joint potential to enhance and augment the fullness of life, can give ground for new hope.

We need ideas to think and work with, to inspire and transform us. To consciously develop spiritual literacy by providing spiritual education and fostering spiritual awakening is one such idea.

Another one is that of a *pneumatophore*, an idea drawn from a word in the plant kingdom that is pregnant with ecological meaning. Botanists use this word for the air roots of plants growing in water. Such roots, sticking out into the air, are carriers of *pneuma*, of air or spirit, if this word is translated literally. If we use it metaphorically, we can think of nodes of thoughts, transformative, empowering ideas, and inspirations that can serve as bearers of spirit and new life for the human community on Earth.

Within the secularity of modern society we need many such pneumatophores—ideas that are bearers of spirit that can kindle spiritualities for the life of the human community, whether these ideas are drawn from traditional religions, secular society, the sciences or the arts, whether they emerge from the sacred or the secular, from national, transnational or global contexts—as long as they help to generate heightened awareness and sensibility, a sense of global responsibility, and a new kind of spiritual literacy that can help people to live on the planet without destroying its life-support system or killing each other. Spiritual work is a demanding task, not light activity whose benefits can be gained in an effortless gesture. To lead people to spiritual awakening, to a deeper awareness, to a self-reflective spiritual consciousness where the energy waves of the universe resound within us, is the great calling of our time. It demands great integrity, deep honesty and truthfulness, and a passionate commitment to the life of the Spirit.

To nurture a truly balanced, holistic spirituality appropriate for our ecological age—a spirituality that can feed the life of people and the planet—is a scientific, practical, educational, and mystical task. It presents the human Earth community with a tremendous challenge—but a challenge that holds great hope and promise for our world. Only if we can make this promise come true will humanity and the earth flourish.

The exuberantly rich and diverse forms of spirituality that now exist and are still emerging prove beyond doubt that spirituality is not the exclusive exploration of personal interiority and inwardness, but is closely interwoven with all dimensions of human experience, including social, political, and economic life. Spirituality is not a permanent retreat from the world into the monastery, desert, or cave, not even into the silence of one's own heart, or the depth of one's mind. Rather, arising out of the midst of lived experience, spirituality implies the very point of entry into the fullness of life by giving meaning, value, and direction to all that humans do and are.

It is in the crucible of life that spirituality is born, emerges, and unfolds, so that human life, and life on Earth, can fully blossom and flourish.

NOTES

One: SEARCHING FOR SPIRITUALITY

P. 5   The "*psyche, pneuma, thumos, nous*" discussion draws on Steven G.
Smith, *The Concept of the Spiritual*. Philadelphia: Temple University
Press, 1988, chapter 1, "Historical Introduction to the Concept of the
Spiritual."

P. 7   Spirituality defined as "the quality or condition of being spiritual . . .":
The Oxford English Dictionary. Oxford: Clarendon Press, 1970: vol. 10, p.
624; the spiritual described as "of or pertaining to, affecting or concerning,
the spirit . . .": p. 622.

P. 10   "These new zealots . . . rather than be seized upon to plug the gap":
Libby Brooks, "Spiritual Tourism," *The Guardian*, December 8, 2003.

PP. 10-11   "Spiritual seeking . . . to spiritual growth": Robert Wuthnow, *Creative Spirituality: The Way of the Artist*. Berkeley: University of California Press,
2001, p. 269.

P. 12   "Creating a satisfactory spiritual life . . . to teach us all": Wuthnow,
ibid., p. 276.

P. 13   "Attention, taken to its highest degree . . .": Simone Weil, *Essential
Writings*. Maryknoll, NY: Orbis Books, 1998, p. 91; "Waiting patiently
. . .": p. 91.

P. 13   "Mindfulness is the miracle . . .": Thich Nhat Hanh, *Essential Writings*.
Maryknoll, NY: Orbis Books, 2001, p. 47.

P. 14   "When I say spirituality . . .": Interview with the Dalai Lama on CD *The 14th Dalai Lama in Hawaii*. Produced by Edgy Lee and Karma Lekshe Tsomo.

P. 15   "All religious life may be presumed spiritual . . .": Peter H. Van Ness, ed., *Spirituality and the Secular Quest*. New York: Crossroad, 1996, p. 7; "what followers of established religious spiritualities might learn . . .": p. 13f.

P. 16   "A radical split": David Tacey, *The Spirituality Revolution*. Hove, U.K. and New York: Brunner-Routledge, 2004, p. 30; see the whole of chapter 2, "Spirit without form"; spirituality as referring "to our relationship with . . .": p. 38; Religions have now "been downgraded to subsets . . .": p. 43.

P. 17   "Desire for spirituality-beyond-religion": Diarmuid Ó Murchú, *Reclaiming Spirituality*. New York: Crossroad, 1998, p. 164.

P. 17   The "discourses of religion and spirituality . . .": Mary N. McDonald, "Spirituality," in *Encyclopedia of Religion. Second Edition* (ed. Lindsay Jones). Chicago: Thomson Gale, 2005: vol. 13, p. 8720.

PP. 17-18   Public worship "of enormous significance in nurturing spirituality . . .": Agneta Schreurs, *Psychotherapy and Spirituality*. London and New York: Jessica Kingsley Publishers, 2002, p. 26; "spirituality in exile," p. 56.

P. 18   "Exploding core of spirit": Tacey, *The Spirituality Revolution*, p. 35.

Two: SPIRITUALITY AS IDEAL AND PRACTICE

P. 25   "Besides the phenomena of heat, light . . .": Pierre Teilhard de Chardin, *Human Energy*. London: Collins, 1969, p. 93.

P. 26   The dimensions of spirit "are the dimensions of the universe itself": ibid., p. 95.

P. 26   "The phenomenon of the spirit is coextensive with . . .": ibid., p. 98.

P. 26   The true name for spirit is "spiritualization": ibid., p. 96.

P. 26   "Cosmic *change of state*": ibid., p. 97.

P. 26   The hypothesis of a cosmos "in spiritual transformation": ibid., p. 110.

P. 32   "An intense form of other-worldliness" until "ordinary men and women": Evelyn Underhill, *The Spiritual Life*. Oxford: Oneworld, 1993, pp. 7-8.

P. 32   "Not a peculiar or extreme form of piety . . . real life for which humanity is made": ibid., p. 33.

PP. 32-33 "The prevalent notion that spirituality and politics . . .": ibid., p. 63.

P. 39   "It is our lives as lived . . .": Victor L. Schermer, *Spirit and Psyche: A New Paradigm for Psychology, Psychoanalysis, and Psychotherapy*. London and New York: Jessica Kingsley Publishers, 2003, p. 122.

Three: SPIRITUALITY IN A GLOBAL WORLD

P. 46   "Will the growing awareness of 'one earth' and . . .": Indira Gandhi quoted by David L. Gosling, *Religion and Ecology*. London and New York: Routledge, 2001, p. 120.

P. 48   Haeckel described ecology as "the body of knowledge concerning the economy of nature . . . its inorganic and organic environment": quoted on website on "Ecology, History of" under "Darwin and Haeckel"; see www.bookrags.com/sciences/biology/ecology-history-of-plsc-02.html (accessed 9/19/2005).

PP. 48-49 "Who is Gaia? What is she . . .": James Lovelock, *The Revenge of Gaia*. London and New York: Penguin Books, 2007, p. xiii; "The Earth system behaves as . . .": p. xiv.

PP. 49-50 "Our environmental, economic, political, social . . .": The Earth Charter; see www.earthcharter.org.

P. 54   "Grow vigorously . . . be active": *The Concise Oxford Dictionary*. Oxford: Clarendon Press, 1990, p. 452.

P. 55   "Nothing less than the *energy of universal evolution*": Pierre Teilhard de Chardin, *Activation of Energy*. London: Collins, 1970, p. 231, 232.

Four: SPIRITUALITY AND INTERFAITH DIALOGUE

P. 67   "Dialogue and spirituality . . . Can we pray together?": S. Wesley Ariarajah, *Not Without My Neighbour: Issues in Interfaith Relations*. Geneva: WCC, 1999, p. 26; see the whole chapter pp. 26-58.

P. 70   "When we see someone overflowing with love and understanding . . .": Thich Nhat Hanh, *Living Buddha, Living Christ*. London: Rider, 1995, p. xvii.

P. 71   "Engaged Buddhism": Thich Nhat Hanh, *Essential Writings*. Maryknoll, NY: Orbis Books, 2001, p. 7.

P. 71   He "is more my brother than many . . . ": Thomas Merton on Thich Nhat Hanh, quoted on frontispiece of *Living Buddha, Living Christ*.

P. 72   "Enduring, daily interfaith cooperation to end religiously motivated violence . . . ": Preamble of United Religions Charter. See www.uri.org.

P. 74   The "more open we are, the more spiritual" we are: Samuel Rayan, "The Search for an Asian Spirituality of Liberation," in Virginia Fabella, Peter K. H. Lee, and David Kwang-sun Suh, eds., *Asian Christian Spirituality: Reclaiming Traditions*. Maryknoll, NY: Orbis Books, 1992, p. 22.

P. 75   "The assimilation of insights . . . to one's own inner life and development": Wayne Teasdale, "The Interspiritual Age: Global Spirituality in the Third Millennium," in Wayne Teasdale and George F. Cairns, eds., *The Community of Religions: Voices and Images of the Parliament of the World's Religions*. London and New York: Continuum, 1996, p. 209.

Five: SPIRITUALITY WITHIN LIFE'S DANCE

P. 78   "The joy of the cosmic dance . . . ": Thomas Merton, *Seeds of Contemplation*. Wheathampstead, U.K.: Anthony Clarke, 1972, p. 230.

P. 79   Language witnessing "to the godlikeness of the human spirit": Michael Mayne, *Learning to Dance*. London: Darton, Longman and Todd, 2001, p. 35.

P. 79   "Initially spirituality is seeing . . . ": Maria Harris, *Dance of the Spirit*. New York and London: Bantam Books, 1991, p. 65.

P. 84   "At the outset of the twenty-first century people are faced with a spiritual dilemma . . . ": Routledge catalogue for Religion, 2001-2002, advertising Polly Young-Eisenrath, *The Psychology of Mature Spirituality*. London: Routledge, 2000.

P. 90   "The ways of living the married life . . . ": Monica Sandor, "The Rise of Marital Spirituality," *INTAMS Review*, vol. 10, issue 2 (2004), p. 153.

P. 92   "Speak to the great miracle of life . . . ": Elizabeth J. Tisdell, *Exploring Spirituality and Culture in Adult and Higher Education*. San Francisco: Jossey-Bass, 2003, p. 76.

P. 97   "The need to receive and give *love* . . . ": Albert Jewell, ed., *Ageing, Spirituality and Well-being*. London and New York: Jessica Kingsley Publishers, 2004, pp. 18-19.

P. 102   "The dance will never be perfected . . . ": Michael Mayne, *Learning to Dance*. London: Darton, Longman and Todd, 2001, p. 138.

Six: SPIRITUALITY, EDUCATION, AND HEALTH

P. 106   "Must transcend material, scientific and intellectual achievements . . . to eternity and to God": Robert Muller, "The Need for Global Education," in *New Genesis: Shaping a Global Spirituality*. New York: Doubleday, 1982, p. 8.

P. 106   "Must perceive his right . . . We must manage our globe . . . human fulfilment on planet Earth is only now about to begin": ibid.

P. 108   "None of these ways of thinking . . . a story that is all his, all hers": Robert Coles, *The Spiritual Lives of Children*. Boston: Houghton Mifflin Company, 1990; London: HarperCollins, 1992, p. 308.

P. 110   "Relational consciousness . . . to things, other people, him/herself, and God": Rebecca Nye, in David Hay and Rebecca Nye, *The Spirit of the Child*. London: HarperCollins, 1998, p. 113.

P. 112   "(1) Spirituality and religion are not the same . . . often happen by surprise": Elizabeth J. Tisdell, *Exploring Spirituality and Culture in Adult and Higher Education*, p. xi (see details under Notes chapter 5).

P. 120   "Psychospiritual self" . . . important empirical evidence exists to show . . .: Victor L. Schermer, *Spirit and Psyche*, p. 107f. (see details under Notes chapter 2).

PP. 120-21 "The structural differences between a house of worship . . . all occur spontaneously within psychotherapy": ibid., p. 181.

Seven: SPIRITUALITY AND GENDER

P. 127   "The opposition still felt . . . women in the Christian pulpit": This and the following quotations from the women's speeches at the 1893 World's Parliament of Religions are taken from Ursula King, "Rediscovering Women's Voices at the World's Parliament of Religions," in Erich J. Ziolkowski, *A Museum of Faiths: Histories and Legacies of the 1893 World's Parliament of Religions*. Atlanta: Scholars Press, 1993, pp. 325-343.

P. 127   And "that the sex of the worker is not a bar to good work": ibid.

P. 139   "We are still measurably ignorant of the nature of woman . . . ": ibid.

Eight: SPIRITUALITY, NATURE, AND SCIENCE

PP. 142-43   "Nature—the source of all life . . . true wisdom found in a sustainable relationship with nature": quoted from the Expo publicity brochure.

P. 145   "You bathe in the spirit beams . . . part and parcel of nature": With this sentence ends the essay "Twenty Hill Hollow," in John Muir, *Wilderness Essays* (ed. Frank E. Buske). Salt Lake City, UT: Gibbs-Smith, 1980 (repr. 1989), p. 88.

P. 151   "Amazed to find boundary lines . . . an orderly universe" and "In my scientific research . . . the desire to question and understand": the Bose quotations are from David L. Gosling, *Religion and Ecology in India and Southeast Asia*. London and New York: Routledge, 2001, p. 43 and p. 44.

P. 151   "Have you ever felt a presence or power . . . ": quoted on the Alister Hardy Society website www.AlisterHardySociety.org; see also Alister Hardy, *The Spiritual Nature of Man*. Oxford: Oxford University Press, 1979.

P. 152   "Matter is one of God's languages . . . ": Austin Farrer quoted in Michael Mayne, *Learning to Dance*. London: Darton, Longman and Todd, 2001, p. 127.

P. 152   "At the heart of matter a world-heart, the heart of a God": Pierre Teilhard de Chardin, *The Heart of Matter*. London: Collins, 1978, and San Diego and New York: Harcourt Brace, 1979, p. 15.

P. 155   "But while experience indicates . . . room for imagination and enthusiasm": David Knight, *Science and Spirituality: The Volatile Connection*. London and New York: Routledge, 2004, p. 190.

P. 155   "In essence, science and spirituality . . . ": The Dalai Lama, *The Universe in a Single Atom: How Science and Spirituality Can Serve Our World*. London: Little, Brown, 2005, p. 220.

P. 157   "This marvelous display of beauty . . . ": Thomas Berry, *The Dream of the Earth*. San Francisco: Sierra Club Books, 1988, p. xv; "among the most sustained meditations . . . ": p. 18; "we seldom notice how extensively we have . . . ": p. 80; "is the greatest religious, moral, and spiritual event . . . ": p. 98; "in between stories": p. 123.

P. 158   "A covenant with Mystery": Ursula Goodenough, *The Sacred Depths of Nature*. Oxford and New York: Oxford University Press, 1998, p. 167.

P. 158   "Wisdom phase": Brian Swimme, *The Hidden Heart of the Cosmos: Humanity and the New Story*. Maryknoll, NY: Orbis Books, 1996, p. 3.

PP. 158-59 "First, the nature that is full of wonder . . . ": Holmes Rolston III, "Scientific Inquiry," in Peter H. Van Ness, ed., *Spirituality and the Secular Quest*. New York: Crossroad, 1996, p. 388; "the secret of life biochemically . . . to the phenomenon of life": p. 395; "the matter that first took on life . . . ": p. 399; "a marvelous endowment . . . ": p. 401; "responsible, creative beings . . . ": p. 402; "virtually all biologists . . . ": p. 406.

Nine: SPIRITUALITY, THE ARTS, AND THE PLANET

PP. 162-63 "Art as spiritual practice": Robert Wuthnow, *Creative Spirituality*, p. 107; "only a slight exaggeration . . . ": p. 266; "to suggest realms of personal experience . . . ": p. 23; "these writers, musicians . . . ": p. 262 (see details under chapter 1).

P. 164 The mystic as "creative artist": Evelyn Underhill, "The Mystic as Creative Artist" in R. Woods, ed., *Understanding Mysticism*. London: The Athlone Press, 1981: pp. 400-414; "mystics are closer to the musician . . . ": p. 408; "in his suggestive and allusive language . . . ": p. 403; "another kind of mystic, naturally inclined to visualization . . . or the lyric poet"; p. 408; "the corporate spiritual consciousness . . . the common world of daily life": p. 402.

P. 166 "Everybody needs beauty . . . ": see "Quotations from John Muir," www.sierraclub.org/john_muir.exhibit/ (accessed on 3/10/2008). See also Peter Browning, comp. and ed., *John Muir in His Own Words: A Book of Quotations*. Lafayette, CA: Great West Books, 1988.

P. 166 "This earth you stand on . . . to take care and protect us we are a dead race": statement from the Navajo Nation Historic Preservation Dept. quoted as book motto in James A. Swan, *The Power of Place and Human Environments*. Wheaton: Quest Books, 1991.

P. 167 "Spiritual ecology": Carolyn Merchant, *Radical Ecology*. London and New York: Routledge, 1992, p. 129.

P. 169 "Forests came to be seen . . . resource as food or medicine": David Kinsley, *Ecology and Religion: Ecological Spirituality in Cross-Cultural Perspective*. Upper Saddle River, NJ: Prentice Hall, 1995, p. 134.

P. 170 "If religions are willing . . . to their full participation": John Grim and Mary Evelyn Tucker, "The Greening of the World's Religions," *The Chronicle Review*, vol. 53, issue 23, quoted online at http://chronicle.com, vol. 53, issue 23 of February 9, 2007. I have drawn extensively on this article.

P. 170 "The common ground is the earth itself . . . flourishing human-earth relations": ibid.

P. 171   "Because it defends the integrity . . . ": John F. Haught, *The Promise of Nature: Ecology and Cosmic Purpose*. Mahwah, NJ: Paulist Press, 1993, p. 92.

P. 171   "Sustainability education": The Earth Charter, 14b; see www.earth charter.org; "the importance of moral and spirituality education . . .": 14d; "recognize that peace . . . all are a part": 16f.

P. 172   "The renewal of religion . . . in the human community": Thomas Berry, "Ecology and the Future of Catholicism," in Albert J. Lachance and John E. Carroll, eds., *Embracing Earth: Catholic Approaches to Ecology*. Maryknoll, NY: Orbis Books, 2004, p. xii.

P. 172   "The protection of Earth's vitality . . . ": The Earth Charter, Preamble "Earth, Our Home."

PP. 172-73 "The monotheistic traditions . . . of bioregions and species": Grim and Tucker, "The Greening of the World's Religions," quoted online (see details above).

P. 173   "Suddenly from behind . . . this is Earth . . . home": Edgar Mitchell's comment on seeing Earthrise is quoted by Holmes Rolston III, in Peter H. Van Ness, ed., *Spirituality and the Secular Quest*. New York: Crossroad, 1996, p. 407.

P. 174   "Our human participation in the grand liturgy of the universe": Thomas Berry, *The Dream of the Earth*. San Francisco: Sierra Club Books, 1988, p. 215.

P. 175   "To create a mutually enhancing mode . . . ": Thomas Berry, *The Great Work: Our Way into the Future*. New York: Bell Tower, 1999, p. ix; "agree in the intimacy of humans . . . ": p. 193.

Ten: SPIRITUALITIES FOR LIFE

P. 179   "The summons to life . . . to discover the spiritual path": Martin Israel, *Summons to Life: The Search for Identity Through the Spiritual*. London and Oxford: Mowbrays, 1974, p. 123.

P. 180   The "spiritual imperative": see Satish Kumar's 2004 Schumacher Lecture, "Spiritual Imperative—elegant simplicity is the way to discover spirituality," *Resurgence*, No. 229: March/April 2005, pp. 6-12.

PP. 181-82 "Spirituality as a soothing nourishment . . . ": Donal Dorr, *Time for a Change: A Fresh Look at Spirituality, Sexuality, Globalisation and the Church*. Dublin: The Columba Press, 2004, p. 154; "generative theme": p. 155; "these are: (1) the need . . . or of the environment": p. 168.

PP. 186-87   World Community for Christian Meditation: see www.wccm.org.

P. 187   Spirit in Education Movement: see www.sulak.sivaraksa.org.

P. 187   "Humanistic Buddhism": Wei-Yi Cheng, *Buddhist Nuns in Taiwan and Sri Lanka: A Critique of the Feminist Perspective*. London and New York: Routledge, 2007, p. 48; see pp. 47-51 on Foguangshan, a well-known Asian Buddhist social action movement with 200 temples worldwide, and members from Asia, Africa, America, and Europe.

PP. 187-88   "Spirituality, and interspirituality . . . help avoid such situations from arising": see website of The Edinburgh International Centre for World Spiritualities (EICWS); www.eicws.org.

P. 189   "Is the extra breath . . . Look well to the growing edge": Howard Thurman, *Meditations of the Heart*. Boston: Beacon Press, 1981; see p. 134.

PP. 189-90   "The unfolding of . . . ": Donal Dorr, *Integral Spirituality: Resources for Community, Justice, Peace, and the Earth*. Maryknoll, NY: Orbis Books, 1990, p. 268; "that the deeper significance is . . . ": p. 272.

PP. 191-92   "The human 'world market'": Pitirim A. Sorokin, *The Ways and Power of Love*. Philadelphia and London: Templeton Foundation Press, 2002, p. 39; "great power stations producing love . . . ": p. 40; "love, radiated by culture . . . from the cradle to the grave": p. 45; "from Buddha and Jesus . . . the great Muslim altruist and mystic": p. 127.

P. 192   "By the mysterious forces of destiny . . . which of the two road we prefer to choose": ibid., p. 489.

REFERENCES AND SUGGESTIONS
FOR FURTHER READING

One: SEARCHING FOR SPIRITUALITY

The Classics of Western Spirituality is an ongoing series consisting of over 116 titles published since 1977 by Paulist Press (New York and Mahwah, NJ). The series covers a wide range of textual sources by saints, mystics, philosophers, and theologians from early, medieval, and modern Christianity, Judaism, and Islam. Each volume has been translated and edited by a competent scholar. The complete series is in print and available from www.paulistpress.com and through bookstores.

Philippa Berry and Andrew Wernick, eds., *Shadow of Spirit: Postmodernism and Religion*. London and New York: Routledge, 1992. An illuminating set of essays that explore the fascination with the "sacred," "divine," and "infinity" in contemporary thought. Philosophy, politics, ethics, and gender all provide examples of the striking affinity between innovative aspects of postmodernism, religion, and mysticism.

Jeremy Carrette and Richard King, $*elling Spirituality: The Silent Takeover of Religion*. London and New York: Routledge, 2005. A critical attack on the commodification of spirituality as big business in the global market. The authors argue that spirituality, offered as an antidote to shallow materialism, has come to embody the complete privatization of religion in the modern West. They present a justified critique of the "shadow side" of commercially offered spirituality, but omit to acknowledge that other forms of spirituality exist and can be of great significance for the flourishing of people and planet.

Kenneth J. Collins, ed., *Exploring Christian Spirituality: An Ecumenical Reader*. Grand Rapids, MI: Baker Books, 2000. An overview of the wide variety of past and present spiritualities of different Christian denominations. Also included are discussions on spirituality and the Trinity, spirituality and scripture, and spirituality and feminism.

Ewert Cousins, editor of the series World Spirituality: An Encyclopedic History of the Religious Quest. New York: Crossroad, 1985-2003 (25 volumes). This amazingly wide-ranging series has been described as the best treatment of spirituality on an interreligious basis. It is a marvelous resource that covers, among others, archaic and indigenous spiritualities; African and Oceanic spiritualities; South American, Meso-American, and North American Indian spiritualities; classical Mediterranean spirituality; Jewish spirituality (2 vols.); Buddhist spirituality (2 vols.); Hindu spirituality (2 vols.); Christianity (3 vols.); Islam (2 vols.); and information on the spiritualities of Jainism, Sikhism, Taoism, Confucianism, as well as on modern esoteric movements and the contemporary secular quest.

Robert Ellsberg, editor of the Modern Spiritual Masters Series, Maryknoll, NY: Orbis Books. Published from 1998 onwards, this series of well over thirty titles provides valuable extracts from the spiritual texts of twentieth-century authors from different religious backgrounds, together with short introductions to their lives and essential writings. These include Simone Weil, Henri Nouwen, Bede Griffiths, John Main, Anthony de Mello, Thomas Merton, Pierre Teilhard de Chardin, Oscar Romero, Thich Nhat Hanh, Mother Teresa, Mohandas Gandhi, Evelyn Underhill, Mother Maria Skobtsova, Sadhu Sundar Singh, Howard Thurman, and Swami Abhishiktananda, among many others.

Antoine Faivre and Jacob Needleman, eds., *Modern Esoteric Spirituality*. New York: Crossroad, 1995. Volume 21 of World Spirituality: An Encyclopedic History of the Religious Quest. It presents valuable information not easily found elsewhere on the ancient and medieval sources of modern esoteric movements, including alchemy, Renaissance Kabbalah, Rosicrucianism, Freemasonry, Theosophy, Rudolf Steiner's Anthroposophy, and C. G. Jung's association with Christian esotericism.

Bradley C. Hanson, ed., *Modern Christian Spirituality: Methodological and Historical Essays*. Atlanta: Scholars Press, 1990. Deals with different aspects of Christian spirituality, mainly from the perspective of the academic study of spirituality. It discusses the major problems in the definition of spirituality, and also its connection with the study of theology.

Ursula King with Tina Beattie, eds., *Spirituality and Society in the New Millennium*. Brighton, U.K. and Portland, OR: Sussex Academic Press, 2001. Written by a group of international scholars for a millennium conference on spirituality, these essays include some fascinating topics under the headings of spirituality, tradition, and change; spirituality, health, and education; spirituality, culture, and politics. They include discussions on the biological basis of spiritual awareness, human spiritual development, masculine spirituality and addiction, Palestinian spirituality of liberation, Jewish feminist spirituality and the Holocaust, interpreting texts and traditions in Christian spirituality, and aspects of contemporary spirituality relating to the mind, body, spirit movement.

Frank N. Magill and Ian P. McGreal, eds., *Christian Spirituality: The Essential Guide to the Most Influential Spiritual Writings of the Christian Tradition*. San Francisco: Harper and Row Publishers, 1988. A wonderful resource for the initial exploration of the great variety of Christian writers and themes through the ages. The volume is chronologically organized from ancient to modern times, gives a brief sketch of each author's life and works, followed by the analysis of one major writing. It also summarizes the main themes, editions, and secondary sources, so that a reader can gain a first taste and be guided to other, more detailed works.

Alister E. McGrath, *Christian Spirituality: An Introduction*. Oxford and Malden, MA: Blackwell Publishers, 1999. A helpful, concise introduction to Christian spirituality which stresses its biblical and theological foundations, the different types of Christian spirituality, its symbolism and practices, and some of its major historical figures. Particularly useful from a pedagogical point of view, with valuable information on spirituality resources on the Internet, a comprehensive glossary, and a compact bibliography. A book for teaching and study.

Thich Nhat Hanh, *Essential Writings*. With an introduction by Sister Annabel Laity. Modern Spiritual Masters Series, Maryknoll, NY: Orbis Books, 2001. A wonderful introduction to the wide range of writings by a great contemporary Buddhist monk and spiritual leader who has a large following. The writings are drawn from more than twenty of his books.

Diarmuid Ó Murchú, *Reclaiming Spirituality: A New Spiritual Framework for Today's World*. New York: Crossroad, 1998. This book argues that spirituality is, and perhaps always has been, more central to the experience of the human species than religion. It seeks to reclaim the long-lost subverted tradition of spirituality from the past, and reestablish its primary significance for the present. The new vision of spirituality for the contemporary world encompasses perspectives on the new cosmology, feminism, sexuality, the collective shadow, and the kingdom of God. Packed with ideas, this stimulating read can spark off many debates.

Benjamin B. Page, ed., *Marxism and Spirituality: An International Anthology*. Westport, CT and London: Bergin and Garvey, 1993. The editor admits that to include Marxism and spirituality together in one book may appear like an exercise in contradiction. Yet its relevance lies in the insights, challenges, and questions Marxism raises regarding spiritual issues and the spiritual dimensions of human life. The international contributors look at such themes as the classical visions of Marxism, the debate on Marxism and spirituality in early twentieth-century Russia, the spiritual crisis of Western Marxism, the dialogues between Marxism and Christianity in Eastern Europe and Latin America, and also the relationship between Marxism, Buddhism, and human suffering. A very unusual and thought-provoking book.

Agneta Schreurs, *Psychotherapy and Spirituality: Integrating the Spiritual Dimension into Therapeutic Practice*. London and New York: Jessica Kingsley Publishers, 2002. An excellent example of the growing number of books that interweave perspectives of psychotherapy, religion, and spirituality. The book deals with "ordinary" spirituality as the phenomena inherent in the processes of spiritual awakening and development. It shows with much sensitivity how the entanglement of psychological and spiritual problems represent a complex field that therapists have to deal with.

Philip Sheldrake, *Spirituality and History: Questions of Interpretation and Method*. London: SPCK, 1995. A major study on the importance of the historical process for understanding Christian spirituality, provided by one of its well-known historians. Insights are drawn from discussions on the nature of history and its usages; two case studies on Christian monasticism and the Beguines are also included. The book also contains nuanced debates on interpreting different spiritual texts and on different types of spirituality, showing the richness of the Christian spiritual tradition.

David Tacey, *The Spirituality Revolution: The Emergence of Contemporary Spirituality.* Hove, U.K. and New York: Brunner-Routledge, 2004. An exuberantly written book by one of Australia's foremost thinkers on spirituality, it is concerned with the emerging spirituality revolution that characterizes the twenty-first century, when ancient beliefs seem to have lost much of their plausibility. Yet a spontaneous movement in society points to a significant new interest in the reality of spirituality and its healing effects on life, health, community, and general well-being. Tacey draws extensively on the spirituality experience of Australian youth.

David Tacey, *Re-Enchantment: The New Australian Spirituality.* Sydney: Harper-Collins Publishers, 2002. This earlier title by the same author focuses more specifically on the significance of spirituality for building a more harmonious and integrated Australian society. A large part of this is concerned with the task of Aboriginal reconciliation, ecospirituality and environmental awareness, and the recognition of youth spirituality.

Peter H. Van Ness, ed., *Spirituality and the Secular Quest.* New York: Crossroad, 1996. Volume 22 of World Spirituality: An Encyclopedic History of the Religious Quest. A fascinating volume covering the history, major themes, and practices of secular spirituality. It discusses the classical sources of secular spirituality in ancient Greece and Rome and places outside Europe; its links with the European Enlightenment, with Romanticism, and with contemporary postmodernism, including New Age spirituality. The book's themes of "Self, Society, Nature, and Culture" include holistic health practices, psychotherapies, feminist spirituality, gay spirituality, social justice struggle, scientific inquiry, and ecological activism.

Simone Weil, *Essential Writings.* Selected with an introduction by Eric O. Springsted. Modern Spiritual Masters Series, Maryknoll, NY: Orbis Books, 1998. See pp. 91-97 for her famous essay "Reflections on the Right Use of School Studies with a View to the Love of God."

Richard J. Woods, *Christian Spirituality: God's Presence through the Ages.* Maryknoll, NY: Orbis Books, 2006. A wide-ranging and engagingly written survey of the major stages and figures of Christian spirituality from its beginnings to the third millennium. The rich perspectives of this book include early Christian pluralism, monastic and lay spirituality, women saints and mystics, aspects of Celtic spirituality, modern ecumenism and interfaith dialogue, ecospirituality, contemporary discussions of religion versus spirituality, and many other topics.

Robert Wuthnow, *Creative Spirituality: The Way of the Artist.* Berkeley: University of California Press, 2001. A masterful, unusual work exploring contemporary spirituality through the wide-ranging activities of artists drawn from the visual, performing, and literary arts in Pennsylvania, northern California, New Mexico, and

New York City. Through their work, the artists narrate spirituality, each describing experiences of spiritual quality. The themes covered include art as spiritual practice, the circle of life, body and spirit, the one earth.

PHILOSOPHY AND SPIRITUALITY:

John Cottingham, *The Spiritual Dimension: Religion, Philosophy and Human Value*. Cambridge: Cambridge University Press, 2005. Lucidly written, this book shows how a religious worldview is best understood as intimately related to spiritual praxis and to the search for self-understanding and moral growth. It touches on many philosophical issues, but also on scientific cosmology, religion and psychoanalytic thought, psychotherapy and spirituality, religion and the good life.

Michael McGhee, *Transformation of Mind: Philosophy as Spiritual Practice*. Cambridge: Cambridge University Press, 2000. A practicing Buddhist and philosopher, McGhee returns to the ancient notion of philosophy as praxis and love of wisdom, and discusses the notion of life, human flourishing, the meaning of spiritual friendship, and what makes life a "good life."

Steven G. Smith, *The Concept of the Spiritual: An Essay in First Philosophy*. Philadelphia: Temple University Press, 1988. Like the two titles above, this is one of the few books that discuss spirituality from a philosophical perspective, thus blazing a new trail. It offers a lucid historical and theoretical analysis of the different definitions, affirmations, and arguments surrounding the concept of the spiritual. Philosophically inclined readers will find it very illuminating.

Two: SPIRITUALITY AS IDEAL AND PRACTICE

Annice Callahan, *Spiritual Guides For Today*. New York: Crossroad, and London: Darton, Longman and Todd, 1992. This book deals with twentieth-century Christian figures (Dorothy Day, Karl Rahner, Thomas Merton, Henri Nouwen, Evelyn Underhill) and Simone Weil, whose background was Jewish.

Harvey D. Egan, *Christian Mysticism: The Future of a Tradition*. Collegeville, MN: The Liturgical Press, 1984. A fine introduction to the themes and practices of Christian mysticism with emphasis on particular figures (St. Teresa of Avila, St. John of the Cross, Thomas Merton, Pierre Teilhard de Chardin).

Roger Housden, *Retreat: Time Apart for Silence and Solitude*. San Francisco: HarperSanFrancisco, 1995. A beautifully illustrated guide to retreat centers from different religious and spiritual traditions across the world. It explores silence, mindfulness, and meditation. These can be followed under a spiritual guide, in a group, or in a solitary retreat; so can be the way of the heart, the body, of art, and of sound.

Information on Christian retreat centers in the United States is supplied by Retreats International (www.retreatsintl.org), and in Great Britain by the UK Retreat Association (www.retreats.org.uk).

Annemarie Kidder, *The Power of Solitude: Solitude as a Spiritual Discipline.* New York: Crossroad, 2006. Kidder explores the promise and power of solitude in ancient and contemporary contexts, revealing it as a physical and spiritual quest born out of the deepest longings for connections. She draws on psychological, theological, mystical, and poetic sources in illuminating the landscape of the soul, the search for wholeness of body, mind, and spirit, the tension between union and separateness, connection and community, in ourselves and others. Written from deep insight, and a strong Christian commitment.

Ursula King, *Christian Mystics: Their Lives and Legacies throughout the Ages.* Mahwah, NJ: HiddenSpring, 2001. An introduction to the lives and writings of 60 men and women from early Christianity to the twentieth century, including many medieval mystics, Eastern Orthodox, and Protestant mystics. The book explains the background, history, and major themes of Christian mysticism.

Donald W. Mitchell, *Spirituality and Emptiness: The Dynamics of Spiritual Life in Buddhism and Christianity.* With a foreword by Keith J. Egan and a preface by Masao Abe. Mahwah, NJ: Paulist Press, 1991. Written from the deep experience of Zen Buddhism and Christianity, Mitchell shows how Buddhist-Christian dialogue through the path of the spiritual life leads to expressing Christian belief in new terms.

Victor L. Schermer, *Spirit and Psyche: A New Paradigm for Psychology, Psychoanalysis, and Psychotherapy.* London and New York: Jessica Kingsley Publishers, 2003. Schermer presents psychospirituality as a paradigm shift linked to new perspectives in science, psychology, and medicine. He deals with spiritual development throughout the life cycle, the psychospiritual self, spirituality and psychological healing. The book includes chapters on the spiritual journey and the therapist as mystic.

Margaret Silf, *The Gift of Prayer: Embracing the Sacred in the Everyday.* New York: BlueBridge, 2005. A well-known spiritual writer and retreat leader looks at the many facets of prayer and asks, What is prayer? Why do we desire it? Who am I praying to? This book emphasizes the benefits of using prayer in everyday situations. Guided by both ancient traditions and contemporary experiences, it explores the abiding qualities of prayer and shows how prayer can deepen and enrich daily life.

James W. Skehan, *Praying with Teilhard de Chardin.* Winona, MN: Saint Mary's Press, 2003. Profoundly moving meditations and a guided retreat based on Teilhard de Chardin's cosmic vision of Christ, written by a fellow Jesuit.

Pierre Teilhard de Chardin, *Writings.* Selected with an introduction by Ursula King. Modern Spiritual Masters Series, Maryknoll, NY: Orbis Books, 1999. This volume introduces Teilhard's spiritual experience and vision. It groups the major themes of Teilhard's spirituality under several themes that run through his works: Discovering the Divine in the Depths of Blazing Matter; Living in the Divine Milieu; Christ in All Things; The Awakening and Growth of the Spirit in the World; The Heart of Teilhard's Faith Questioned and Reaffirmed.

Pierre Teilhard de Chardin, *The Human Phenomenon.* A new edition and translation of *The Phenomenon of Man* by Sarah Appleton-Weber. Brighton, U.K. and Portland, OR: Sussex Academic Press, 1999. Teilhard's magnum opus, first published in 1955, traces the rise of life and thought from prelife to a higher form of life. Its perspective of coherence, energy, and love can provide much hope and inspiration.

Pierre Teilhard de Chardin, *Human Energy.* London: Collins, 1969; see for "The Phenomenon of Spirituality," pp. 93-112. The same volume contains other essays on spirituality, on the significance of suffering, on the nature of human energy, especially the energy of love, and on the mysticism of science.

Pierre Teilhard de Chardin, *The Divine Milieu.* Translated by Siôn Cowell. Brighton, U.K. and Portland, OR: Sussex Academic Press, 2004. A modern spiritual classic. Teilhard explains spiritual practice as a divinization of human activities and passivities, and as learning to live in the "divine milieu."

Evelyn Underhill, *The Spiritual Life: Great Spiritual Truths for Everyday Life.* Oxford: Oneworld, 1993. A slim volume of four radio talks given in 1936. They have lost nothing of their freshness and wisdom.

Evelyn Underhill, *The Essentials of Mysticism and Other Essays.* Oxford: Oneworld, 1995. A very readable selection of some of Underhill's best-known essays on the ideals of the spiritual life.

Rowan Williams, *The Wound of Knowledge: Christian Spirituality from the New Testament to St. John of the Cross.* London: Darton, Longman and Todd, second revised edition, 1990. This penetrating psychological and intellectual analysis of Christian spirituality is from the pen of the current archbishop of Canterbury. It was originally published in 1979, when he was still a professor of divinity at Oxford University, and appears now in the series of DLT Classics.

John R. Yungblut, *The Gentle Art of Spiritual Guidance.* New York: Continuum, 1995. Yungblut founded and directed the Guild for Spiritual Guidance, Wainwright House, in Rye, NY. He links Christian spiritual guidance to Jungian depth psychology and Teilhardian ideas.

John R. Yungblut, *Rediscovering Prayer.* Rockport, MA and Shaftesbury, Dorset: Element Books, 1991. Written for people of all religious backgrounds, this book encourages its readers to rethink prayer, to return to the ultimate ground for confidence in its practice, and to find a significant place for it within their changing lives.

SPIRITUALITY AS AN ACADEMIC SUBJECT OF STUDY:

Dominic Corrywright, *Theoretical and Empirical Investigations into New Age Spiritualities.* Bern: Peter Lang, 2003. It contains a wealth of details about individuals and organizations that reflect the diverse and dynamic nature of New Age spiritualities. The author uses different frameworks for studying this diversity, and perceives them as connected through a weblike network.

Elizabeth A. Dreyer and Mark S. Burrows, eds., *Minding the Spirit: The Study of Christian Spirituality.* Baltimore and London: The Johns Hopkins University Press, 2005. Brings together leading essays from the former *Christian Spirituality Bulletin* (1993-2000) grouped under such headings as "Spirituality as an Academic Discipline," "The Self-Implicating Nature of the Study of Spirituality," "Spirituality and Healing," "Spirituality and Aesthetics." A strong North American rather than global orientation.

Cheslyn Jones, Geoffrey Wainwright, Edward Yarnold, eds., *The Study of Spirituality.* London: SPCK, 1986. A very informative and wide-ranging reference work. Although mainly focused on major Christian traditions and spiritual figures, this handbook also contains valuable chapters on the spiritualities of Judaism, Islam, Hinduism, Buddhism, African religions, and Amerindian spirituality. Separate essays on such themes as the nature of spiritual development, spiritual direction, spirituality and social justice, Christian spirituality and healing are also included.

David B. Perrin, *Studying Christian Spirituality.* New York and London: Routledge, 2007. A comprehensive introduction to the contemporary study of Christian spirituality, presented from an ecumenical and interdisciplinary perspective. This handbook provides many helpful references to both method and content in the contemporary academic study of spirituality.

Kees Waaijman, *Spirituality: Forms, Foundations, Methods.* Leuven, Paris, Dudley, MA: Peeters, 2002. The most comprehensive reference book for the comparative study of spirituality currently in existence. Written from within a Christian framework, this massive study of almost 1,000 pages contains a wealth of systematic presentations, theories, and bibliographical references that are indispensable for the academic study of spirituality but not easily accessible to the general reader. Waaijman organizes his magisterial reference work around three basic forms of spirituality: lay spirituality, schools of spirituality, and countermovements.

For other books on spirituality as a subject of academic study see the titles by Cousins, Hanson, McGrath, and Sheldrake listed under chapter 1.

Three: SPIRITUALITY IN A GLOBAL WORLD

Yann Arthus-Bertrand, *The Earth from the Air.* London: Thames and Hudson, 1999; third revised edition, 2005. The most amazing aerial pictures of every corner of the globe, accompanied by environmental comments. Informative and inspiring.

Thomas Berry, *The Dream of the Earth.* San Francisco: Sierra Club Books, 1988. A masterly introduction to the new ecological age and the earth community, outlining the task of developing an ecologically sensitive spirituality and a cosmology of peace (for additional information see under chapter 8).

Peter Beyer, *Religion and Globalization.* London, Thousand Oaks, New Delhi: Sage Publications, 1994. Beyer examines different approaches to globalization, and five case studies of religion in global society: the New Christian Right in the United States, the liberation theological movement in Latin America, the Islamic Revolution in Iran, new religious Zionism in Israel, and religious environmentalism.

James Conlon, *The Sacred Impulse: A Planetary Spirituality of Heart and Fire*. New York: Crossroad, 2000. This book is written for the present generation in search of a spirituality that can guide, inspire, and energize their lives. It helps individuals and groups to relate to the new universe story, to find deeper meaning, and work for more justice on Earth. A practical workbook with many lessons and insights.

Clive Erricker and Jane Erricker, eds., *Contemporary Spiritualities: Social and Religious Contexts*. London and New York: Continuum, 2001. Here are informative essays on influential spiritual writers and thinkers (Bede Griffiths, Thomas Merton, Krishnamurti, the Dalai Lama, Teilhard de Chardin) and on different faith communities (Thai Buddhist Forest Retreat Order, ISCON, the Amish, African American Pentecostals, the Taizé community, the Khoja Shi'a Ithnasheeries from East Africa).

David L. Gosling, *Religion and Ecology in India and Southeast Asia*. London and New York: Routledge, 2001. This book explores the ecological resources of Hinduism and Buddhism and looks at contemporary environmental issues in India and Thailand within the socio-political context of religious change.

Ursula King, *The Spirit of One Earth: Reflections on Teilhard de Chardin and Global Spirituality*. New York: Paragon House, 1989. Teilhard de Chardin was a pioneer in thinking about spirituality within a large global context. This is shown in relation to his understanding of Western and Eastern mysticism, interreligious dialogue, the convergence of religions, and his ideas about the future of humanity, which has many parallels in Sri Aurobindo's work.

James Lovelock, *Gaia: A New Look at Life on Earth*. Oxford: Oxford University Press, 1979. Lovelock's famous book which first presented his theory of Gaia—the earth—as a self-regulating system.

James Lovelock, *The Revenge of Gaia: Why the Earth is Fighting Back—and How We Can Still Save Humanity*. London and New York: Penguin Books, 2007. A provocative and terrifying book that shows how Gaia, the living earth, is fighting back humans who have for millennia exploited the planet without counting the cost. What must the human species do to survive its greatest crisis?

Robert Muller, *New Genesis—Shaping a Global Spirituality*. New York: Doubleday, 1982. An inspiring vision by a former assistant secretary-general of the United Nations, dealing with the global transcendence of humanity, human values, and religions. This vision emerged out of the practical experience of serving the United Nations for more than thirty years and is influenced by "five Teilhardian enlightenments." The essays reflect Muller's deep desire for global peace.

Martin Redfern, *The Earth: A Very Short Introduction*. Oxford: Oxford University Press, 2003. Fascinating details about the history and nature of our planet are presented together with facts about the earth.

Elizabeth Roberts and Elias Amidon, eds., *Earth Prayers from around the World: 365 Prayers, Poems, and Invocations for Honoring the Earth*. San Francisco: HarperSanFrancisco, 1991. A marvelous collection of prayers from around the world which, in Thomas Berry's words, can awaken us "to the presence of the divine that comes to us through the Earth and the entire natural world."

Roland Robertson and William R. Garrett, eds., *Religion and Global Order*. New York: Paragon House, 1991. It covers different aspects of religion and globalization, including some case studies, mostly written by sociologists. Robertson has contributed the concluding essay on "Globalization, Modernization, and Postmodernization: The Ambiguous Position of Religion."

Paul R. Samson and David Pitt, eds., *The Biosphere and Noosphere Reader: Global Environment, Society and Change*. London and New York: Routledge, 1999. This is an outstanding collection of excerpts on the biosphere and noosphere, drawn from scientists around the world, showing the different ways in which these concepts are understood and have evolved, especially since Teilhard de Chardin first suggested the idea of the "noosphere." These perspectives will be new to most, and will make readers conscious of the importance of the noosphere in relation to contemporary global issues.

Manfred B. Steger, *Globalization: A Very Short Introduction*. Oxford: Oxford University Press, 2003. A very accessible introduction to the economic, political, cultural, and ideological dimensions of globalization.

Brian Swimme and Thomas Berry, *The Universe Story: From the Primordial Flaring Forth to the Ecozoic Era—A Celebration of the Unfolding of the Cosmos*. New York: HarperCollins, 1994. A magnificent synthesis of the new story of the evolution of life, combined with a deep concern for restoring the ecological balance on our planet. For this to happen we have to bring together our scientific knowledge with the wisdom of the classical philosophical and religious traditions from East and West, North and South.

Pierre Teilhard de Chardin, *Human Energy* (see details under chapter 2). For "The Spirit of the Earth," see pp. 19-47. A pioneering essay, written in 1931.

Pierre Teilhard de Chardin, *Activation of Energy*. London: Collins, 1970. See especially the essay written in 1950, "The Zest for Living," pp. 229-253. Other essays deal with the role of energy in human life, the spiritual energy of suffering, and energy in evolution.

The Earth Charter. See www.earthcharter.org. An important document outlining global human responsibility for the earth. Several religious groups have already published statements in response to this charter.

Four: SPIRITUALITY AND INTERFAITH DIALOGUE

Swami Abhishiktananda, *Essential Writings*. Selected with an introduction by Shirley du Boulay. Modern Spiritual Masters Series, Maryknoll, NY: Orbis Books, 2007. This book provides a good introduction to Abhishiktananda's immersion into Hinduism, his reflections on Advaita, on East and West, prayer and awakening, and on his reinterpretation of Christianity in the light of Hindu spirituality.

Tosh Arai and S. Wesley Ariarajah, eds., *Spirituality in Interfaith Dialogue*. Geneva: WCC Publications, 1989. Valuable interfaith reflections from a consultation held by the World Council of Churches in Japan in December 1987.

S. Wesley Ariarajah, *Not Without My Neighbour: Issues in Interfaith Relations*. Risk Book Series. Geneva: WCC Publications, 1999. A thoughtful discussion of major interfaith issues by the former Sri Lankan director of the WCC's dialogue program.

Shirley du Boulay, *The Cave of the Heart: The Life of Swami Abhishiktananda*. Maryknoll, NY: Orbis Books, 2005. Retracing the extraordinary religious experience of a French Benedictine monk who became an Indian sannyasi, this is a story of spiritual transformation and adventure.

Shirley du Boulay, *Beyond Darkness: A Biography of Bede Griffiths*. London: Rider, 1998. The inspiring life of a great contemplative spiritual leader, an English Benedictine who immersed himself in Hinduism. He lived at the Christian Shantivanam Ashram in South India, where he became a guru for many people from West and East.

Stuart Brown, *Meeting in Faith: Twenty Years of Christian-Muslim Conversations Sponsored by the World Council of Churches*. Geneva: WCC Publications, 1999. A documentary record of Christian-Muslim dialogue sponsored by the WCC, listing themes, participants, and programs. It includes basic texts for further exploration of the different dimensions of dialogue. An encouragement in fostering understanding and peace.

Beatrice Bruteau, *The Other Half of My Soul: Bede Griffiths and the Hindu-Christian Dialogue*. Wheaton, IL: Quest Books, 1996. An inspiring set of essays and tributes by many who knew Bede Griffiths. It explores his multireligious experience, his search for a bridge between East and West, and for a holistic spirituality of the future.

Bede Griffiths, *Essential Writings*. Selected with an introduction by Thomas Matus. Modern Spiritual Masters Series, Maryknoll, NY: Orbis Books, 2004. This book describes another Christian encounter with Hinduism, very different from Swami Abhishiktananda's. It reflects on the awakening to the Feminine, the vision of nature, the coming of a new age, and the meeting of religions.

Whalen Lai and Michael von Brück, *Christianity and Buddhism: A Multi-Cultural History of Their Dialogue*. Maryknoll, NY: Orbis Books, 2001. A wide-ranging, informative study of the encounter between Buddhism and Christianity in India, Sri Lanka, China, Japan, Germany, and the United States, with a foreword "On Buddhist-Christian Dialogue" by Hans Küng.

Jonathan Magonet, *Talking to the Other: Jewish Interfaith Dialogue with Christians and Muslims.* London and New York: I. B. Tauris, 2003. Both Jews and Muslims are minorities in Europe. This important book by the well-known rabbi and former principal of London's Leo Baeck College, who has been involved in interfaith dialogue for more than thirty years, addresses Christians, Muslims, and Jews. It challenges the Jewish community to broaden its commitment to interfaith dialogue in a rapidly changing world.

Thomas Merton, *Essential Writings.* Selected with an introduction by Christine M. Bochen. Modern Spiritual Masters Series, Maryknoll, NY: Orbis Books, 2000. A powerful selection of major passages from some of Merton's best-known books, letters, and notes. Organized under "a call to contemplation," "a call to compassion," and "a call to unity," these texts provide a very good introduction to Merton's complex personality and deep spiritual insights.

Thomas Merton, *The Asian Journal of Thomas Merton.* New York: New Directions, 1973; London: Sheldon Press, 1974. Well-annotated diaries of Merton written during his visit to Asia in October and November 1968, where he tragically died. They record his thoughts on traveling in India, Sri Lanka, and Thailand; on meeting the Dalai Lama, and other monks; on monasticism, Marxism, and on the monastic experience and East-West Dialogue.

Thomas Merton, *The Seven Storey Mountain.* San Diego and New York: Harvest Books, Harcourt Brace, 1999. The famous autobiography of Father M. Louis, as Thomas Merton was called in his Trappist monastery at Gethsemani, Kentucky, which brought him first to public attention. Originally published in 1948, this "odyssey of a soul" has become a modern spiritual classic, and is still an engrossing read.

The Merton Institute for Contemplative Living: see www.mertoninstitute.org.

Thich Nhat Hanh, *Living Buddha, Living Christ.* London: Rider, 1995. This book shows Thich Nhat Hanh's great sensitivity and closeness to the central experiences and insights of Christian spirituality, and the parallels he draws between Buddha and Christ.

Thich Nhat Hanh, *Essential Writings* (see details under chapter 1).

Raimon Panikkar, *The Unknown Christ of Hinduism: Toward an Ecumenical Christophany.* London: Darton, Longman and Todd and Maryknoll, NY: Orbis Books, revised and enlarged edition, 1981. A pioneering book and in-depth exploration of the encounter of Christianity and Hinduism, first published in 1964, by a well-known spiritual writer and thinker who was born into a family of Catholic and Hindu background.

Raimon Panikkar, *The Intrareligious Dialogue.* Mahwah, NJ: Paulist Press, 1999. A small, pioneering work of visionary sweep which explores dialogue, encounter, and multireligious experience from the perspective of philosophy, theology, Christianity, Hinduism, Buddhism, and humanism.

Aloysius Pieris, *Love Meets Wisdom: A Christian Experience of Buddhism.* Maryknoll, NY: Orbis Books, 1988. A Sri Lankan Jesuit who has been immersed in Buddhism and studied it throughout his life writes about dialogue with Buddhism in East and West, the spirituality of the Buddhist monk, and the Buddhist political vision.

Pontifical Council for Interreligious Dialogue, *Guidelines for Dialogue between Christians and Muslims.* Prepared by Maurice Bormans. New York and Mahwah, NJ: Paulist Press, 1990. These contain very informative and helpful texts intended to assist the development of dialogue between Christians and Muslims.

Samuel Rayan, "The Search for an Asian Spirituality of Liberation," in Virginia Fabella, Peter K. H. Lee, and David Kwang-sun Suh, eds., *Asian Christian Spirituality. Reclaiming Tradition.* Maryknoll, NY: Orbis Books, 1992: pp. 11-30. An inspiring essay in a book that deals with several aspects of Asian spiritualities of liberation in Korea, Indonesia, India, the Philippines, Sri Lanka, and Hong Kong.

Wayne Teasdale, *The Mystic Heart: Discovering a Universal Spirituality in the World's Religions.* Novato, CA: New World Library, 1999. A great visionary book whose central theme is the new age of interspirituality we are now approaching, by a spiritual teacher with a radical vision that links mystical experience with interreligious dialogue. Foreword by the Dalai Lama.

Wayne Teasdale, "The Interspiritual Age: Global Spirituality in the Third Millennium," in Wayne Teasdale and George F. Cairns, eds., *The Community of Religions: Voices and Images of the Parliament of the World's Religions.* London and New York: Continuum, 1996, pp. 209-219. Teasdale discusses the meaning of "interspirituality" and the elements of global spirituality.

Pierre Teilhard de Chardin, "The Zest for Living," in *Activation of Energy,* London: Collins, 1970, pp. 231-243. An inspiring essay, originally given as a talk to an interfaith group in postwar Paris in 1950. It looks at the importance of the zest for life, the role of religions in feeding it, and the new religious needs of the world today.

Five: SPIRITUALITY WITHIN LIFE'S DANCE

Shirley du Boulay and Marianne Rankin, *Cicely Saunders: The Founder of the Modern Hospice Movement.* London: SPCK, 2007. A biography of the founder of St. Christopher's Hospice and of the modern hospice movement, first published by Shirley du Boulay in 1984. As Dame Cicely lived until 2005, Marianne Rankin has provided a further three chapters to cover the time until her death. Dame Cicely Saunders's work transformed the management of pain and care for the dying. She established the field of palliative medicine and thereby changed medical practice.

Sarah Coakley, ed., *Religion and the Body*. Cambridge: Cambridge University Press, 2000. A comparative study on the body and its relation to society and the Divine. The contributors explore the distinctive ways in which Western and Eastern religions have approached the body in their texts and devotional practices. Includes essays on Judaism, different forms of Christianity, Hinduism, Buddhism, Sufism, Taoism, Japanese religions, Zoroastrianism, and Sikhism.

Kenneth J. Doka and John D. Morgan, eds., *Death and Spirituality*. Amityville, NY: Baywood Publishing Company, 1993. A book of extraordinarily rich resources for dealing with the spiritual needs of the dying, with spiritual issues of bereavement, spiritual care in hospice, in the case of perinatal death, suicide, or AIDS. Distinct perspectives on death are presented in Jewish, Roman Catholic, and Protestant thought, in Eastern religions, African American communities, and among those without conventional religious beliefs.

Dody H. Donnelly, *Radical Love: An Approach to Sexual Spirituality*. Minneapolis, MN: Winston Press, 1984; Fremont, CA: Dharma Cloud Publishers, 1992. Here spirituality is grounded in the full affirmation of the body, the goodness and beauty of sexuality. The author shows how we have to love with a radical love, rooted in cosmos, nature, and body, and ultimately grounded in the experience of God's loving touch.

Elizabeth A. Dreyer, *Earth Crammed with Heaven*. Mahwah, NJ: Paulist Press, 1994. Written from a Christian perspective, this book shows the paradigm shift from traditional clerical and monastic spirituality to new forms of lay spirituality practiced in everyday existence, not in withdrawal from the world. It discusses spirituality in relation to sexuality, childbearing, work, the marketplace, the earth, and the cosmos.

Kathleen Fischer, *Winter Grace: Spirituality and Aging*. Nashville, TN: Upper Room Books, 1998. Fischer draws on theology, literature, and the social sciences to explore the spirituality of life's later years. With much sensitivity and wisdom, but also humor and hope, she takes us into the heart of the paradoxical Christian mystery of death and resurrection.

Margaret Guenther, *Toward Holy Ground: Spiritual Directions for the Second Half of Life*. Boston: Cowley Publications, 1995. This book explores the practical aspects of spirituality in midlife: prayer, the need for community, lightheartedness, detachment, preparing for aging, and a good death. The author—wife, mother, teacher, Episcopal priest—was the director of the Center for Christian Spirituality of the General Theological Seminary in New York City.

Alister Hardy, *The Spiritual Nature of Man: A Study of Contemporary Religious Experience*. Oxford: Clarendon Press, 1979; Alister Hardy Research Centre, 1991. An empirical study by an Oxford scientist who collected a large number of reports on people's religious experiences. The book discusses the varieties of spiritual awareness, with their sensory, behavioral, cognitive, and affective elements, and concludes with a chapter on "What is spirituality?" (for additional information see under chapter 8).

Maria Harris, *Dance of the Spirit: The Seven Steps of Women's Spirituality*. New York and London: Bantam Books, 1991. Women's spirituality is explored here in terms of successive steps of awakening, discovering, creating, dwelling, nourishing, traditioning, and transforming. An imaginative, nourishing book full of questions, suggestions, poems, and prayers for practical use.

David Hay and Rebecca Nye, *The Spirit of the Child*. London: HarperCollins, 1998. This is based on a three-year investigation of children's spirituality that shows that children are capable of having profound beliefs and meaningful spiritual experiences from a very early age. They emerge from infancy with a spiritual awareness that is richly open and creative, yet the world of schooling is often destructive of this dimension. What can we do to nurture the spirit of the child? A thorough and thought-provoking study.

INTAMS Review, published since 1995 by the International Academy for Marital Spirituality, located in Sint-Genesius-Rode near Brussels, Belgium. This is a center for teaching and research, encounter and dialog for scholars and practitioners; see www.intams.org. In 2005, INTAMS established a Chair for the Study of Marriage and Spirituality at the Theology Faculty of the Catholic University of Leuven, Belgium, which is dedicated to research and teaching.

Lisa Isherwood and Elizabeth Stuart, *Introducing Body Theology*. Sheffield: Sheffield Academic Press, 1998. Helpful survey on current discussions about embodiment, embodied theology, spirituality, ecology, and gender relations from a largely Christian perspective. Includes a chapter on women, spirituality, and embodiment.

Albert Jewell, ed., *Spirituality and Ageing*. London and Philadelphia: Jessica Kingsley Publishers, 1999. A fine set of essays to raise awareness of the spiritual needs of older people and encourage interest in the spirituality of aging and "sageing." Discusses issues of spiritual care with regard to sufferers of dementia and Alzheimer's disease, experiences of gender, community care, and death. It also deals with spirituality and age among British Hindus, Sikhs, and Muslims.

Albert Jewell, ed., *Ageing, Spirituality and Well-being*. London and New York: Jessica Kingsley Publishers, 2004. Another set of essays from the same editor, based on the second International Conference on Ageing, Spirituality and Well-being, held in 2002 at Durham University, England. Contributors from medicine, theology, and the social sciences provide guidance on how the spiritual needs of people moving into the "fourth age" of life can be met, and how having a purpose in life and continual spiritual growth are vital elements in the well-being of older people.

Elizabeth MacKinlay, *The Spiritual Dimension of Aging*. London and Philadelphia: Jessica Kingsley Publishers, 2001. Based on in-depth interviews with people of the so-called third age, i.e., sixty-five years and over, the participants in this fascinating study are of an either Christian or nonreligious background and are living independently in the community. The author is an experienced gerontological nurse and priest in the Anglican Church who explores with great sensitivity how the spiritual dimension of aging can contribute to well-being and health in later life.

Michael Mayne, *Learning to Dance.* London: Darton, Longman and Todd, 2001. An enchanting book full of wisdom by the dean emeritus of Westminster Abbey, London. It approaches spirituality under the theme of the dance: the dance of life, of the cosmos, the natural world; the dance of the arts, of relationships, of dancing in the dark; the dance of faith, and the hidden dance that some call heaven.

Parker J. Palmer, *The Active Life: A Spirituality of Work, Creativity, and Caring.* San Francisco: HarperCollins, 1992. Palmer, a well-known Quaker activist and higher education teacher, explores spirituality in action, and what it means to be fully alive. What spiritual sources can we draw upon for our lives in a world of action? Palmer uses a variety of religious traditions, including Taoist, Jewish, and Christian sources.

Edward Robinson, *The Original Vision: A Study of the Religious Experience of Childhood.* Oxford: Religious Experience Research Unit, Manchester College, Oxford University, 1977; New York: Seabury Press, 1983. It discusses various accounts of religious experiences that occurred in childhood and examines the authenticity, authoritative quality, and interpretation of these experiences in later life. Robinson's findings call into question several earlier theories of children's religious understanding.

Monica Sandor, "The Rise of Marital Spirituality," in *INTAMS Review* vol. 10, issue 2 (2004), pp. 153-176. A discerning, comprehensive discussion of the nature and practice of spirituality in marriage. It examines the new interest in marital spirituality as linked to the contemporary experiential turn, to a spirituality of creation, of the body, to lay spirituality, and the vocation of marriage.

Barbara Smith-Moran, *Soul at Work: Reflections on a Spirituality of Working.* Winona, MN: Saint Mary's Press, 1997. Six weeks' meditations on central attitudes to work, from vocation and calling to success and setback, transformation and transfiguration. Inspired by Biblical readings and ideas from Teilhard de Chardin, this book is suitable for personal and group retreats.

Elizabeth J. Tisdell, *Exploring Spirituality and Culture in Adult and Higher Education.* San Francisco: Jossey-Bass, 2003. An authoritative study on spirituality and culture in adult meaning-making, identity formation, and spiritual development. The findings are applied to transformative teaching practice in adult and higher education, inviting teachers and students to work toward personal and social transformation.

Six: SPIRITUALITY, EDUCATION, AND HEALTH

EDUCATION AND SPIRITUALITY:

Ron Best, ed., *Education, Spirituality and the Whole Child.* London and New York: Cassell, 1996. A wide range of essays concerned with awakening spirituality through education, spiritual development, the relation between childhood spirituality and developmental psychology, spiritual education and public policy, including the development toward a secular concept of spirituality.

Robert Coles, *The Spiritual Life of Children*. Boston: Houghton Mifflin Company, 1990; London: HarperCollins, 1992. A pioneering study by an eminent psychiatrist and writer who, during more than thirty years of talking and listening to children, was able to explore their inner lives, record their thoughts and feelings about the meaning of life, and discover their penetrating insights into the religious beliefs of the adults around them. These relate to Christianity, Islam, Judaism, and secular soul-searching. The book concludes with a chapter on "The Child as Pilgrim" and includes some wonderful drawings in color.

Elizabeth M. Dowling and W. George Scarlett, eds., *Encyclopedia of Religious and Spiritual Development*. Thousand Oaks, CA: Sage Publications, 2006. This large, ambitious publication brings together many facets of different religious traditions and spiritualities in a single volume. Some 265 short key entries have been contributed by more than 100 specialists from a range of disciplines and professions. Like *The Handbook of Spiritual Development in Childhood and Adolescence* published alongside this title (see entry under Roehlkepartain et al. below), this *Encyclopedia* belongs to the SAGE Program on Applied Developmental Science. "Spiritual development" is understood to be "about becoming a whole person, someone who stands for something that defines and gives meaning to being human" (p. xxiii). Religion is viewed as one route to spirituality, but not the only one.

Jane Erricker, Cathy Ota, and Clive Erricker, eds., *Spiritual Education: Cultural, Religious and Social Differences—New Perspectives for the 21st Century*. Brighton, U.K. and Portland, OR: Sussex Academic Press, 2001. This volume emerged from the First International Conference on Children's Spirituality, held in Chichester, England, in 2000. It discusses religious, theological, psychological, anthropological, and pedagogical approaches to spiritual education. It presents the latter as a distinctive field in its own right and argues that spiritual education is beginning to offer a radical challenge to our contemporary values.

David Hay and Rebecca Nye, *The Spirit of the Child* (see details under chapter 5).

Robert Muller, "The Need for Global Education," in *New Genesis: Shaping a Global Spirituality*, pp. 3-9 (see details under chapter 3). This inspiring essay is found in an exceptionally inspiring book that reflects the deep influence of Teilhard de Chardin on Muller's own thinking.

Robert Muller, *The Birth of a Global Civilization: With Proposals for a New Political System for Planet Earth*. Anacortes, WA: World Happiness and Cooperation, 1991. Published when Muller was chancellor of the University of Peace in Costa Rica, it is full of stimulating proposals for global renewal and reorganization including "Dreams for Peace Education," "Global Networking," and "Emerging New Global Human Rights." Also included is a reprint of "The Need for Global Education" (pp. 40-45), followed by "A Recommended Global World Core Curriculum" (pp. 46-66).

Eugene C. Roehlkepartain, Pamela Ebstyne King, Linda W. Wagener, Peter L. Benson, eds. *The Handbook of Spiritual Development in Childhood and Adolescence.* Thousand Oaks, CA: Sage Publications, 2006. Published alongside the *Encyclopedia of Religious and Spiritual Development* (see entry under Elizabeth M. Dowling above), this multi-author volume contributes to the newly emerging science of child and adolescent spiritual development, discussing its foundations, methods, and findings. It examines the intersections and divergences of spiritual and religious development and the place of spirituality in general human development.

Elizabeth J. Tisdell, *Exploring Spirituality and Culture in Adult and Higher Education* (see details under chapter 5).

Peter H. Van Ness, ed., *Spirituality and the Secular Quest* (see details under chapter 1).

Andrew Wright, *Spirituality and Education.* London and New York: Routledge-Falmer, 2000. A fine study of the main approaches and debates surrounding spiritual education, including the problems of defining spirituality, empirical research, theories of childhood spiritual development, secular and religious manifestations of spirituality in contemporary society. It looks at spiritual education as nurture and as critique, and is lucidly written, informative, and very helpful.

HEALTH AND SPIRITUALITY:

Herbert Benson with Marg Stark, *Timeless Healing: The Power and Biology of Belief.* New York: Scribner, 1997. The message of this book is that faith heals. Drawing on his long experience as physician and researcher, Dr. Benson reveals how affirming beliefs, particularly belief in a higher power, can have an important impact on physical health. We are not simply nourished by meditation and prayer but, in essence, we are "wired for God." He shows how people can use their beliefs and self-care methods to heal over 60 percent of their medical problems, and also discusses wellness, medicine's spiritual crisis, and his use of relaxation response.

David Kinsley, *Health, Healing, and Religion.* Upper Saddle River, NJ: Prentice Hall, 1996. Kinsley explores the relationship between modern scientific medicine and earlier or alternative forms of medicine in traditional cultures and religions. The section on Christianity includes a chapter on Jesus as healer, saints and healing shrines, and contemporary Christian faith healers. The last part looks at modern medical culture, the search for meaning in modern medicine, and the healer's/therapist's role in modern psychotherapy.

Harold G. Koenig, *Spirituality and Patient Care: Why, How, When, and What.* Philadelphia and London: Templeton Foundation Press, 2007. Part of the growing literature that demonstrates the influence of one's spiritual beliefs on one's general health and well-being. The book argues that, in addition to physical and lifestyle assessments, medical practitioners need to do a religious/spiritual profile on patients in order to develop the best plan for their health and healing. Koenig is director and founder of the Center for the Study of Religion/Spirituality and Health.

Ronald L. Numbers and Darrel W. Amundsen, *Caring and Curing: Health and Medicine in the Western Religious Traditions*. London and Baltimore: Johns Hopkins University, 1998; first published in 1986. Twenty informative essays give overviews on how Western religious traditions have understood human well-being, healing, rites of passage, madness, suffering, and caring. Also provided is a data bank of information for health-care professionals in surveying Judaism, Roman Catholicism, Eastern Orthodoxy, main-line Protestant denominations, Christian Science, Latter-Day Saints, Jehovah's Witnesses, African American traditions, Adventism, and modern Pentecostalism.

Fazlur Rahman, *Health and Medicine in the Islamic Tradition: Change and Identity*. Chicago: ABC Group International, 1998. A world-renowned expert on Islam, a philosopher and liberal reformer who taught at the University of Chicago, shows what value Islam attaches to spiritual, mental, and physical well-being. Included are discussions on wellness and illness in Islam, suffering and destiny, medical education and health care institutions in the Islamic world, medical ethics, sexual ethics, attitudes to death and dying. A most informative book with much information not easily found elsewhere.

Simon Robinson, Kevin Kendrick, and Alan Brown, *Spirituality and the Practice of Healthcare*. Basingstoke, U.K.: Palgrave Macmillan, 2003. This book discusses different meanings of spirituality and provides a working definition in relation to health, illness, and suffering. It looks at spirituality from cradle to grave, especially with regard to childhood, aging, dying, and bereavement. Separate chapters deal with spirituality and mental health, spirituality and learning disability, spirituality and the nursing profession, and hospital chaplaincies.

Lawrence E. Sullivan, ed., *Healing and Restoring: Health and Medicine in the World's Religious Traditions*. New York: Macmillan, 1989. The fifteen essays of this volume demonstrate how religion and medicine have long shared a special kinship, although their responses to illness and suffering are not identical. Four perspectives are explored here: health and illness, the human life-cycle with its rites of passage and their impact on well-being, healing and maintenance of health, and the impact of ethics and justice. Among the religious traditions included are Mahayana Buddhism, Chinese and Sri Lankan Buddhism, Japanese religions, Hinduism, Islam, African cultures, Haitian Vodou, Native American beliefs, and religions of Mesoamerica and South America. This informative reference work complements the one on *Health and Medicine in the Western Religious Traditions* by Numbers and Amundsen (see details above).

John Swinton, *Spirituality and Mental Health Care*. London and Philadelphia: Jessica Kingsley Publishers, 2000. Based on an interdisciplinary approach to contemporary mental health practice, the author explores the therapeutic significance of spirituality for clients with such problems as psychotic disorder, depression, Alzheimer's disease, and AIDS. He discusses both the positive and negative aspects of spirituality and mental health care, and suggests an understanding of spiritual care that will enable spiritual healing.

PSYCHOTHERAPY AND SPIRITUALITY:

Dalai Lama and Howard C. Cutler, *The Art of Happiness: A Handbook for Living*. New York: Riverhead Books, 1998. Based on interviews of the Dalai Lama by the psychiatrist Howard Cutler, this book blends psychology with Buddhist meditation and stories. The Dalai Lama explains how to defeat depression, anxiety, anger, and jealousy through meditation. There are fine chapters on the purpose of life, the value of compassion, facing suffering, overcoming obstacles, and on living a spiritual life.

David Fontana, *Psychology, Religion, and Spirituality.* Oxford and Malden, MA: BPS Blackwell Books, 2003. This book by a much-published British writer on the psychology of spirituality explores the effects of religious and spiritual belief on behavior, physical, and psychological health. He links religion and spirituality to the major psychological theories, examines different approaches to religious experience, and looks at spiritual practices such as prayer, meditation, and ritual. Examples are drawn from Buddhism, Confucianism, Christianity, Hinduism, Jainism, Judaism, Islam, Shamanism, and Taoism.

Thomas Hart, *Hidden Spring: The Spiritual Dimension of Therapy.* Minneapolis, MN: Augsburg Fortress, 2002. Written by a therapist and theologian, this book shows how much richer therapy is when it calls attention to spirituality in addressing human struggles. It argues that psychology and spirituality unite in a common goal of healing, searching for growth and fulfillment. Six case studies demonstrate how to integrate therapy and spirituality in practice.

Victor L. Schermer, *Spirit and Psyche* (see details under chapter 2).

Agneta Schreurs, *Psychotherapy and Spirituality* (see details under chapter 1). An illuminating study of spirituality from the perspective of a practicing psychotherapist. It examines the cultural and spiritual root metaphors of modern Western consciousness and discusses the existential, cognitive and relational aspects of spirituality.

William West, *Psychotherapy and Spirituality: Crossing the Line between Therapy and Religion.* London: Sage Publications, 2000. This book encourages psychotherapists and counselors to consider the relationship between spiritual experiences and therapeutic practice while arguing that therapists need training in dealing with spiritual issues. Moreover, therapy itself can be seen as a spiritual process, although there remains a clear distinction between spiritual direction and specific therapies. The author concludes with a discussion on the future of therapy as a spiritual activity.

Seven: SPIRITUALITY AND GENDER

Carol J. Adams, ed., *Ecofeminism and the Sacred.* New York: Continuum, 1993. Ecofeminism covers a wide, and sometimes contradictory, range of interests in the revaluation—and resacralisation—of woman and nature, reflected in this collection of essays on women, religion, and ecofeminism. A third of the essays are devoted to ecofeminist spiritualities.

Lorraine Anderson, ed., *Sisters of the Earth: Women's Prose and Poetry about Nature.* New York: Random House Vintage Books, 1991. These eloquent writings sing of nature as mother and sister, healer and victim, filled with wild and beautiful spaces. Stirring reflections, poems, and prayers by women in response to the natural world present an alternative vision where humans are not estranged from their planet.

Tina Beattie, *Woman.* London and New York: Continuum New Century Theology series, 2003. A very accessible, well-informed, and provocative theological reflection that critiques Christian patriarchal and androcentric values. It suggests imaginative alternative ways for understanding woman, man, and God from within the Christian tradition.

Carol P. Christ, *Diving Deep and Surfacing: Women Writers on Spiritual Quest.* Boston: Beacon Press, second edition 1986. A landmark book—based on the writings of Kate Chopin, Margaret Atwood, Doris Lessing, Adrienne Rich, and Ntozake Shange, it reveals how these writings can take the place of traditional religious texts in women's search for spiritual renewal.

Carol P. Christ, *Rebirth of the Goddess: Finding Meaning in Feminist Spirituality.* London and New York: Routledge, 1997. Christ explores the practices and beliefs of contemporary feminist spirituality centered on the divine as female and demonstrates with fine discernment the revolutionary effects of worshiping the goddess for women and men around the world.

Carol P. Christ and Judith Plaskow, eds., *Womanspirit Rising: A Feminist Reader in Religion.* San Francisco: Harper and Row 1979, 1992. A classic text that brings together historical, theological, and ritual contributions to feminist thinking on religion and spirituality. These essays give powerful witness to the maturity, complexity, diversity, and richness of the women's spirituality movement.

Elizabeth A. Johnson, *She Who Is: The Mystery of God in Feminist Theological Discourse.* New York: Crossroad, 1992. A highly acclaimed study of the Christian doctrine of God that combines the best of classical insights with the critical, liberating concerns of contemporary feminist theology. The author leads readers into a sophisticated exploration of God as Spirit-Sophia, Jesus-Sophia, and Mother-Sophia, but also into the relational mystery of the Trinity that addresses us through the rich symbols of a living and suffering God. This vividly written text celebrates God as "She Who Is," the "creative, relational power of being who enlivens, suffers with, sustains, and enfolds the universe."

Beverly J. Lanzetta, *Radical Wisdom: A Feminist Mystical Theology.* Minneapolis, MN: Fortress Press, 2005. A refreshingly daring feminist revision of mysticism going beyond both the positive and negative paths of the mystical journey. This meditative study explores with deep sensitivity and urgent social concern the innermost spiritual oppression of women's souls and bodies while proposing a new "via feminina" to heal the deep spiritual wounds of patriarchy.

Jo Ann Kay McNamara, *Sisters in Arms: Catholic Nuns Through Two Millennia.* Cambridge, MA and London: Harvard University Press, 1996. A highly acclaimed history of Catholic nuns in the Western world, telling their spiritual struggles and remarkable achievements. Women created their own space in religious communities where they could evolve spiritually, intellectually, and emotionally, but also had to work continually against male church hierarchies and the restrictions of their gender roles by society.

James B. Nelson, *The Intimate Connection: Male Sexuality, Masculine Spirituality*. Philadelphia: The Westminster Press, 1988. An innovative and influential book that shows that men can gain from feminist thought a renewed understanding of male sexuality and masculine spirituality. It stimulates discussion of masculine and feminine spirituality and of the true meaning of love.

James B. Nelson, "Masculine Spirituality and Addiction: A Personal Journey," in Ursula King with Tina Beattie, eds., *Spirituality and Society in the New Millennium* (see details under chapter 1), pp. 93-106. A moving personal account of Nelson's journey from alcoholism to recovery, involving a new understanding of his manhood, masculinity, and spirituality.

Judith Plaskow and Carol P. Christ, eds., *Weaving the Visions: New Patterns in Feminist Spirituality*. San Francisco: Harper and Row, 1989. A sequel to *Womanspirit Rising* (see entry under Christ and Plaskow above), these essays reflect the great diversity of approaches to feminist spirituality from white, black, Chicana, Asian American, and Native American women representing Jewish, Christian, Goddess, Native American, Yoruba, Vodou, and other perspectives.

Elizabeth Puttick and Peter B. Clarke, eds., *Women as Teachers and Disciples in Traditional and New Religions*. Lewiston, NY: Edwin Mellen Press, 1993. Fascinating studies of women's religious leadership, from early Christian Egypt to contemporary new religious groups in Hinduism, Buddhism, and Islam, to Bahian Candomble, esoteric groups in Italy, and modern Paganism.

Melissa Raphael, *Thealogy and Embodiment: The Post-Patriarchal Reconstruction of Female Sacrality*. Sheffield: Sheffield Academic Press, 1996. Raphael examines spiritual feminism that takes the female body seriously as a medium of divine creative activity. She sees the Goddess not as a personal divinity but as a symbol of rebellion against patriarchal religion's construction of femininity. An important contribution to contemporary debates in feminist theology and spirituality.

Melissa Raphael, *Introducing Thealogy: Discourse on the Goddess*. Sheffield: Sheffield Academic Press, 1999. A lucidly written, very accessible and succinct account of the revival of Goddess religion among feminists in Europe, America, and Australasia.

Rosemary Ruether, ed., *Women Healing Earth: Third World Women on Ecology, Feminism, and Religion*. Maryknoll, NY: Orbis Books, 1996. Essays by Latin American, Asian, and African women on ecotheological issues, on an Earth-based spirituality, and Earth-healing; reveals the experiences and perspectives of ecofeminists in the South and the importance their thinking has for those in the North.

Articles on other themes of feminist spirituality from the Third World can be found in **Ursula King**, ed., *Feminist Theology from the Third World*. London: SPCK, and

Maryknoll, NY: Orbis Books, 1994. See pp. 303-394 for essays on "A Newly Emerging Spirituality."

Charlene Spretnak, ed., *The Politics of Women's Spirituality: Essays by Founding Mothers of the Movement.* New York: Doubleday, 1994. A feminist classic with a chorus of voices on different themes of feminist spirituality: the Goddess and her meaning; developing consciousness, personal energy, and power; applying spirituality as a political force.

Starhawk, *The Spiral Dance: A Rebirth of the Ancient Religion of the Great Goddess.* San Francisco: HarperSanFrancisco, special twentieth anniversary edition, 1999. Influential in launching the American Goddess movement, this is a classic of feminist spirituality full of rituals, invocations, exercises, and magic.

Karma Lekshe Tsomo, ed., *Innovative Buddhist Women: Swimming Against the Stream.* Richmond, Surrey: Curzon, 2000. This volume documents the extraordinary changes that are taking place among Buddhist women around the world since the foundation of Sakyadhita, the global Buddhist women's movement, in 1987. This has led to a revival of full ordination for Buddhist nuns, an engagement in compassionate social action, a growth of women's nunneries, and the reinterpretation of traditional texts and spiritual teachings, all of which contribute to giving women a new spiritual authority and leadership in ways unknown before.

Ellen M. Umansky and Dianne Ashton, eds., *Four Centuries of Jewish Women's Spirituality: A Sourcebook.* Boston: Beacon Press, 1992. Diary entries, letters, prayers, poetry, sermons, speeches, and rituals are brought together in this wonderful sourcebook, revealing the great variety of spiritual paths that Jewish women have taken from the past until today. More than half of the book is devoted to twentieth-century voices.

Pieternella van Doorn-Harder, *Women Shaping Islam: Reading the Qur'an in Indonesia.* Urbana and Chicago: University of Illinois Press, 2006. A groundbreaking book that reveals the active role Muslim women leaders and scholars play in Indonesia, the largest Muslim-majority country in the world. It discusses the large networks led by women who interpret sacred texts and exercise powerful religious influence, thus utilizing Islam as a significant force for societal change.

Joann Wolski Conn, ed., *Women's Spirituality: Resources for Christian Development.* Mahwah, NJ: Paulist Press, second edition, 1996. Another amazingly rich anthology of spiritual texts, this time from the Christian tradition; a rich selection of essays on traditional and contemporary issues in Christian spirituality, with a focus on the specificity of women's spirituality.

Serinity Young, ed., *An Anthology of Sacred Texts by and about Women.* New York: Crossroad, 1994. The most comprehensive selection on women, religion, and spirituality from the sacred writings of the world's religions. It contains a helpful introduction on the major genres of sacred literature and the most significant cross-cultural themes on women in religious texts.

For an introductory overview and discussion of the major themes on feminist spirituality, see **Ursula King**, *Women and Spirituality. Voices of Protest and Promise.*

London: Macmillan, and University Park, PA: Penn State Press, second edition, 1993. For brief biographies of Christian women mystics, see **Ursula King**, *Christian Mystics* (see details under chapter 2).

Eight: SPIRITUALITY, NATURE, AND SCIENCE

Ian G. Barbour, *Nature, Human Nature, and God*. Theology and the Sciences Series. Minneapolis, MN: Fortress Press, 2002. Deals with a wide range of questions in the contemporary dialogue between scientists and theologians, including God and nature from a process perspective, the Holy Spirit in nature, the redemption of nature, and the sacred in nature. Environmental and globalization issues are also considered.

Thomas Berry, *The Dream of the Earth* (see details under chapter 3). A book of exceptional quality and insight that brings together outstanding essays by one of the foremost and most original ecological thinkers. It is full of enchantment and critical vision, showing us the Earth community in the ecological age and pointing to the possibilities of our way into the future. A book that is as spiritual as it is practical, concluding with a "cosmology of peace."

Dalai Lama, *The Universe in a Single Atom: How Science and Spirituality Can Serve Our World*. New York: Morgan Road Books, 2005. A rare, personal investigation by the Dalai Lama, who discusses his vision of science and faith working hand in hand to alleviate human suffering. He explores the parallels and convergences between modern science and Buddhist perspectives on spirituality and humanity.

Oliver Davies with Thomas O'Loughlin, *Celtic Spirituality*. Classics of Western Spirituality. New York and Mahwah, NJ: Paulist Press, 1999. A collection of newly translated texts from Latin, Irish, and Welsh that reflect the rich tradition of Celtic Christianity. An authoritative introduction on debates surrounding the notions of Celtic Christianity and Celtic Spirituality, the place of the body, of nature, creativity in poetry and art, revealing the freshness of an alternative world that challenges and fascinates.

Richard Dawkins, *The God Delusion*. London: Bantam, 2006. The well-known Oxford scientist writes as an atheist for whom God is not only a delusion, but a pernicious one. Religion is attacked in all forms. This fascinating polemic is brilliantly argued, but not convincing to anyone with any knowledge and understanding of how religion and spirituality affect people's lives and shape their worldviews.

Henry A. Garon, *The Cosmic Mystique*. Maryknoll, NY: Orbis Books, 2006. A scientist and committed Christian offers timely reflections on the physical world and the relationship between faith and science. Like few others, this book reveals our intimate, ultimately mystical, relationship with matter, and the discernment of nature as inclusive of ourselves. We discover here a "cosmic mystique" that discloses the dignity of ordinary things, the shepherdhood of matter, the worldliness of God awaiting and meeting us in unexpected ways.

Ursula Goodenough, *The Sacred Depths of Nature.* Oxford and New York: Oxford University Press, 1998. An eloquent book of luminous prose reflections on the origins of Earth, life, evolution, awareness, emotions and meaning, sexuality, death, and speciation by one of America's leading cell biologists. It culminates in a set of emergent religious principles, and a "covenant with Mystery" in response to the epic of evolution.

Pierre Hadot, *The Veil of Isis: An Essay on the History of the Idea of Nature.* Translated by Michael Chase. Cambridge, MA and London: Harvard University Press, 2006. An authoritative philosophical history of the idea of nature in Western thought, with a special emphasis on antiquity. Following Heraclitus's observation that "Nature loves to hide," the author suggests that two contradictory attitudes to this opacity developed: a Promethean, scientific-technical, veil-removing approach, and an Orphic, contemplative-poetic, reverential approach to nature's "mysteries." Neither will do. Instead, we should embrace nature at the level of the sublime, and so come to appreciate fully our own place in the world as neither masters nor underlings.

Alister Hardy, *The Spiritual Nature of Man* (see details under chapter 5). Hardy was an eminent Oxford professor of zoology who devoted himself to the study of religious experience and set up the Religious Experience Research Unit at Manchester College, Oxford, in 1966. This book offers an analysis of the first 3,000 accounts of spiritual/religious experiences collected by the unit, and reflections for the development of a science of natural theology. The research is now being carried on by the Alister Hardy Centre at the University of Wales, Lampeter.

For the current research of the Alister Hardy Society and Centre see their website, www.AlisterHardySociety.org.

John F. Haught, *Christianity and Science: Toward a Theology of Nature.* Maryknoll, NY: Orbis Books, 2007. A thought-provoking study of the relationship between science and Christian theology, especially with regard to the understanding of nature, evolution, cosmology, and creation. Of special interest are the discussions on science and the persistence of mystery, on Teilhard de Chardin's contribution to cosmology and religion, on the need for a new spirituality, and the refutations of the atheistic views of some contemporary scientists. A more developed, popular version of these can be found in Haught's book *God and the New Atheism: A Critical Response to Dawkins, Harris, and Hitchens.* Louisville, KY: Westminster John Knox Press, 2008.

David Knight, *Science and Spirituality: The Volatile Connection.* London and New York: Routledge, 2004. Knight offers a new history of the interaction between Western science and faith, showing that their connection has been volatile and changing rather than being locked in inevitable conflict. He illustrates with subtlety and wit how moral and spiritual values continue to intervene in modern scientific endeavors.

Alister E. McGrath, *Science and Religion: An Introduction.* Oxford and Malden, MA: Blackwell Publishers, 1999. A very helpful, clearly structured text explaining the complex relationship between science and Christian faith from the Middle Ages to the present time. Included are chapters on philosophy of science, philosophy of religion, creation, natural theology and finding God in nature, and contemporary case studies in science and religion that discuss the work of Ian G. Barbour, Arthur Peacocke, Pierre Teilhard de Chardin, and others.

J. Philip Newell, *Celtic Prayers from Iona: The Heart of Celtic Spirituality.* New York and Mahwah, NJ: Paulist Press, 1997. Celtic prayers from the weekly prayer cycle of Iona Abbey in the Western Isles of Scotland, reflecting the spirituality and justice concerns of the contemporary Iona Community and many of its followers.

W. Mark Richardson, Robert John Russell, Philip Clayton, and Kirk Wegter-McNelly, eds., *Science and the Spiritual Quest: New Essays by Leading Scientists.* London and New York: Routledge, 2002. A unique book of interviews with well-known scientists from cosmology, physics, biology, and computer science, answering the question of how their faith has had an impact on their scientific work, followed by an essay from each. They cover a wide religious background: Quaker, Muslim, Catholic, Presbyterian, Anglican, and Hindu. Their personal testimonies provide evidence for seeing how the project of science is part of a wider spiritual quest.

Holmes Rolston III, "Scientific Inquiry," in Peter H. Van Ness, ed., *Spirituality and the Secular Quest* (see details under chapter 1), pp. 387-413. This marvelous essay explores the numerous possible relations between scientific inquiry and the spiritual quest in much detail and depth. It deals with astronomical, microphysical, biomolecular, evolutionary, and ecological spirituality.

James A. Swan, ed., *The Power of Place and Human Environments: An Anthology.* Wheaton, IL: Quest Books, 1991. A fascinating set of accounts about sacred places and their meaning. This includes Native American sacred sites, sacred places in India, holy wells in Ireland, a temple garden in Japan, feng-shui in traditional Chinese and Korean settings, and instrumental and spiritual views on people-environment relations.

Brian Swimme, *The Hidden Heart of the Cosmos: Humanity and the New Story.* Maryknoll, NY: Orbis Books, 1996. A wonderfully inspiring journey through the cosmos. Following the recent scientific discoveries about the origins and nature of the universe, the author shows us how this new way of seeing the world bridges the chasm between science and spirituality.

Pierre Teilhard de Chardin, *The Heart of Matter.* San Diego, New York, London: Harcourt Brace and Company, 1979. A collection of essays that begins with Teilhard's spiritual autobiography "The Heart of Matter," in which he explains how his spiritual vision represents a synthesis of cosmic, human, Christic, and feminine elements. He describes his discovery of evolution, his understanding of the noosphere, his love of the universal Christ, and the *divine milieu.*

See also his works *The Human Phenomenon* and *The Divine Milieu* (details under chapter 2).

B. Alan Wallace, ed., *Buddhism and Science: Breaking New Ground.* New York: Columbia University Press, 2003. Wallace, who is a former monk in the Tibetan Buddhist tradition, a translator, and a Buddhist teacher, has edited the dialogues between the Dalai Lama and a number of Western scientists that have taken place at the Mind and Life Institute in Boulder. The book covers a wide range of issues in the cognitive and physical sciences discussed by Buddhists and scientists; it also includes a substantial history of previous Western writing on the Buddhism-science interface, and complements the Dalai Lama's own writing on this subject (see entry under Dalai Lama, above).

Edward O. Wilson, *In Search of Nature.* Washington, DC and Covelo, CA: Island Press/Shearwater Books, 1996. This collection of seminal, short writings by the eminent Harvard scientist E. O. Wilson is organized under the headings "Animal Nature, Human Nature," "The Patterns of Nature," and "Nature's Abundance." Beautifully illustrated by line drawings, the book has as its central theme that wild nature and human nature are closely interwoven.

Richard J. Woods, *The Spirituality of Celtic Saints.* Maryknoll, NY: Orbis Books, 2000. A marvelous survey of the lives and legacies of the saints of Celtic Britain, Ireland, Scotland, and Brittany, including a calendar of Celtic saints. The author highlights interesting aspects of their lives, such as social justice, the place of women, the importance of art, literature and music, attitudes to nature, and the intriguing use of blessings and curses.

The Metanexus Institute of Religion and Science: see www.metanexus.net.

Nine: SPIRITUALITY, THE ARTS, AND THE PLANET

David Landis Barnhill and Roger Gottlieb, eds., *Deep Ecology and World Religions: New Essays on Sacred Grounds.* Albany: State University of New York Press, 2001. Covered here is a wide range of perspectives from indigenous traditions to Hinduism, Chinese religions, Judaism, Islam, Protestantism, Catholicism, and ecofeminism, concluding with a discussion of Ken Wilber's critique of ecological spirituality.

Thomas Berry with Thomas Clarke, *Befriending the Earth: A Theology of Reconciliation Between Humans and the Earth.* Mystic, CT: Twenty-Third Publications, 1991. This record of a short colloquium between the two authors provides a first succinct outline of Berry's seminal ideas that were later developed in full-length books. These include our present revelatory moment, sacred community, spiritual discipline, the conditions of the ecozoic age, and reflections on Christology, sacrifice, and grace.

Thomas Berry, *The Dream of the Earth* (see details under chapter 3).

Thomas Berry, *The Great Work: Our Way into the Future.* New York: Bell Tower, 1999. Berry explores here the significance of the human presence on planet Earth at the beginning of the twenty-first century and explains where we are, how we got here, and what we have to do to build the future by "reinventing the human." A highly acclaimed book of deep insight and great visionary force. For the chapter on "The Fourfold Wisdom," see pp. 176-195.

Joan Chittister, *In the Heart of the Temple: My Spiritual Vision for Today's World.* New York: BlueBridge, 2004. A passionate and prophetic voice from the Benedictine tradition which addresses today's most pressing questions in the struggle for social justice, feminism, and ecology. She guides us with a bold vision to honor the earth, its people, and all of life.

Lois K. Daly, "Ecological Activism," in Peter H. Van Ness, ed., *Spirituality and the Secular Quest* (see details under chapter 1), pp. 445-462. Daly looks at the development of the ecological movement and at three early American environmentalists. Of special interest are the strands of ecological activism that develop from secular spirituality.

Celia Deane-Drummond, ed., *Pierre Teilhard de Chardin on People and Planet.* London and Oakville, CT: Equinox, 2006. These essays by a group of British and American scholars look afresh at Teilhard de Chardin's views on the cosmos, mysticism, ecotheology, environmental responsibility, and East and West.

Matthew Fox, *Original Blessing: A Primer in Creation Spirituality Presented in Four Paths, Twenty-Six Themes, and Two Questions.* Santa Fe, NM: Bear and Company, 2000. The best-known and most influential book on creation spirituality, originally published in 1983, presented as a journey to readers seeking wisdom and human/earth survival. Fox argues that the human race requires a new religious paradigm, as offered by a creation-centered tradition.

David L. Gosling, *Religion and Ecology in India and Southeast Asia* (see details under chapter 3).

Paulos Mar Gregorios, *The Human Presence: Ecological Spirituality and the Age of the Spirit.* Amity, NY: Amity House, 1987. A fine meditation by the former Syrian Orthodox metropolitan of New Delhi, India, and president of the World Council of Churches for Asia. Well known as a theologian and spiritual father, he presents a universal spirituality of Earth and the Earth community in response to the central problems of our time: the threat to life, nature, and human resources posed by practical atheism; a dualistic consciousness; and instrumental attitudes inherent in an outdated aspiritual science and technology.

John F. Haught, *The Promise of Nature: Ecology and Cosmic Purpose.* Mahwah, NJ: Paulist Press, 1993. This is a rich exploration of the theological perspectives of ecological spirituality. Haught, unlike others, does not consider ecological spirituality entirely secular.

David Kinsley, *Ecology and Religion: Ecological Spirituality in Cross-Cultural Perspective.* Upper Saddle River, NJ: Prentice Hall, 1995. Kinsley argues that many themes about the earth and its people held by contemporary advocates of ecological spirituality are shared by most modern and premodern views and by non-Western spiritual traditions. He looks at a variety of traditional cultures, several Asian religions, and Christianity as providing the background to contemporary debates on religion and ecology. This includes a discussion of the desacralization, domination, and degradation of nature and matter.

Albert J. Lachance and John E. Carroll, eds., *Embracing Earth: Catholic Approaches to Ecology*. Maryknoll, NY: Orbis Books, 2004. These essays by contemporary Catholic spiritual and mystical writers are responding to the planetary crisis by offering theological, philosophical, spiritual, and practical reflections. The concluding chapter, "Toward a Second Axial Age," is by Wayne Teasdale.

James Lovelock, *Gaia* (see details under chapter 3).

James Lovelock, *The Revenge of Gaia* (see details under chapter 3).

Bron R. Taylor, ed., *The Encyclopedia of Religion and Nature*. 2 vols. London and New York: Thoemmes Continuum, 2005. A pioneering, award-winning publication that informs on all ecological issues. Entries include, among many others, Deep Ecology, Earth Charter, Epic of Evolution, Gaia, Nature Religion, and Paganism. For ongoing information see http://www.religionandnature.com.

Mary Evelyn Tucker, *Worldly Wonder: Religions Enter Their Ecological Phase*. Chicago and La Salle, IL: Open Court Press, 2003. A sustained reflection on the relationship between ecology and religion, this book reveals how, at a time when the vast complexity of the evolutionary story of the universe is awakening us to a new consciousness, we are also becoming acutely aware of the growing environmental crisis that is such a threat to all species and habitats around the globe. This perilous situation calls on the world's religions to reawaken the human community to the wonder of the earth and to re-envision our role and responsibilities as citizens of the universe. The author, who has done so much to rediscover and activate the ecological resources of different religious traditions, argues that the world's religions will undergo both a renewal and transformation in responding to the contemporary ecological crisis. The book includes important environmental statements issued between 1990 and 2002, the Earth Charter among others, and lists a helpful bibliography on religion and ecology. An excellent resource for activists and thinkers and for the nurturing of an ecological spirituality.

Evelyn Underhill, "The Mystic as Creative Artist," in R. Woods, ed., *Understanding Mysticism*. London: The Athlone Press, 1981, pp. 400-414. This brief, perceptive essay is unfortunately little known or rarely cited. Based on quotations by mystics of different faiths and ages, Underhill reflects on their suggestive and allusive language that reflects "the landscape of Eternity," and reveals the mystic as "a creative artist of the highest kind" (ibid., p. 400f.).

Robert Wuthnow, *Creative Spirituality* (see details under chapter 1).

Mary Yakush, ed., *Frederick Hart: The Complete Works*. Louisville, KY: Butler Books, 2007. This illustrated catalog was published on the occasion of a comprehensive exhibition of Hart's sculptures—the largest so far—organized in 2007 at the University of Louisville, Kentucky. The rich visual documentation, including many color plates, is complemented by interpretive essays from Donald Kuspit, Frederick Turner, and Hart's wife, Lindy Lain Hart.

The Earth Charter: see www.earthcharter.org.

Ten: SPIRITUALITIES FOR LIFE

Tissa Balasuriya, *Planetary Theology*. Maryknoll, NY: Orbis Books, and London: SCM Press, 1984. A truly prophetic and visionary book by a Sri Lankan theologian and activist who takes into account the spiritual needs of the whole world, of North and South as well as East and West. Rooted in Asian experience and perspective, this book advocates above all a spirituality of justice.

Nikolai Berdyaev, *Spirit and Reality*. London: Geoffrey Bles, The Centenary Press, 1939. Important reflections by a renowned Russian religious thinker and philosopher who explores the attributes of spirit in relation to individual and society. Included is a discussion of the contradictions and achievements of mysticism and a vision of the realization of spirit in what he called already in the late 1930s "the new spirituality."

Thomas Berry, *The Dream of the Earth* (see details under chapter 3).

Marcus Braybrooke, ed., *Stepping Stones to a Global Ethic*. London: SCM, 1992. A very useful survey on the search for a global ethic, the relationship between human rights and religious traditions, and the various meetings and documents that preceded the Global Ethic Declaration of the Parliament of the World's Religions in 1993. Also included is an earlier version of the Earth Charter (see details under chapter 3).

Beatrice Bruteau, *The Grand Option: Personal Transformation and a New Creation*. Notre Dame, IN: University of Notre Dame Press, 2001. Bruteau argues that the next step in evolution will be a radical novelty, an altogether "new creation" involving deep personal and social transformations. Inspired by Teilhard de Chardin's ideas on human energy and convergence and by feminist thinking on radical changes in human consciousness, Bruteau invites us to enter into deep engagement with the "grand option" of creating a future linked to a new image of humanity animated by the living spirit of love, both human and divine.

Donal Dorr, *Time for a Change: A Fresh Look at Spirituality, Sexuality, Globalisation and the Church*. Dublin: The Columba Press, 2004. With a background of teaching philosophy and theology in Ireland, and pastoral work in Africa and Latin America, Dorr presents a powerful, at times radical, spiritual and practical vision. He looks at sexuality as a key component in spirituality, explores the need for spirituality in the workplace, and makes radical proposals for change in the Catholic Church so that it can offer people a spirituality that is true to the gospel.

Donal Dorr, *Integral Spirituality: Resources for Community, Justice, Peace, and the Earth*. Maryknoll, NY: Orbis Books, 1990. Dorr begins with "down-to-earth" spirituality, explores prayer, how it puts people in touch with their own power, and how this power is used with integrity. Dorr's vision of integral spirituality brings together personal healing, economic and social justice, concern for the earth, intimacy with God, and life in the community. He introduces the enneagram and discusses its uses for self-discovery and personal, religious, and political growth.

Martin Israel, *Summons to Life: The Search for Identity through the Spiritual.* London and New York: Continuum International, 2001 (originally London and Oxford: Mowbrays, 1974). This book is a classic, written by a distinguished pathologist who is also a priest, spiritual guide, and retreat leader. It provides an in-depth analysis of the spiritual dimension and argues that life, in the ultimate sense, can be found only through awareness of the spiritual. It discusses what is the spirit in the human being and how it works, the mystery of love, prayer, mysticism and spirituality, and questions of human identity found through the spiritual.

William Johnston, *Mystical Theology: The Science of Love.* Maryknoll, NY: Orbis Books, 1995. Johnston argues that theological reflections on mysticism must engage in dialogue with both science and Eastern religions. He gives an example of this by drawing on Einstein's theories as well as Zen Buddhism, which he knows well through his long life in Japan. The "science of love" of the mystical journey today must engage the whole person and lead to social action. It cannot remain an eso-teric discipline for religious professionals, such as monks and nuns, but must be a path open to all who are wrestling with the problems of our age.

William Johnston, *Mystical Journey: An Autobiography.* Maryknoll, NY: Orbis Books, 2006. An intensely personal account where the themes of *Mystical Theology* (see above) are further explored and developed. He describes encounters with other spiritual guides and leaders, such as Thomas Merton, Bede Griffiths, and the Dalai Lama, and advocates the practice of "global meditation" in working toward peace in the world.

Ursula King, "Love—a Higher Form of Human Energy in the Work of Teilhard de Chardin and Sorokin," in *Zygon: Journal of Religion and Science* 39/1 (March 2004), pp. 77-102. Compares the remarkable parallels and distinctive differences that exist between Teilhard's understanding of the phenomenon of love and Sorokin's approach to creative, altruistic love. Both thinkers advocate systematic scientific research on the production and application of "love-energy" for the change of cul-ture, social institutions, and human beings.

Paul F. Knitter, *One Earth Many Religions: Multifaith Dialogue and Global Responsi-bility.* Maryknoll, NY: Orbis Books, 1995. Knitter addresses the global crisis by arguing that the center of gravity of the world's religious traditions must shift from an inward-looking preoccupation with their own faith to a globally responsible and responsive dialogue that is centered on justice, responsibility, and liberation.

Hans Küng, *Global Responsibility: In Search of a New World Ethic.* London: SCM Press, 1991. Küng's program for a global ethic; it preceded the Global Ethic Decla-ration of the Parliament of the World's Religions in 1993. Its original German title is "Projekt Weltethos," a designation under which Küng's program is still working today. The book is organized around three succinct statements: (1) No survival without a world ethic; (2) No world peace without religious peace; (3) No religious peace without religious dialogue.

See also the work of the Institute for Global Ethics (IGE), Camden, Maine, and its affiliate The Institute for Global Ethics UK Trust, and IGE Canada in Van-couver: http://www.globalethics.org.

Hans Küng and Karl-Josef Kuschel, eds., *A Global Ethic: The Declaration of the Parliament of the World's Religions.* London: SCM Press, 1993. This book contains the full text of the declaration and a commentary by the two editors. The declaration is based on two principles: (I) No new global order without a new global ethic; (II) A fundamental demand: Every human being must be treated humanely. This is articulated in detail in four irrevocable directives or commitments to a culture of (1) nonviolence and respect for life; (2) solidarity and a just economic order; (3) tolerance and a life of truthfulness; (4) equal rights and partnership between men and women. A concluding section points to a transformation of consciousness and a conversion of the heart, needed among the human community on the planet.

Beverly Lanzetta, *Emerging Heart: Global Spirituality and the Sacred.* Minneapolis, MN: Augsburg Fortress, 2007. This begins with the author's account of her own spiritual experience, followed by probing reflections on the mystical heart of world faiths, the significance of interreligious dialogue, and a newly emerging global spirituality. An inspiring read full of new insights, born out of the compelling depths of experience of a seasoned scholar, meditator, and spiritual director.

John Main, *Essential Writings.* Selected with an introduction by Laurence Freeman. Modern Spiritual Masters Series, Maryknoll, NY: Orbis Books, 2002. Main was an English Benedictine monk who through his retreats and books pioneered the practice of Christian meditation as a way for people today to develop a deeper spiritual life. This selection of writings, chosen by Laurence Freeman, who founded the World Community for Christian Meditation inspired by Main's work, includes such themes as "Holy Mystery"; "Being with God"; "Letting Go"; "Embracing the World"; "One Hundred Sayings on Prayer, God, and Love."

Mary John Mananzan, Mercy Amba Oduyoye, Elsa Tamez, J. Shannon Clarkson, Mary C. Grey, Letty M. Russell, eds., *Women Resisting Violence: Spirituality for Life.* Maryknoll, NY: Orbis Books, 1996. Based on a global conference of women theologians from North, South, East, and West, this publication discusses women's spirituality as a struggle for life, which includes resistance to cultural, ecological, domestic, physical, economic, and military violence. It also explores aspects of ecofeminism.

Thierry Meynard, ed., *Teilhard and the Future of Humanity.* New York: Fordham University Press, 2006. These essays explore different aspects of Teilhard de Chardin's work in relation to the human spirit, ecology, economic globalization, and modern science. An inspiring set of readings.

Pitirim A. Sorokin, *The Ways and Power of Love: Types, Factors, and Techniques of Moral Transformation.* Introduction by Stephen G. Post. Philadelphia and London: Templeton Foundation Press, 2002 (first edition, 1954). A masterly work of great originality, substance, and size (552 pages). It deserves to be studied with dedicated attention, passion, and commitment in order to learn how "love-energy" can transform the human community.

Howard Thurman, *Essential Writings.* Selected with an introduction by Luther E. Smith, Jr. Modern Spiritual Masters Series, Maryknoll, NY: Orbis Books, 2006.

Thurman was a Christian minister, philosopher, and civil rights activist whose writings influenced Martin Luther King, Jr. This carefully chosen selection from his classic works begins with an introduction on "The Call to Prophetic Spirituality," followed by "Religious Experience; Encountering God," "The Hunger for Community," and "The Authentic Self."

World Community for Christian Meditation: see www.wccm.org.

Spirit in Education Movement: see www.sulak.sivaraksa.org.

The Edinburgh International Centre for World Spiritualities (EICWS): see www.eicws.org.

INDEX